Gloria has gathered the umpteen moving parts of planning and delivering critical business events and engineered them into a blueprint for your organization to perform as a well-oiled machine. Clear, concise, and uncompromisingly complete, Gloria's book, *The Art of Professional Connections: Event Strategies for Successful Business Entertaining*, patiently guides readers through every crucial aspect of creating a successful event. From considering the purpose, to creating a theme, to all the meticulous logistics, to post-event strategies, Gloria has crafted a chapter to cover each detail. Laid out in an easy-to-use format, including comprehensive checklists, readers can choose to examine the entire process or dive directly into the aspect of events that interests them most. I only wish this book was available when my teams hosted Hollywood celebrities, presidents, and royalty. Everyone involved in organizing events could use this supporting guide for the essential details, keeping in mind Gloria's point: the goal of any event is to create a memorable experience that demonstrates appreciation, builds goodwill and loyalty, and treats each participant like the royalty they are to your organization.

> **Dolores McKay**, President, The Leadership Firm
> international award-winning experience designer

Gloria Petersen packed *Event Strategies for Successful Business Entertaining* with advice and resources for anyone appointed with the unexpected task of planning an event. It's a guide for putting together a meeting or event that provides insights on everything from hiring the caterers to hiring the speaker. Reading this book gives you a point of reference and leaves you free to create an event with your own special touch. Plus, you will feel more informed when dealing with meeting professionals and bureaus.

> **Rob Carsello**, Lecture Agent and President
> Speaker Resource Center

Event Strategies for Successful Business Entertaining is a must-have for any well-stocked business reference library. Graduates, new managers, executives and their spouses, event planners—this book is for you! Gloria presents the clear guidance, tools, and resources essential to successful business entertaining. From a framework of time-tested, fundamental protocol, Gloria has masterfully woven in current social trends to deliver a relevant and powerful guide. As an experienced professional event sponsor and social hostess, I find the comprehensive approach Gloria presents a fantastic refresher and a recipe for success.

Tina LaCroix-Hauri, former Director,
Enterprise Risk Management and Operational Risk,
Discover Financial Services

Event Strategies for Successful Business Entertaining provides readers a great foundation for what it means to be a planner or a guest at major business events and provides useful strategies, tools, and templates for making a favorable and memorable impression. Meetings, social and business-oriented events, celebrations, and even trade shows present unique face-to-face opportunities with clients, prospects, and contacts. *Event Strategies* shows you how to build relationships and connect with others in a broad spectrum of social situations.

Nancy Sanders, MBA, Founder, Three Dog Marketing,
a strategic marketing, sales and communications firm

Gloria has compiled an easy first-step checklist to consider and follow when presented with planning any event. As a 30-plus-year veteran meeting planner, I especially appreciate the advice on invitations, what to do with uninvited guests, and the protocol that every meeting planner needs to know. Every meeting planner is a protocol officer and this book gives the reader, no matter what stage of experience they have achieved, a good checklist to consider when producing any type of event or meeting.

Cynthia W. Lett, CPP, CEP, CTP, Executive Director, The Lett Group,
and the International Society of Protocol & Etiquette Professionals

Event Strategies for Successful Business Entertaining is an essential tool designed for young professionals to seasoned executives who entertain prospects, clients, and employees. Gloria's comprehensive approach not only allows the host to have a successful event, but in turn allows the guests to enjoy a memorable experience that will solidify relationships for the mutual benefit of all involved.

Nicole Roberts, former Corporate Event Planner

THE *Art* OF
PROFESSIONAL
CONNECTIONS

**Event Strategies
for
Successful
Business
Entertaining**

Gloria Petersen

COPYRIGHT STATEMENT

Library of Congress Cataloging-in-Publication Data is available.

ISBN: 978-1-60494-855-4
LCCN: 2013930063

Printed in the United States of America

For information or to report unauthorized usage, contact publisher:
Wheatmark®
1760 East River Road, Suite 145
Tucson, Arizona 85718 U.S.A.
www.wheatmark.com

Cover design by MullinsCreative.com
Illustrations by Michel Wentling, media@azcaprint.com

To order, contact:

Wheatmark, Inc.
1760 East River Road, Suite 145
Tucson, Arizona 85718 USA
Tel: 520-798-0888 Ex. 103
Fax: 520-798-3394
www.wheatmark.com

Or

Global Protocol, Inc.
2415 East Camelback Esplanade, Suite 700
Phoenix, Arizona 85016
Tel: 602-553-1046
Toll Free: 866-991-2660
www.GlobalBusinessProtocol.com
www.GloriaPetersen.com
www.ArtofProfessionalConnections.com

A NOTE ABOUT THE SERIES

The Art of Professional Connections is a series of four books designed to enhance the leadership qualities and effectiveness of corporate CEOs, company presidents, and their management teams. It also serves as a practical guide for new hires to prepare for leadership roles in their respective careers, especially when interacting with clients and peers, both domestic and international.

This book, *Event Strategies for Successful Business Entertaining*, addresses the basics of organizing business events—everything from cultural events and sporting activities to educational conferences and trade shows. You will learn what you need to know about staging, hosting, and participating in events. It will guide you step by step from the initial planning stages to the last and most important step afterward: the debriefing. It will make you comfortable being the host or being a guest, being a participant or merely a spectator. Most importantly, this book and this series is about being prepared, about creating the right conditions and the best atmosphere for solidifying relationships with clients, customers, prospects, and employees.

The *first* book, *Seven Steps to Impressive Greetings and Confident Interactions*, serves as a guide to project a professional presence, to upgrade the quality of your interactions with others, and as the foundation for all four titles.

The *second* book, *Success Strategies for Networking in Person and Online*, identifies a wide range of mingling and networking options. It will address not only your in-person interactions and present success strategies, but also the importance of building your online presence with care, and protecting your reputation as you do so. It is strongly recommended that you use this book as a preparation tool to ensure successful interactions at networking events and receptions.

The *third* book, *Dining Strategies for Building and Sustaining Business Relationships*, will take you step by step through the details of a successful business meal. It will address orchestrating and managing the logistics of a business meal, showcasing manners, and handling mishaps. The book will also give you tips on everything from setting up the appointment and securing a strategic seating arrangement to wine pairings, the ritual of toasting, and global dining Use this book to ensure a successful business meal experience, whether casual or formal.

The entire series, including this *fourth* title, *Event Strategies for Successful Business Entertaining*, will groom you to be an asset to your company and prepare you for career advancement in domestic and international markets.

To my clients and associates:

Corporate executives,
small-business owners,
and all those who participated
in the development and endorsement of
my four-title book series,
The Art of Professional Connections.

**Satisfied clients and new career opportunities are
the end result of every successful business interaction.**

TABLE OF CONTENTS

PREFACE

Is business entertaining on the rise, or are companies becoming averse to entertainment and gifts? There seem to be mixed feelings about business entertaining today, due to the scrutiny that corporations now receive. While some companies are cutting back to avoid accusations of lavish spending, or to prevent the possibility of a backlash for inappropriate behavior, or to negate any conflicts of interest that may arise from such events, others are increasing the level of their entertaining, changing from sporting events to formal events, or becoming more creative at lesser expense.

On the other side of the equation is the question of customer loyalty. Today's business climate shows that customer loyalty is not to be based on the type of entertainment received, but instead on how the event or gesture made the customer feel. Customer loyalty cannot be built on creating a feeling of obligation. It has to be based on feelings of appreciation.

Business entertaining will never totally go away because too many business opportunities would be lost and organizations or institutions that accommodate entertainment needs would suffer as a result. It would create a domino effect: the restaurant, hotel, airline, sporting events, cultural events, and overall meeting planning industries depend to some extent on the entertainment industry. Plus, guests and customers expect to be made to feel appreciated and special. Employees need to keep their training, their new-product awareness, and their service techniques up to date. Business entertaining and company- or association-sponsored conferences accomplish that best.

Just what is the answer? Go ahead and entertain, but do it for the right reason, and be sure that your social skills and professionalism are intact and your motive is ethical. Also, realize that employees are customers too. The future of your guest relationships and the morale of your employees are influenced by how they are treated and made to feel special.

ACKNOWLEDGMENTS

Thank you to our
Fact-Checkers and Contributors

This was a community effort. No one person can know every-thing there is to know about how to plan or participate in an event; therefore, a select group of fact checkers and contribu-tors was involved in the development of this book. Each checker selected a chapter or section and read it to be sure it reflected current trends and contained valuable information, and in some cases added tips based on his or her experiences.

Neelum T. Aggarwal, MD
Associate Professor of Neurology
Rush University Medical Center
Fact checker: *Personal Concierge; The Arts and Other Cultural Events*

Cheryl Valdez Barsanti
Community Relations Director
Formerly Corporate Sales, BAI
Fact checker: *Laying the Foundation for a Successful Event; Mastering the Logistics; Conferences, Conventions and Trade Shows*

Larry P. Canepa, CCE
Certified Culinary Educator, American Chef Federation
Director of Training and Development, Dinner at Eight
Fact checker and contributor: *Banquet Setup; Hiring Caterers versus Catering Yourself; Food and Beverage Checklist*

Tranda Covington
Business Operations Manager
Motorola
Etiquette and Protocol Expert*
Fact checker: *Office Soirées and Holiday Gatherings*

Angela Gregory
Wedding Planner
The Riverside Church in the City of New York
Protocol and Etiquette Expert*
Contributor: *Weddings and the Workplace*

Donna Hoffman
President
Women on Course
Fact checker: *Sporting Events/Golf*

Dan Hotchkin
Golf Pro
Palatine Hills Golf Club
Fact checker: *Sporting Events/Golf*

Lisa James
Managing Director
Lisa James and Associates
Protocol and Etiquette Expert*
Fact checker: *Invitation and Hosting Details*

Christine Jurich
National Director of Recruiting
Fact checker: *entire manuscript*

Zak Kimble
Director of Sales and Marketing
Marriott Denver
Fact checker: *Company Outings; Travel Tips*

Patricia Leupp
Co-Owner
Mr. Formal of Phoenix
Fact checker: *Interpreting Business Dress and Formal Attire*

Paul A. Logli
President and CEO, United Way of Rock River Valley
Formerly Winnebago County State's Attorney, Rockford, IL
Fact checker: *Master of Ceremony*

Jennifer Longdon
Writer, speaker, and policy advocate on issues impacting people with disabilities
Fact checker and contributor: *Accommodating Guests with Disabilities*

David Medrano
Training Manager
Major Southern California utility company
Formerly Assistant Dean, University of Toyota
Fact checker: *Cultural Events*

Greg Nosek
Greg Nosek "Show Ready" Audio Visuals
Audiovisual Specialist and Video Journalist
Fact checker and contributor: *Audio/Video Checklist*

Haydee Pampel
President and CEO
MeetingLink, LLC
Fact checker and contributor: *Mastering the Logistics; Food and Beverage Checklist*

Maripat Quinn, Ph.D.
Public Relations Director
Heritage Trust, Mt. Sinai, New York
Fact checker: *The Arts and Other Cultural Events; Creating the Theme*

Susan Ratliff
Speaker and Author
Exhibit Like an Expert
Fact checker: *Conferences, Conventions, and Trade Shows*

Diane Roundy
Director of Business Development
Schenck
Fact checker: *Name Tags, Badges, and Security Passes*

Jackie Sanborn
Instructor
Fullerton College
Protocol and Etiquette Expert*
Fact checker: *Unraveling the "What to Wear" Dilemma; Theater Policies; Gestures of Appreciation*

Amy Suess-Garcia
Senior Director of Global Customer Service
Taylor Company
Fact checker: *Creating the Experience; Mastering the Logistics; Theater Policies; Gestures of Appreciation*

Steve Teeple
President
Safe Air Testing, Inc.
Fact checker: *Encouraging Camaraderie and Building Morale*

Paula West
Chief of Protocol, City of Phoenix
Executive Director, Phoenix Sister Cities Commission
Fact checker: *Receiving-Line Protocol*

Quotes and Tips from Business Professionals

- Letitia Baldrige, Author, *New Manners for New Times*
- Anita Brick, Career Services, University of Chicago School of Business
- Tania Carrière, Advivum, Canada
- Wallie Dayal, Dayal Resources
- Bruce Hodes, President, CMI Experiential
- Horace, poet (BC)
- John F. Kennedy
- Hilka Klinkenberg, Etiquette International, Inc.
- François de La Rochefoucald, French author, 1613–1680
- David Rydell, president, and Elaine Markou, director, HR, Bergstrom Manufacturing
- George Bernard Shaw, playwright, 1856–1950
- Shania Twain, singer

*Train The Trainer Certification from Global Protocol, Inc.

LETTER FROM THE AUTHOR

A new university graduate was hired by a large Chicago bank as a loan officer. When cutbacks took place and their in-house meeting planner was eliminated, he was given the responsibility of organizing events. He did not want to admit that he did not have the right background. Instead, he sought out a business entertaining seminar that I was presenting at a private club in Chicago and signed up. Afterward, he asked, "Why don't you write a book on this and make life easier for the rest of us?" *Good point!* I thought. I stored that idea away but took no immediate action.

A Fortune 500 technology company hired a top honors university graduate as an account executive and gave him their high-profile clients to entertain. He came from small-town USA and had never been to the opera or to a symphony, yet he was expected to entertain at these venues. His manager arranged a private session with me to help acquaint him with business entertaining. He asked the same question: "Why don't you write a book that can serve as a resource for this type of entertaining?" *Good point,* I thought again, but I took no action.

I never forgot their requests, and I kept putting the idea on the back burner. To be honest, I thought that if I wrote books, then I would not get seminar work or certification training opportunities. That was selfish thinking. Then life took some dramatic turns, and I knew that now was the time. After over twenty-five years as a specialist in professional presence, business etiquette, and international protocol, I decided it was time to share my knowledge, experiences, and research in this series of books. Why? Because life is unpredictable, and each morning I wake up, I thank God for that day. In 2004, I was a victim of a stabbing in an upscale department store—a simple matter of being at the wrong place at the wrong time. In 2010, I learned that I had cancer. In both situations, I came close to losing my life. I am grateful that I have this opportunity to put my legacy into a series of books that will help you, the reader, achieve success. I not only survived, but I also have full use of my left leg, and I am now cancer-free. I am blessed.

I have attended and I have helped plan numerous banquets, conventions, cultural events, and sporting activities—sometimes as a participant, sometimes as the speaker, and sometimes merely as spectator. Whenever I received a unique request, I would create a file of my tasks, experiences, and observations on that event, and I would use it later for a seminar handbook. This habit has helped me create seminars that better prepare my clients to receive international visitors, to serve as a protocol logistic adviser, and to organize business entertaining and educational events of all kinds. Admittedly, I do not have all the experience or all the expertise needed to write a comprehensive book on business entertaining on my own, so I engaged help from a long list of experts who plan or work with business events. Without them, this book could not have happened.

Every event and every situation is unique and has different needs. So make life easier for yourself, and use this book as your personal guide to create your own strategies and to customize the planning, organizing, and carrying out of your own successful event.

OVERVIEW OF THE BOOK

Whether you are planning a business event or simply participating, knowing all the behind-the-scenes preparation that goes
into it will give you a better appreciation for the event itself, and
for the people involved. Before you can begin planning, you will
need a road map: a guide that outlines all the different paths you
can take and highlights any detours you may face, based on your
needs and the desired outcomes.

 **To begin the process,
consider the following options:**

1. A *meeting* is a gathering of people for a *discussion* that typically
   takes place over a meal at a conference or small-event meeting
   room.

2. An *event* is something that is planned months in advance and
   happens for the purpose of education, for introducing new
   products or services, or for a celebration. Like a meeting, an
   event takes place on specific days and at specific times.

3. An *activity* or *exercise* involves direct experience and participation for enjoyment, for making introductions or creating new
   relationships, or for reinforcing a learning skill.

Protocol plays a major role in planning events, while the etiquette involved may vary. As with any industry, etiquette/
protocol experts and meeting professionals will differ on their
advice. This does not necessarily mean that someone is right
and someone is wrong. It means that at times there are different approaches based on different experiences. When faced with
conflicting information, ask for the history or strategy behind
the approach. Then select the approach that matches your expertise, needs, and industry.

Based on the premise that "one size does not fit all," event
planning is equally complex. There are many variables that

involve regional expectations, personality challenges, and levels of formality. Overall, you must use your best judgment and be willing to seek advice. Although I recommend the engagement of a professional meeting planner, I understand that budgets often do not allow those responsible the extra expense. So I've designed this book to serve as your *event development guide*. It offers comprehensive guidelines and addresses the principles and strategies for planning business entertaining events, everything from the most elaborate formal events to simple outings. You will find it a highly valuable resource.

Chapter 1

LAYING THE
FOUNDATION FOR A
MEMORABLE EVENT

> *The essence of you*
> *— your presence, charisma, and demeanor —*
> *is best showcased when socializing.*

Entertaining customers, company celebrations, and employee outings are integral parts of running a successful business, solidifying client relationships, and rewarding employees. When a company invests in entertainment, the expectation is that there will be a return on its investment. This often takes time. Consequently, it is very important that events are planned carefully and every risk of failure is eliminated. Record keeping is a must!

 The objectives of this chapter are . . .

1. To address the principles and strategies of business entertaining, from a small conference to the most elaborate event;

2. To review the steps necessary to utilize your social-ability to create an energizing social environment that helps you build solid professional relationships; and

3. To impress upon you the importance of setting goals, creating plans, and assembling the right team to make your business social event purposeful and memorable.

The nuts and bolts of doing business fill the core hours of the workday. Social events and after-hours activities provide the best opportunities to reach out to colleagues, clients, and prospects. These occasions are especially suited to broadening one's visibility, expanding business contacts, building relationships, and encouraging loyalties. Having a plan and inspiring "social-ability" contributes greatly to the success of this effort.

A Solid Foundation Starts with a Plan

The *creative side* of planning involves the theme, the décor, and the food. The *planning side* involves the budget, programming, and logistics. *Honoring special people* involves tributes and roasts. Your *social-ability* puts the team in teamwork, and contributes to the successful of any endeavor.

Consider this: as your customer commitment increases, vendors or suppliers may want to invite you to a dinner and include your spouse or date, or treat you to a play or a sporting event. Perhaps you are a vendor seeking ways to show appreciation.

The theory behind such invitations is that special treatment is a wonderful way to show appreciation and create loyalty. Although some may find these functions more of a chore than pleasure, they are nonetheless part of doing business. Not making the effort to build a relationship at a social event may limit your chance to expand your contact base or other business opportunity. To do this effectively, you need a plan.

WHICH ONE ARE YOU?
Do you fire and then aim?
(Do you scatter your seeds and then watch to see which ones will grow?)

Or do you aim and then fire?
(Do you strategically plan where you will plant which seeds and then monitor their growth?)
Careful planning produces the results!

If you do not know where you are going or how to get there, you will end up lost. Be clear about your purpose, and then aim for the result you want. If your target audience cannot discern the purpose of your event, they will not understand their ROI (return on investment), and they will not make the investment of time and money to attend. Worse yet, if your clients attend and feel misled, they will consider your efforts a waste of their time.

There are many options, but it is up to you to decide which kind of social activity works best and will deliver the intended outcome. While some people prefer an active environment and new experiences, others prefer to keep things simple and private. Start with a "getting to know you" leisurely coffee or meal. This is the time to utilize small talk to find out where a prospect's or new client's interests lie. Learn their preferences by researching on the web, visiting social media sites, talking to staff, and networking. Then consider the type of activity or event that helps you achieve your goals. There are three popular ways to achieve this:

1. With a celebration (or recognition) banquet
2. With an unusual (or memorable) experience
3. With an exciting (sporting) activity

Whatever the occasion, maintain a social presence and make it memorable. (Refer to step five in *The Art of Professional Connections: Seven Steps to Impressive Greetings and Confident Interactions*. It offers a DNA approach to conversation that will help you learn interests.)

Social Media Knows!

> It only takes one negative incident
> to ruin what you have spent years building.

People share stories and post YouTube video clips of behavior (rude or impressive) for the world to see. Your privacy is not so private anymore, because once posted, it cannot be retracted. More than ever before, respectful behavior is paramount. Behave in the manner in which you want to be seen on the Internet.

In Summary

There are many different things to consider when planning or participating in an event. This book will address the principles and strategies of business entertaining, from theater to sporting events, and from conferences or conventions to trade shows. *The Art of Professional Connections: Seven Steps to Impressive Greetings and Confident Interactions* serves as a prerequisite for building this skill set. Read it first!

> Inspire, build loyalty, and show appreciation.
>
> Entertaining Does It Best!

①

EXPANDING ON YOUR SOCIAL-ABILITY AND DEFINING THE PURPOSE

In too many situations, respecting planning decisions, adhering to proper conduct, and extending simple courtesies have become low priority among people of all levels of intellect. People have become careless and do not think about how an event or a meal is affected by their inconsideration or inappropriate behavior, because they are more focused on their personal agendas than on consideration for others. Therefore, it is very important that behavioral expectations and protocol advisement are included in the planning process.

By utilizing effective protocol when planning and adhering to professional etiquette when interacting, you will have a successful event. As the old saying goes, it is all about *dotting one's I's* and *crossing one's T's*: Protocol creates a plan that removes distractions, and etiquette monitors behavior.

This is why establishing the proper protocol is so vital. The protocol will lead you step by step from conception to completion. You need to ensure that proper protocol is followed and promoted throughout the event. Everyone involved in the planning process should have a copy of the protocol.

> Protocol helps create a distraction-free environment that enhances the experience.

Whether your event is casual or formal, people who are organized project visual poise, display respectful manners, and have interactive social skills have more impact on event success than those who do not. Developing these skills produces self-confidence, enhances self-respect, and contributes to your company's ROI (return on investment).

There is a right way and a wrong way to establish the rapport that builds loyalty. It starts by focusing on the comfort level of your guests, by knowing their interests, involving careful planning, and by going out of your way to make everyone feel special.

Feeling Socially Inept?

If you feel you are not ready to launch into entertaining business clients, or if you have had a chance to participate in a company event but have had very little opportunity to develop your social skills, *meetups* are a great way to start establishing your social skills and to get event ideas.

A *meetup* group (meetup.com) is a local community of people that sponsor face-to-face gatherings around a special interest. You can get background information and register online. There is something for everyone; these gatherings can range from social purposes to strictly business networking. They give you the opportunity to select your activity and start developing your social skills before you begin making that all-important professional impression by planning an event or party.

The first two books in this series, *Seven Steps to Impressive Greetings and Confident Interactions*, and *Successful Networking Strategies for Building and Sustaining Business Relationships*, are written specifically to help you develop your social-ability. You will want to refer to them often for the social skill set you need to establish a greater comfort level and build confidence.

Connecting Is a Learned Skill

The ability to socially connect with people in a wide range of venues is a learned skill. Some people are natural-born socializers, while others need to develop this skill. The whole idea of socializing is to expand one's knowledge of others, increase mutual comfort, and develop trust.

Being social means that you have to step away from your computer (or comfort zone) and interact with people face to face. If you are someone who refrains from organizing or attending an event because of your internal "what ifs," think ahead and prepare so that you can relax, enjoy, and reap the benefits. The following questions will introduce great ways to check or enhance your "social-ability."

When you are mingling, you are socializing.

You are socializing best when you are taking the initiative.

■ Do you stake out your claim at a table of familiar people by putting your folder on the seat (or table) and stand there waiting for the other members of your party to show up? Or do you mingle in the crowd and just take whatever seat you get when it's time to be seated? If you are sitting with people you do not know, you are expanding your social circle.

■ Have you spoken with your management team ahead of time to inquire about your duties during social events? For example, are you expected to make table introductions during the event breakfast, lunch, or dinner? If so, have you practiced the pronunciation of names, learned titles, and put together some background? If you have, you will project impressive leadership skills.

Another often-overlooked social skill is the art of introducing one person to another. During social events, it's always nicer to be able to add some small details about the person, besides just a name and where they work. Point out any commonalities you have found during your sleuthing. Did someone attend the same school, are they both tennis buffs or perhaps also enjoyed a trip to China recently? This gives your guests some conversational landmarks and increases the sense that you are bonding together.

—Maripat Quinn, Ph.D., public relations director at Heritage Trust, Mt. Sinai, New York

- Is the gala dinner a showcase dinner where awards are being presented? If so, are members of your party among those receiving awards? Are you showing or offering your support? By doing so, you are participating in the celebration.

- Are any of your guests people with whom you have business to conduct? If so, have you planned the right time and spot for this conversation? If yes, you are making valuable use of your time.

Socializing allows you to learn what others think and what they like and dislike, and over time to transform contacts into long-term business relationships. By getting to know your target audience (or customer) and organizing the event carefully, you will create an energizing event that will help you turn new and renewed contacts into solid business relationships and at the same time build employee loyalty, which improves retention.

Moreover, making people feel special is one of the most effective means of gaining insights into the personalities of customers and colleagues alike, and learning their personal goals.

Define the Purpose

Why are you holding the event or activity? It is important to make this a win-win opportunity. Determining the purpose is an important step that is too often bypassed.

Is the purpose to …?

- Acknowledge a success.
- Honor an individual or group?
- Enhance learning?
- Celebrate a contract?
- Show appreciation to employees, customers, or suppliers?

By knowing the reason, you will be able to match the right customer with the right activity. When you plan an event to build customer loyalty or show appreciation, it can be simple or complicated. Stating the purpose, having a plan, and incorporating a theme are important to building continued relationships. It is the theme that makes the event memorable and provides you or your event planner with the starting point for creating the appropriate atmosphere and entertainment. Do not overlook any detail.

A global accounts manager for a Fortune 500 technology company breaks down the *purpose* for his events into four categories:

1. *Closing a Deal Event:* Finishing a project and saying "thank you."

2. *Relationship Event:* Building a relationship with customer that includes his or her spouse or date. (This type of event can range from attending the symphony or formal theater to going to a ball game.)

3. *Team Event:* Combining customers with team members at an event to offer everyone an opportunity to learn each other's personalities and goals and how needs can be met.

4. *Brand-New Person Event:* Introducing a new client or team member (especially if it is an international client or team member) to the staff—may include a corporate tour.

Perhaps you want to give a client an update on your products or services. Invite your client to your corporate headquarters. Arrange for your client to meet with every department and talk about how each discipline sees the account. Then have a catered buffet for lunch, or spend the afternoon in a private box at a sporting event such as a ball game, or plan an evening opera outing. You have just created a memorable event that not only kept your client abreast of new products or services, but also gave them the memory of a wonderful time.

This opportunity to get to know colleagues, management, and clients outside the normal business environment is just as important as the proposal you have spent days developing, the e-mail dialogue you have been engaged in, and any phone conversations you have conducted.

> The proposal or e-mail dialogue shows you in *print.*
> The phone conversation communicates your *tone.*
> A social event reveals you in person—the *real* you.

Regardless of the venue or the reason for the event, there are several decisions to make when selecting the appropriate way to entertain a client or hold a business meal. Whichever you choose, it is always about getting together and sharing ideas in a relaxed, fun-filled atmosphere. The ultimate goal is to strike a balance between being friendly and concentrating on business.

Since meals are always a part of the planning, you will find additional guidance on determining the purpose by reading *The Art of Professional Connections: Dining Strategies to Building and Sustaining Business Relationships.*

> Strike a balance between your social-ability
> and planning process.

❷

SELECTING YOUR TEAM AND DETERMINING THE FIVE "WS"

 The Basic Three

1. What is the event and *theme*?
2. Who is the *sponsor* or host?
3. Who are the guests, and is there a *guest of honor*?

Planning a large event or receiving visitors for a corporate event or activity takes attention to detail, a professional demeanor, and the right planning skills. It is the best way to make everyone feel special; offer education, product, and service updates; develop public support; and show appreciation. All this starts with a carefully selected team.

Select and Engage Your Team

No one person can truly handle all the details from start to finish. Select committee members with varying backgrounds and experience. The more diverse the committee, the more ideas you will garner; however, you will also encounter resistance to ideas. When personalities or ideas clash, it is a time to "agree to disagree" and engage in diplomatic solutions; therefore, your committee chair should have "Grade A" people skills, strong leadership experience, and the ability to engage a diplomatic solution when ideas clash.

The committee will be in charge of all the arrangements, from selecting the venue and handling the logistics to working with the vendors. Everyone's organizational skills and social behavior will have a direct effect on the outcome.

You and your committee should ask the following six questions and record the responses:

1. What is your motivation or justification?
2. What do you expect or want to accomplish?
3. How do you want your guests or participants to feel?
4. What are your key takeaways?
5. What follow-up actions will you take once the event accomplishes your goals?
6. What steps do you need to take if the event does not accomplish your goals?

If the budget is tight, survey your staff to see if you have individuals with meeting-planning backgrounds. Then assemble your planning team, making sure that it has a diversity of talents, expertise, and resources. Also consider the mix of personalities, genders, ages, and cultures in the group. This will help you address any special considerations that may arise? This can include cultural beliefs and dietary habits that will influence the type of activities planned, the food selections, and the overall décor.

Use your imagination, and engage the right mix of people to ensure success. Consider including everyone from support help to upper management. This is not about titles; it is about creating a fun and memorable event. You might even want to consider asking the spouses and teenage children to take part. This is especially effective if the event involves evenings and weekends away from home. You have now turned the planning into a family event. This also creates a better balance of everyone's time; plus fresh ideas are bound to surface. (Refer to chapter 7 for more ideas on involving the family.)

Note the "Five P's": Prior Planning Prevents Poor Performance

To make sure that your event experience is worry-free and profitable, you must have a plan of action. This plan starts by establishing a protocol for a smooth-running event and honoring basic etiquette to avoid conflicts and missteps. Utilize a procedure that defines the sequence of events so that everyone is on the same page.

Start by selecting a few calendar dates and possible venues. There are a number of considerations to keep in mind when selecting a date for your event. Venue availability and local holidays are very important. If you are inviting multinational guests, consider the holidays related to your guests' nationalities and cultural affiliations. Allow yourself plenty of time to book a venue. Three to six months in advance is ideal; more time is needed if you are booking close to the holidays.

Include the "Five W's": Who, What, When, Where, Why

The more elaborate the event, the more information the invitation, event flyer, or social media campaign should include. Most importantly, make sure your marketing materials and invitation includes the "Five W's" (Who, What, When, Where, Why).

1. **Who** is doing the inviting, whom are you inviting, and how many will be invited?
2. **What** is the theme or purpose of the event?
3. **When** will the event be held?
4. **Where** will the event be held?
5. **Why** are you holding the event?

Use the following eleven points as a guide when developing your campaign and invitation:

1. *Name of Host and/or Sponsor(s):* Name of your company and/ or sponsors.
2. *Type of Event:* Holiday party, reception, lunch, dinner, outing, retirement, employee recognition, etc.
3. *Purpose of Event:* To celebrate, get acquainted, learn new skills, celebrate a new contract, etc.

4. *Date of Event:* Include month, day, and year.

5. *Time of Event:* Include AM or PM and time zone. Including the time zone is very important for those who will be traveling from a different region or country to your event.

6. *Location:* Include a complete address and directions. Insert a map or diagram with instructions in the invitation. Be specific about where everyone should meet or gather upon arrival.

7. *Attire:* State the dress code (e.g., semiformal, business dress, casual). Be prepared to describe attire expectations if this is designated on the invitation. If an outdoor event and a dinner are both planned, make sure that the appropriate attire is understood for both activities. One's attire should not be too casual or too revealing.

8. *Special Needs:* Include a clause on the invitation addressing special needs (e.g., wheelchair access and seating, dietary or culture/religion-based alternative menu choices, etc.).

9. *Response:* Include response date and method of response. To help ensure a response, include a self-addressed, stamped envelope for postal mailed invitations. Or, offer an email option.

10. *Security Arrangements:* If the event is to be held in a high-security building, be sure your guests are aware of the protocol required and identification needed to gain admittance to the building. For example, are picture IDs required? Will your name be on the security's event client list?

11. Other Details Pertinent to the Event: Include additional information that will help in the preparation and arrival. Here are some examples:

   ■ Lobby entrance (if there is more than one lobby entrance).

   ■ Valet service (or where to park).

   ■ Elevator instructions (especially if the event is in a multi-tower, high-rise building with multiple elevator locations).

- Ticket instructions (if needed).

- Alternate gathering place. (If it is an outdoor event, always add an alternate gathering place in the event of inclement weather.)

You now have the basic foundation for organizing a tour, party, or other event. Be aware that there are bound to be some steps unique to your industry for the type of activity you choose. The larger the event, the more the steps involved.

> A successful event is a team effort
> that requires careful planning.

CREATING THE THEME FOR THE RIGHT EXPERIENCE

All events, including networking events, need a theme to set the tone and spark interest. In fact, some people say that they will not attend an event unless the theme is clearly stated.

The first and most important step in selecting a theme is to create a memorable experience. Then consider the logistics, the type of entertainment that complements the theme, and cultural norms (if international guests will be present).

> *When choosing themes, always consider cultural norms and other "politically correct" barriers a particular theme may pose. Our company once held a seminar for European delegates based on a "regal" theme. We wanted our international guests to feel like royalty. Unfortunately, the French guests felt that we were favoring the guests from England because of our references to kings and queens. Unless your entire audience is of the same age, gender, and culture, it is best to work with something that is culture-neutral, such as a nautical theme, a superhero theme, a jungle theme, or a space theme. Even the most conservative events can be made memorable with small, theme-related details. We have found that conference guests often remember such themes for decades after the event.*
>
> —Amy Suess-Garcia, senior director of global customer service,
> Taylor Company

Your ultimate goal should be to create a non-offending experience that strengthens the relationship.

Match the Event to the Needs of the Client

By planning an event that will be specifically targeted to your client's range of interests, you will show yourself and your company in the best light. You will be seen as someone who is forward thinking and driven by quality, someone who understands the interests of your clients—you'll be doing great. This is your opportunity to gently steer the conversation to those items that are important for your work, flattering to the client, and enjoyably memorable to all, and this is how you guarantee success.

−Maripat Quinn, Ph.D., public relations director at
Heritage Trust, Mt. Sinai, New York

When planning an event, think, "What kind of experience do I want my clients to have? What kind would they like to have?" Entertaining is about your clients; it is not about you. Ensure that the activities planned are of interest to your clients or customers. Activities can range from the traditional to the very elaborate or unusual. Know as much as possible about your clients' interests prior to the event. For example, if your client has eclectic tastes, make it unusual. If your client has traditional tastes, make it simple.

Never make a selection based on your personal interests alone. It would be disastrous to invite the wrong client to a concert or to a baseball game. Again, plan a win-win experience by putting your client's interest ahead of your own. Sometimes it is possible to compromise with something you both will enjoy.

For example:

If you prefer comedies and your client or employees prefer musicals, select a musical, or perhaps compromise with a musical comedy.

Everyone enjoys a good laugh, so if you select a comedy, make sure that the comedian's style and content and your client's sense of humor are in sync. Once a client is offended, it is difficult to remove the discomfort, and it is a reflection on your company.

Golfing may be one client's favorite activity, while another client may prefer the theater. To avoid awkward moments, do not invite anyone to play a participatory sport such as golf or tennis unless you know you are both competent at the game. Otherwise, stick to being spectators—or consider noncompetitive activities such as the theater, the arts, or a festival. You will learn more about these options in upcoming chapters.

With the advent of the Internet and social media, it is fairly simply to find out the interests of another person. If you happen to be in charge of entertaining a person who does not have any online presence, you can often find out where they attended school. The school clue might bring you to that college's website or, better yet, the person's yearbook, which often lists early interests, clubs, hobbies, and associations. Do they belong to a country club known for golf or tennis? There are many avenues to do sleuthing; you just need to think creatively. No one would like to be surprised to find out that their client doesn't drink, while on a day tour of wineries.

—Maripat Quinn, Ph.D., public relations director at Heritage Trust, Mt. Sinai, New York

You might consider using a use a gala as an opportunity to create an atmosphere of elegance and raise money for a favorite charity or cause. This also showcases the fact that the company is fulfilling a valuable community service role. Know as much as possible about your clients' interests prior to the event. Find an event that works for everyone. Be creative.

Determine the Theme

Once you have determined the experience, the theme will evolve. The themes for more playful events often include novel accessories like unusual hats, masks, or costumes. For example, technology is used to wow the guests; balloons and gimmicky toys are used to make everyone feel like a kid again. These events can range from a Mardi Gras party to playful themes such as a circus with clown costumes. Competition among corporations also contributes to some of the uncommon ways in which businesses choose to entertain. The theme needs to be in good taste as well as fun. It is extremely important that the amusement selected does not embarrass the guests.

Avoid events like the one that involved a clown who chased the clients with his mechanical barking dog. Some guests were amused, but others were embarrassed or felt humiliated.

A theme can also be created around an activity involving the theater, a golf outing, a featured museum exhibit, or a restaurant's celebrity chef. It does not have to be complicated. Use what is already available. Check your local or the intended location's newspaper entertainment section, magazine, or community event calendar website for ideas.

If appropriate, the welcome team can be dressed in theme costumes that reflect the theme. For example, the welcome team for a horse-racing theme can be dressed like jockeys, or the welcome team for a Western theme can be dressed like cowboys or cowgirls.

Consider the following traditional events, and then add a new twist:

- Executive club luncheons (feature a high-profile CEO as speaker)
- Biz talks (offer updates on new products and services)
- "Lunch 'n Learn" (put a surprise in a boxed lunch)
- Industry-related clubs (e.g., Technology Club)

- Sporting events
- Casino and tracks
- Customer appreciation dinners
- "Executive of the Year" celebrations

Combine a theme with a tasting. A *tasting* is a chance to compare and sample a variety of beverages and foods. This does not just involve food; it often refers to a wine tasting or food and wine tasting. Here are some examples:

- Menu tasting
- Wine tasting
- Caviar tasting or sampling
- Chocolate tasting
- Cheese and crackers tasting

Offering a tasting session is actually not new. Meeting planners have been using it as a way to determine a menu for an event. It is also referred to as a "food sampling." What is new is how it is listed on the menu to give the diner the same opportunity without ordering a full-course menu. You might see them referred to as "a la carte," "prix fixe dining," or "appetizer" menu options. A chef may refer to it as a "bento box," which is simply a Japanese lunchbox or packed lunch. Any number of items may be inside.

My most memorable experience was at a chocolate tasting at which the chocolates were paired with dessert wines. Chips of dark chocolate and chips of milk chocolate were placed on individual saucers representing cacao beans from different countries. (The dark chocolate was lined up on one side of the table and the milk chocolate on the other side.) We were then given a rating sheet to determine our favorite chocolate and preferred region. The pairings included a dessert wine for the dark chocolate and a dessert wine for the milk chocolate. Small cubes of bread were available to help cleanse or neutralize the palate periodically.

> *Did you know that chocolate is properly tasted (and dissolved) on the roof of the mouth and that both dark and milk chocolate have nutritional value? It was also a wonderful opportunity to learn more about dessert wines that paired beautifully with chocolate. The conversation and interaction were phenomenal because it was a new experience for everyone.*

The list of options is endless. Also, international guests often favor anything that is unique to our culture or lifestyle.

> *Don't make the mistake of stereotyping interests to a particular sex, race, or cultural group. Some men will enjoy fashion shows more than some women, and fishing trips can be ideal for interested parties of either sex. All people are individuals first but members of groups only by accident of birth, not necessarily by choice. Research the individual, not a group of individuals.*
>
> —Maripat Quinn, Ph.D., public relations director at Heritage Trust, Mt. Sinai, New York

As you plan, remember to include a "rules of behavior" guide or briefing that compliments your theme. When involved in an activity (especially out of doors), it is easy for members of your client group to become lost, confused, or unruly. Do not lose sight of the real purpose: to learn more about your client, secure goodwill, find out information, and show appreciation. You have a job to do, and part of that job is to make the activity beneficial for everyone and to allow opportunities for conversation.

 Here is a checklist of ideas:

- Amusement parks
- Architectural boat tours
- Auto shows
- Backyard cookouts

- Bingo games
- Boat tours
- Career centers and libraries at local colleges and universities
- City and state government buildings
- A tour of the changing seasonal landscape colors (especially in the fall)
- Cowboy and Indian theme (e.g., rodeos, native dances, rope tricks)
- Cultural attractions
- Demolition derbies
- Factory tours
- Fashion shows
- Fishing trips
- Giant or specialized supermarkets (e.g., organic)
- Live television tapings
- Local courtrooms
- Ranch or farm visits
- Potluck dinners
- Regional food harvests
- Seasonal art and food fairs
- Shopping tours (e.g., grocery stores, outlet malls, fashion squares)
- Sporting events such as soccer and racing State and county fairs
- Symphonies, operas, theater productions
- Trade shows
- … As you can see, the list is endless

Plan a debriefing for the conclusion of your activity. The guidelines and forms are in chapter 10.

Considerations when Using a Professional Event Planner

Many companies turn over their business entertainment functions to professional event planners (currently more and more referred to as "event or meeting professionals"). These event planners often handle especially complicated (or larger) events such as business galas, dinner cruises, corporate anniversaries, and retirement parties. Be careful! There must be clear, concise, and constant communication between the company and outside event planners.

> A certain pharmaceutical company hired an event planner to arrange a scenic architectural tour along the Chicago River as part of its regional sales conference's afternoon activity. The company was expecting a riverboat tour, but the event planner scheduled a ground tour on a trolley. This misunderstanding created a lot of confusion and dissatisfaction with the event planner—not to mention how embarrassed the company was when the clients inquired why they were on a noisy ground tour when they understood that they were going to be on a more serene boat tour. While both parties used the word "tour," they were not specific about the type of tour.

Meeting planners are a great source of ideas when you want to know about current trends or have an unusual theme in mind; however, clear communication among all involved (in-house personnel and outside contractors) during the planning stage avoids misunderstandings. When an event planner is involved, it is still important to double-check every detail to ensure that your expectations are met, and that the activities planned are appropriate for your clients and employees. Some event planners have become so used to bizarre requests (or budget concerns) that they may inadvertently plan something inappropriate for your theme or for your guests. Competition among corporations also contributes to some of the uncommon ways in which businesses choose to entertain. The theme still needs to be in good taste, and the execution needs to result in a fun event.

Make sure that your event planner is very specific and advises you of any last-minute changes or substitutions. They are working for you, and you should work very closely with them.

> Above all, plan a fun, relaxing, and
> memorable event.

PACING YOURSELF TO AVOID BURNOUT

Planning business events and activities can take a toll, so be mindful of your time and energy. Constant entertaining at restaurants, participating in outings, or organizing events can take a toll physically, mentally, emotionally, and financially. It is work. Still, it should never become tedious or interfere with the balance of work and your personal life. If you are getting home late and getting up early, the stress of trying to do it all will interfere with your busy day and your mental state. Know what is involved and what is expected of you as you evaluate your options and start planning.

There will be times when focusing more on just having a conversation and less on trying to impress with an event will suffice. Sometimes meeting with a small group of people for a simple beverage and snack is adequate. But if it is meant to be an occasion to educate and inspire employees, bring your market up to date on products or services, or demonstrate appreciation, an event will do it best.

Respect Your Limits

Do not try to be all things to all people. Consider partnering with a team member who can stand in for you on occasion. You do not want your workload to pile up or other contacts to suffer. If you are organizing a client-related event and will be alternating with another team member, make sure this is okay with your client. If your partner and the client have not met, include them at a few meals (or coffee meetings) so that they may become familiar with one another. Let your client know that there may be times when extenuating circumstances do not allow you to attend a planning meeting but that when that occurs, your associate will be there to answer questions or address concerns.

Tread Lightly When Encountering Freeloaders

Learn how to recognize individuals who are really just freeloaders. They are not interested in your service or product. They simply want a free meal or to be seen at your event, or they just like tagging along. Although this type of individual can become a nuisance and waste a lot of your time, he or she might be someone who could be a valuable connection for you one day. Therefore, you need to find a diplomatic way to discourage this individual from being a nuisance; your kind approach will be remembered.

You can accomplish this by being appreciative of their interest, keeping the communication door open and departing with grace without offending or cutting the individual short. Yes, this can be a delicate situation; however, you still need to respect your time and your budget.

Webinars: Socializing from Afar

Alternating a live event with a webinar (Internet seminar) is another way to avoid burnout. Webinars offer the capability of reaching the widest range of people through various social networks, and is a great resource when distance is a barrier. Plan a *Webinar* when an in-person demonstration or product update is not an option due to distance.

Put together a series of PowerPoint slides and video clips that are entertaining and informative based on your knowledge of your client or prospect's interest. These could include photos of your city's architecture, video clips of staff members at an activity, or photos of an event they missed. The options are endless. If you do not know how to put together a webinar, there are books on the market that will take you through the process step by step, or you can hire someone to assist you.

The beauty of webinars is that they can be conducted and enjoyed from a private area of your corporate office or home office. Developing a webinar, however, can be another time-consuming task, so be mindful that you will need to pace yourself very carefully. However, once it is developed, it is show time. You do not have to worry about logistics.

> Maintain a work-life balance.

Chapter 2

MASTERING
THE LOGISTICS

> *If you want to get a point across, entertain.*
> —George Bernard Shaw, 1856–1950

There is more to celebrating doing business with a client than saying thank you. Planning a dinner party, staging an event, receiving out-of-town office visits, or scheduling a special outing can be incorporated into the price of doing business. The steps that you take to make clients, customers, and prospects feel appreciated and special give you the best competitive edge.

☞ The objectives of this chapter are …

1. To help you consider all the logistics and create your own protocol for hosting a small or large event;

2. To provide you with an understanding of all the details behind staging a successful business event or banquet, from table decorations and seating to hiring caterers, all of which will have a direct bearing on creating a memorable experience; and

3. To give you a complete perspective on what it takes to create a memorable event for entertaining guests, from knowing the expectations and protocol, to covering all the details, to avoiding distractions and pitfalls.

Whether you are hosting a lunch or a special event, your goal should be to come away with information and insights that will keep your best customers in place and be useful to you as you seek new customers. This is the perfect time to ask why your clients prefer to do business with your company, where your company is strong, and what you can do better to serve them.

Each event should have its own unique approach or planning system; however, when a planning system is not in place or you are new to the planning process, you need a guide sheet. This chapter will get you started by helping you create your own protocol. You will experience flaws as well as successes at first events. Review these experiences and debrief those involved to assist you in making each event more successful than the last, and to provide a valuable aid for the next person in line to make event arrangements.

Identify the Type and Size of the Event

Although every planner will have his or her own unique interpretation of the type of event and the expected number of attendees, the following will get you started:

Company Retreats or Sales Conferences: Company retreats are project meetings that are not going to fit into a two-hour or half-day meeting and are typically held off-site. They are used for strategic planning, stimulating new thinking, launching a new project, visioning, team building, reorganizing with new role clarifications, etc. The goal is to get team members to think outside the box and to think a little bit differently about the way the staff members communicate with each other and their clients. They often involve indoor or outdoor interactive activities that keep the event fun and energized.

 Additional characteristics include:

- A motivational speaker to set the tone or for a kickoff
- An inside or outside facilitator to keep the discussion on track
- Typically less than a hundred participants
- A merging of domestic and international branch locations (e.g., sales, marketing, or management team)
- Corporate tour, product or service demonstrations, and brainstorming sessions
- A duration of up to three days

Educational Seminars: Educational seminars can be held in person or online (e.g., a teleseminar or webinar). When held in person, they can also utilize Skype video for those speakers and attendees who cannot attend a live event.

 Additional characteristics include:

- An opening speaker to introduce the education topics
- Speakers covering specific professional development and industry update topics
- As few as fifty or up to four hundred attendees (unlimited if a teleseminar or webinar)
- One topic per training time, or the option of two or three topics selected for each track
- Table setup for support material and literature
- Typically a one-day event

Symposium or Conference: The terms *symposium* and *conference* are somewhat synonymous. They are both meetings whereby several speakers are engaged to present or discuss a topic or a collection of topics. While a symposium might focus on differences of opinion on one topic, a conference offers a range of topic options. Symposia or conferences tend to be for a target audience (e.g., the sales team).

 Additional characteristics include:

- A keynote speaker to open the event
- A select group of speakers discussing a specific topic or sharing opinions with an audience, or the option of two or three topics selected for each track
- As few as a hundred or up to four hundred attendees
- Vendor exhibits
- Typically a one-day to three-day event

Convention: A convention is a very large conference and involves a variety of entertainment. They are either corporate-based or association-based and draw attendees from a wide range of positions (e.g., entry-level to upper management). They also draw individuals who are considering entering a particular field or trade to learn more about career opportunities.

 Additional characteristics include:

- A keynote speaker (or speakers) at breakfast and lunch
- A select group of speakers presenting on a wide range of topics during tracks or breakout sessions where participants can select their preferred topic
- Over five hundred attendees
- An award or foundation dinner
- Trade show vendor exhibits
- Typically a three-day to five-day event

Planning Points

Making conference meetings relevant requires a great deal of thought. Once the type and size of the event has been determined, the following points will help your committee with the planning. (Also, review chapter 1.)

1. *Establish a goal, and have a purpose:* Having a goal and identifying the purpose is a key element when developing marketing materials. If there is more than one goal, identify the three most important goals and make sure that they are intertwined.

2. *Develop a theme:* The theme creates the excitement and is the motivating factor for attendance. It should also identify a logical succession of presentations and workshops that illustrate key points. Bottom line, the theme should make the conference relevant.

3. *Do Your Research:* Before you map out the beginning, the middle, and the end, check to see if there is an event journal

with a visit or event history to use as a reference or guide to avoid repeating past mistakes and to incorporate helpful suggestions. Then bring your team of planners together and provide a forum for brainstorming. Some use storyboards or sticky notes to help the planning team visualize the event in its entirety. Each session should build upon the previous one and keep the theme intact.

4. *Utilize a "parking lot" flipchart.* There will be suggestions that might not fit in with the overall goals. Simply record these ideas on a flipchart (or sticky notes on poster board), thus parking them, and revisit them at the midpoint or conclusion of the development process. It is important to keep the ideas flowing. Some of these ideas can be used for future conferences. The "parking lot" concept helps keep everyone on track and controls randomness.

5. *Consider including pre-conference homework with registration confirmation.* Once you receive a registration, send optional homework with the confirmation. Do not just depend on the three-ring binder that the attendee will receive upon arrival. This will help the attendee to prepare and to get into the conference mindset prior to arrival.

6. *Provide a speaker guide sheet for the presenters.* Note when they can set up their equipment, how their session introductions will be handled, and the amount of time that should be dedicated to a question-and-answer period (most prefer ten to fifteen minutes). The Q&A is extremely important because it allows the attendees to zero in on what is relevant to them or to get clarity on something that was presented.

7. *Collect evaluations and follow-up:* Make it easy for attendees to fill out evaluations and turn them in. Also send out a post-conference e-mail survey of how the conference was valuable and relevant. Feedback serves as your planning guide for the next conference.

8. *Keep track of publicity:* Assign someone to watch for publicity

in the local periodicals, online, and in your respective trade magazine. Then send hard copies of (or e-mail links to) any publicity that appeared (with reprint permission) over the next three to six months to the attendees. It will serve as a wonderful reminder of your event and encourage future attendance.

Planning encompasses the location, theme, and budget. The logistics will depend on the type and size of your event. The larger the event, the more details will be involved. The upcoming chapters will go into greater detail.

Checklists and forms to help you create a good record-keeping system are in chapter 11. For small, meal-related gatherings, refer to *The Art of Professional Connections: Dining Strategies for Building and Sustaining Business Relationships*.

Your planning points are your roadmap.

TACKLING BASIC LOGISTICS FOR LARGE EVENTS

In these times of multitasking and budget cuts, you may find yourself being asked to add the duties of "event manager" to your already busy schedule. In this case, do not panic. This book includes planning steps that will make you feel like a pro. Be sure to ask if anyone on the staff has had experience handling events, and recruit them to assist you or use the tips in chapter 1 to help assemble a planning team.

If the budget allows, hire an event manager (or event professional) for large productions, because this is their field of work and they know all the ins and outs of making a large event successful. Since they do not know your business, you will need to brief them and guide them to some degree. Some companies have in-house event managers who are certified specialists in their field. Your job is to offer assistance when asked, but leave the details to them.

Consider the following when working with professional planners:

- Overall budget
- Cost of airfare and lodging for the attendees
- Security concerns from the airport to the hotel
- Availability of AV and business center support services
- Event entertainment
- Accessibility to local nightlife

Depending on the size of your event, you may require setup by an exhibit house with experienced staff to communicate and manage your logistic needs. There is a lot involved, and it is important to be ready for anything and everything. The following is broken down into ten main points to help you understand the details for each category.

Ten Preparation Steps	
1. Language Code	**6.** Equipment Compatibility
2. Facility	**7.** Security
3. Meeting Room	**8.** Safety Tips for Leisure Time
4. Parking	**9.** Smoking Notice
5. Transportation	**10.** Flag Protocol for Formal Events
Other important areas are discussed throughout this book. Refer to chapter 10 for a detailed checklist.	

1. *Language Code*

Encourage the use of common, everyday language. This means avoiding colloquialisms, acronyms, and clichés. These can be very confusing for individuals for whom English is their second language. Here is an example:

> A new employee with limited English was assigned to assist with an event. When he contacted his supervisor with a problem, the supervisor commented, "We are putting out a fire. I will get back to you!" In a moment of panic, the employee pulled the fire alarm, thinking there was a fire. There was no fire! It may sound far-fetched, but situations similar to this one do happen when there is a language challenge.

Become familiar with the language code; that is, the words and acronyms used by vendors and event personnel. You might even consider creating a glossary of terms and commonly used acronyms and sharing it with your team.

2. *Facility*

Maintaining a good working relationship with the venue staff and the vendors adds to the successful organization of any event. Advise the facility holding your event as to the number of exhibitors and vendors, the number of anticipated attendees, and the number of rooms needed for educational sessions. Remember, large conferences are usually booked as much as a year or more in advance. It is also helpful if the event managers clearly understand your objectives. A staff orientation session (in person or virtual) prior to your event will ensure that everyone is clear on all the details.

Notification of the time and location of the event, along with the hours of registration, should be sent to each attending participant at least two to three months in advance. This will allow sufficient time to schedule hotel accommodations and flight arrangements. Again, the larger the event, the more advance preparation time is needed.

Some attendees plan out their travel (or conference) schedule a year in advance. They may want the expense to come from the planning year budget and not the event year budget. This is another reason that advance notice is preferred.

Providing directional signage to the registration area will help guide participants to ensure that they are registered and their badges are processed in a timely manner. Directional signage should include the company logo and the name of your conference at the entrance to the convention facility. In a very large facility, several events may be scheduled at the same time; therefore, signage is important to provide clear and easy access for registrants.

3. *Meeting Room Logistics*

Reserving a meeting room is just the beginning. There are several logistical needs to consider in order to guarantee the comfort of the participants and to meet the needs of your speakers or presenters. Consider the following:

Podium/lecterns: The biggest podium mistake you can make is to place the podium at the front of a long, narrow room. This creates too much distance between the presenter and participants in the back rows. If you are working with a long room, consider positioning the podium on the wide side to accommodate the audience and creating several aisles to make visibility and interaction easier.

If possible, use an acrylic lectern, because it allows the audience to see the entire person—this is especially helpful for short speakers. If the seating is for more than fifty attendees, position the podium on a raised platform.

Lighting: Odd as it may seem, participants feel that if they cannot see the speaker, they cannot hear the speaker. Therefore, it is essential to provide good lighting and to space the chairs with clear lines of sight to the podium. If the lights are lowered for a long period of time in order to accommodate a projector, you might find the participants getting tired—and if they are tired, they are not listening. If possible, only turn off the light above the screen and maintain medium lighting in the rest of the room. Most LCD projectors can accommodate this lighting. A room with windows facing the south or east can also be a problem on a sunny day. You might need to position the projector in an area of the room away from the windows. (Ask if blackout window coverings are available.)

Ambience: Music playing while attendees enter the room always sets a wonderful tone. The music should be appropriate and should complement the theme of the event. If music is not possible, have an icebreaker exercise planned for the opening to help set the mood. Be creative with the meeting room setup. You are setting your stage. Anything you can add to the room to create a sense of fun or a feeling of elegance will enhance the comfort of the room.

Treat: Candy on each table can create a warm feeling. Select candy that is easy to handle, non-messy, and possibly foil-wrapped. Avoid candies with wrappers that are noisy and distracting (e.g., cellophane), hard candy that can clank against the teeth, and candy that is sticky or melts easily on the fingertips.

Assign a team of event or room monitors: These individuals help with the timing and seating, take care of speaker needs, and serve as the "go-to" people when special needs arise or there is a technology issue. They know whom to contact to take care of issues or problems. Provide the room monitor with a "technology survival" bag or box. This is a small bag that has an assortment of battery sizes, in case there is a dead battery during a presentation, and other small items that your planning team feels would be helpful.

Start and end on time: Be fair to those who arrive on time by making sure the program starts on time. There will always be late arrivals. Make an exception if weather or parking conditions contribute to a delay; then only allow a five- to ten-minute delay. You might consider roping off the last row or the last table for late arrivals.

The program should always end on time, even
if there is a late start. If there's been a late
start, the room monitor should check with the
speaker or presenter during the break to see if
there is anything that he or she can do to help
the program end on time. Some room monitors
also serve as "timekeepers" and will discreetly
hold up a countdown card indicating the time
remaining (e.g., fifteen, ten, or five minutes left).

4. *Parking*

As you work through the process of creating your event,
remember that people remember how things end longer
than they remember how they began. This means that your
event has to be thought through very carefully from the time
of arrival (first impression) to how the parking (last impression) is handled.

*When a local bank sponsored an outdoor food fest fund-raising
charity, they received a response much larger than their parking space could accommodate. So they decided to valet park 90
percent of the arriving vehicles (at no charge), and they selected their own valet team. This meant that cars had to be double
and triple parked in order to handle all the traffic, which, unfortunately, generated a 45- to 60-minute wait when retrieving
cars. Needless to say, this disturbed many of the attendees who
became irritated and complained as they endured a long line
and wait. The enjoyment of the event started to diminish in the
long line.*

When accommodating a large turnout with limited parking
for a small event, engage the expertise of a professional valet
service. They know how to anticipate parking time, keep
things moving, and hold wait times down.

For large events, parking requires the assistance of the

facility and security staff. Do you need a special area designated for your clients? If so, the facility will need to block
off parking spaces and add signage to ensure that adequate
space is available. Will you need traffic control by the local
police department, or will you be using corporate security
guards? If you answer yes to either, you will need to plan for
the added cost involved.

Whether the event will be utilizing a public or private
parking facility, advise your clients of the parking fee and
whether or not they will receive validation. If the parking lot
is used for other events, you will need to advise your clients
of parking alternatives.

Parking can be a very frustrating experience for your
clients, so make it easy, affordable (if fees are involved), and
pain-free. If you are using a convention-size facility that
covers several acres, you may want to include a facility map
for your clients.

5. *Transportation*

If your guests will need to use other forms of transportation (e.g., shuttle, taxi or limo), either make arrangements
to cover this expense to and from the event or give them a
detailed list of options with phone numbers and rates. Also,
be prepared to arrange transportation for any guest who has
had too much alcohol to drink at the end of the evening.

6. *Equipment Compatibility*

As a host, it is your responsibility to ensure that the correct
equipment has been delivered. As a speaker, it is your responsibility to have a contingency plan in place at all times for
any equipment shortcomings. It is extremely important to
make sure that your event speaker arrives one to two hours
early and checks the equipment.

Before your event begins, you should always check out
the equipment and the lighting. If the speaker has ordered
an LCD projector, make sure that an overhead projector has

not been provided by mistake. (Although rare today, some older buildings or facilities still work with older equipment.) Lighting needs to be synchronized when the speaker shifts from his or her presentation to the screen. In some cases, the lighted area by the screen needs to be dimmed without putting the audience or the speaker in the dark. If a lavaliere and a handheld microphone are to be used, be sure that they do not interfere with each other. Practice walking and speaking using both mikes. Learn where the interferences occur, and then adjust the volume. Too many microphones in one room may cause a screeching-sound feedback. Consult with your audiovisual technician; he or she may recommend the use of a mixer. (There are more details on AV equipment in chapter 10.)

At least a couple of hours before, if not the day before, arrange for the speakers to perform a check of their equipment. They should be sure, for example, that their laptops are compatible with the equipment and that sufficient extension cords have been provided. It is also extremely important that your speakers have AC adapters for their laptop computer models. A battery may not last through the entire presentation.

If any of the equipment or presentation aids (e.g., clickers) require batteries, speakers should bring extra batteries. If a battery goes dead during the presentation, suggest a five-minute stretch break (your attendees will love the opportunity), change the battery, and begin again. This is another reason why supplying the room monitor with a "technology survival" bag is important. The speaker may have forgotten he or she used the last battery at a previous presentation. (Refer to chapters 8 and 10 for additional preparation steps to consider.)

7. *Security*
When planning an event that involves VIPs or international

clients, make the facility's security team a part of your team. It is your responsibility to take care of your client's safety and security. By involving security, you communicate that you care about your client's safety and well-being. Negative experiences have the greatest long-term impact and can diminish or cancel out all your relationship-building efforts for the visit.

 For example: If a laptop is stolen or lost at the airport or hotel, how you handle this issue will be remembered longer than how great or elaborate the rest of the experience is for your customer.

Check all security procedures and identify the protocol for those procedures. For example, what steps will be taken to protect identities? Will they need the names of your clients for the security desk? Will your clients need picture IDs? Security considerations include the following:

- Hotels are much better now than in the past at being discreet with room numbers. Make sure the staff does not communicate room numbers verbally during check-in. This is especially important for individuals traveling alone. Ask if there is a special floor (or wing) for women traveling alone that is monitored frequently.

- Practice theft prevention by checking out public areas and meeting rooms for accessibility from outside areas. Too much accessibility to the property could mean that there is a risk of outsiders (non-registered) entering your conference areas.

- Make sure the guest room doors have deadbolts or computer locks and peepholes.

- Always ask to see a written security plan. Familiarize yourself with the emergency procedures for the venue. Have the phone number of a contact to call should there be a health-related emergency. Know the location of the nearest hospital or emergency room.

- Know the location of all emergency exits.

If confidentiality or proprietary information is a consideration, find out from the venue if any of your competitors are hosting an event at the same time. There is more on travel security in chapter 8.

8. *Safety Tips for Leisure Time*
   There will be times when customers or clients will want to be on their own. Do not just give them a map of the city and tell them to go have fun! Give your customers a map of the city, mark areas that may not be safe, and note convenient and safe ATM locations. Consider conducting a briefing on how to protect oneself from pickpockets and other unexpected moments.

While en route to a five-star convention center in São Paulo, Brazil, the unexpected happened. While we were at a stoplight, two young men approached my host's car on both sides, with rocks in hand, demanding money. My host said to look like I was searching for money in my handbag, and as soon as the light turned green, we sped off. Certainly this is not unique to Brazil. It can happen anywhere. Desperate people do desperate things, and if you look like a foreigner or a tourist, you are fair game.

Help your guests choose good restaurants versus inferior ones, good nightclubs versus clubs with questionable reputations, and make sure they know how to call for a cab, use public transportation, or rent a car. Awareness is the key preventive element for all security and safety matters. If you and your visitors are aware of what is going on around you, and if you understand what the risks are and adhere to safety precautions given to you by the hotel, you will be able to avoid mishaps or be better prepared if something does happen.

There is an element of risk in everything we do and everywhere we go. Your job is to minimize these risks.

9. *Smoking Notice*

   Although smoking is restricted in most facilities and Americans are accustomed to the restriction, your international guest may not be. You will need to have a designated smoking area and let your guest know where it is located. If reaching the designated smoking area will require guests to go through doors that are normally secured, you will need to coordinate special arrangements with the facility captain and security staff. Also, make sure that safe ashtrays are available in the smoking area.

10. *Flag Protocol for Formal Events*

    A director of international relations for a Fortune 500 company shares an experience he had when preparing for a visit from the president of Malaysia. To receive and honor its client properly, his company had a Malaysian flag made and displayed. Fortunately, the Malaysian press arrived before the president of Malaysia and noticed the flag was incorrect.

Although the Malaysian flag looks similar to the United States flag, there are distinct differences. Like the US flag, their country's symbolic crest is bordered by red and white stripes. It might seem that the flag company simply replaced the US crest with the Malaysian crest. Inside the Malaysian flag's field is a crescent representing the Islamic religion and a star with fourteen points signifying the fourteen states. The US flag's union (or crest) contains fifty stars representing each state.

The flag manufacturer did not notice that the first stripe under the union in the upper left-hand corner is red for the Malaysian flag and white for the US flag. Nor did the manufacturer notice that the Malaysian flag has fourteen stripes and the US flag only thirteen. When told, the director of international relations immediately removed the flag and commented that it is better to have no flag than to display an incorrect flag.

A flag is a symbol of people—whether a nation, city, or corporation. It is often displayed along with other flags at meetings, banquets, and other corporate events. Learning the history and the symbolism of your visitors' native flag will make you more knowledgeable and your conversation more impressive.

It sends a strong message that you value and respect your visitor. Consequently, it is important to learn how to display and handle flags correctly, and to respect the protocol. An inappropriate display of a flag can send an insulting message.

Flags are customarily displayed only in the meeting rooms of an event space (e.g., customer briefing center, corporate boardroom, or convention center conference room). They may also be displayed in dining rooms where the visitors will be—rarely or never in the hallways or entryways. Flag displays are handled by the facility's staff. They will need sufficient lead time and will need to know who will be placing the flags on their poles and taking them down.

When displaying the US flag from a staff projecting from a window, balcony, or other part of a building, the blue field with white stars (union) should be at the peak of the staff unless the flag is at half-mast. When flown with flags of states, communities, or societies on separate flagpoles that are of the same height and in a straight line, the flag of the United States is always placed in the position of honor. The other flags may be smaller, but none may be larger. No other flag should ever be placed above the US flag. (Source: www.usflag.org/flag.etiquette.html.) Also, visit www.ushistory.org/betsy/flagetiq.html for flag rules and regulations.

When mounting the US flag to a building, the union should be on the left. A corporate expert or adviser should always oversee the photographer's staging.

The cover of a high-profile business magazine displayed the flag backward, with two men holding the flag with the blue field on the right instead of on the left. This was noticed, and it conveyed a message that the magazine was careless.

Show pride by taking special care of your flag. It should never look damaged or be handled or displayed in a careless fashion. A flag is a symbol of a country's identity and represents its people.

Show respect at all times. When the national anthem is played, hats should be removed; this includes baseball caps!

You now have a guideline to assist you in planning a successful event from conception to the flag display. Use the checklists in chapter 10 to assist you further.

Leave no stone unturned.

❷
ACCOMMODATING HOME-OFFICE VISITS OR RETREATS

Small company meetings, conferences, or retreats are usually called for the purpose of bringing clients up to date or bringing virtual team members together for an in-person update on new products or services. They are also organized to bring domestic and international company teams together to meet each other and bond. There is only so much that can be accomplished online. Meeting in person and socializing always create a special bond.

Senior managers or relationship managers are normally the key individuals assigned the responsibility of receiving visitors and coordinating private business affairs. (This will vary with an organization's structure.) However, there are times when office personnel have this responsibility.

Consider assigning one person in your office to act as a concierge. His or her responsibilities will include helping guests get theater tickets and dinner reservations and find services such as cleaners, shoe repair, and a doctor or dentist for minor emergencies. (Learn more about the role of a corporate concierge in chapter 4.)

> **Question:** My boss is a regional manager for a Fortune 500 company, and I'm the office coordinator assigned to serve as the company concierge. For the past year, we have had an increasing number of home-office visitors. Are we expected to plan events and host visitors every evening if they're going to be staying in town for three or four days?
>
> **Answer:** You are not obligated to spend every night with visitors. You should, however, make your visitors feel welcome, and you can accomplish this without tying up all of your evenings.

To ensure that there is a smooth and productive interchange, consider the following:

1. How much time has been allocated?

2. What is the theme? Are special props or decorations needed? (Make it fun!)

3. What are the names (with pronunciation guidance if needed), titles, and organizations of the visitors or team members?

4. What is the purpose of the visit?

5. When do they arrive, and what is the length of their stay? (Will some be adding vacation time to their visit?)

6. What types of activities have been scheduled? After a long day of meetings, is there a special activity (e.g., the theater, a dinner, a tour)?

7. Is there a visit history? If so, have there been issues or difficulties in the past that need to be rectified or avoided?

8. What are the two or three most relevant discussion points? (This is important for brainstorming and facilitation sessions.)

 First and Lasting Impressions are in the Details:

- Gifts and how will they be presented. (Will these be presented at the event or sent to the hotel room?)

- Welcome sign and other signage that announces "ABC Regional Offices welcome (name of your guest)." People love to see their name in print.

- Copy of agenda for staff and clients.

- Name badges.

- Notepads and pens or pencils.

- Welcome folder.

- On the day of arrival, all hotel and car rental reservations must be confirmed.

Set aside one night for entertaining special groups at a restaurant. Select one or two places that offer good food, good service, and a nice atmosphere, and use them exclusively. Let the manager and maître d' know that you will be entertaining groups there frequently. This will assure that you always get a warm welcome and VIP treatment. (Refer to "Building Restaurant Relationships" in *The Art of Professional Connections: Dining Strategies for Building and Sustaining Business Relationships.*)

Company-Sponsored Guests

If your organization is sponsoring guests to attend your event and paying for everything, the confirmation mailing and arrival protocol should reflect the following:

- Personalized itinerary.
- Copy of flight tickets with airport/hotel transportation information.
- Rental car and parking information (if needed).
- Shuttle service schedule if event is held at more than one location.
- "Meet and greet" information.
- Key contact phone numbers and e-mail addresses plus other relevant information.
- Packing tips.
- Hotel registration card.
- Hotel brochures.
- Emergency phone numbers and any additional relevant "leave behind" information.
- Name badges, with instructions if the name is incorrect.

 Protocol for Receiving High-Ranking Guests

- Have them met at the airport by someone of equal or higher rank.
- Have a translator and interpreter available if English is a second language or not used.
- Place welcoming flowers, wine (or preferred alcoholic

beverage), soda (if non-drinking), and candy in your guests' hotel room. If you select fruit and cheese, be sure that a small knife is available.

- A personal note of welcome from the CEO or the highest-ranking company person should await them.
- Provide a complete schedule of events, in both English and the guests' language.
- Know whether the guest has medical concerns, and if so, make sure a list of doctors is provided or tell where to get medical assistance (e.g., urgent care facilities) if there is a problem.
- If the guest is a celebrity, make sure you protect his or her privacy. Only allow autographs if the celebrity guest agrees.

You will need to adjust the above checklist to the type and size of event you are planning or sponsoring. Not everything will apply.

If you are arranging for a limo, make sure that your guests or customers know the name of the limo company and where they will be greeted (in most cases, it will be at the airport baggage claim area). If you are greeting customers, e-mail them a photo so you can be easily identified. Limo companies typically have a sign with the guest's name; however, it can be easily overlooked in a crowded airport. A skycap or luggage cart should be secured for moving the luggage. Avoid having the visitors or guests carry their own luggage. The limo driver or taxi driver will take care of loading the trunk of the limo or car.

> *Limos:* If you are using a limo and it becomes crowded, the company greeter should sit in the front seat. A client or high-ranking executive never sits in the front seat of a limo.

> *Taxis:* If there are too many people in your party and one member of your group will need to sit up front with

the taxi or limo driver, this person should be the lower-ranking individual. The curbside seat is best reserved for visiting dignitaries, important clients, or the senior executive.

If your guests will be traveling by coach (bus) or shuttling to and from the hotel to the venue, or if your event is in a large hotel and locating the correct conference rooms can be difficult, consider creating a welcoming committee of greeters whose main responsibility is to direct guests to the coach or conference rooms the first day of the meeting.

Welcome Packets and Baskets

Put together a welcome packet. A welcome package outlining the visit is critical. This should include a map and a listing of public transportation options. Include a brochure from your local tourism and convention bureau. Also include a list of popular restaurants with tips on the food, atmosphere and prices at each.

When you select your guest's hotel, also arrange for a welcome basket of fruit, wine, cheese and crackers, and/or chocolates in the room for your guests.

A small, theme-related gift with a welcome note waiting in the guest's room makes a wonderful first impression. Also read the concierge section of chapter 4 for more welcome packet ideas.

Amy Suess-Garcia, who plans small to large events for Taylor Company, offers the following "welcome package" suggestions for themed events:

Select strawberries or yellow submarine-shaped notepads for a Beatles-themed conference; a deck of cards or dice for a Las Vegas-themed event; or a bag of microwave popcorn for a circus-themed seminar—all are intended to make the guest feel special. A similar gesture can be made upon the guest's departure.

Once you have welcomed your guests, given them a tour of your facility, and entertain them at dinner the first night; then you can make other arrangements for the remainder of their stay. You are not obligated to spend every evening entertaining your guests. Allow them some time on their own to explore your town. Consider making special arrangements for guests traveling alone, especially women.

If your guests will be entertained at more than one dinner, select one or two restaurants that offer food compatible to their tastes, good service, and a pleasant atmosphere. Use these restaurants exclusively. Let the manager and maître d' know that you will be entertaining groups there on more than one occasion. Take this a step further by telling the maître d' (or restaurant manager) that he or she should feel free to offer selections that are particularly unique to the restaurant. Maître d's love to offer their opinion! This will assure a warm welcome and VIP treatment.

If your agenda has people visiting recommended sites on their own, be sure to state a meeting time and place for the beginning of the event and then again at the close. Once your group has arrived, review the instructions and reconfirm the designated time and place for everyone to meet at the end of the event or tour.

> You should be the first to arrive at the meeting place at the beginning and at the end of the event so that you can greet everyone and confirm that they are in the right place and have transportation back to their hotel or your office.

When it comes time for departure, the greeter, planner, or manager should accompany the visitor to the airport and see him off. This time can also be used to recap the visit and establish that last-minute rapport.

These simple suggestions will help your guests feel pampered and entertained even if you do not host them every evening. You will discover that guests do like to have free time to do as they please.

To Recap: Consider This Scenario

Suppose you are planning to celebrate ten years of doing business with your client and you want to combine this visit with an introduction to a new product or service. Arrange an invitation to your facility for an update on your products and services and a tour; pay for their travel expenses if they are coming from out of town. Following the tour, serve a catered meal.

Schedule three hours in the morning for briefings with every department. If you are a manufacturing company, include key shop personnel with office personnel. Allow time for demonstrating any new product or service, but be careful not to oversell. Make it fun and interesting for everyone.

If there will be a variety of people involved, make sure that there are name tags available so that all participants will be well equipped to remember names. For employees who do not typically host guests, brief them to bring their business cards. Those with less visible positions often forget this important detail. A tour of your facility is a good option. Guests enjoy seeing their products being manufactured. If you are conducting a tour, make sure that any preliminary correspondence indicates the dress requirements for a manufacturing facility (e.g., closed-toed shoes, long-sleeved shirts). Have appropriate safety wear such as safety glasses, lab jackets, or hard hats on hand for guests if necessary.

—Amy Suess-Garcia, senior director of global customer service, Taylor Company

Start the morning with product demonstrations leading up to a catered luncheon buffet with unique selections. You might want to include a buffet menu card with a list of the food items for your client to review beforehand. This will ward off any food issues or dietary concerns.

> *If possible, put the guests' names and company name on a marquee or electronic screen in the lobby or other area where the guests will be welcomed. People like to see their names and are complimented by the amount of preparation put in place for their visit. Additionally, if your company has more than one flagpole, fly their country flag or a flag with their company logo if you can obtain one or have one made. You will win big points in the hospitality department.*
>
> —Amy Suess-Garcia, senior director of global customer service, Taylor Company

After lunch, plan a sports activity or a tour of the city's architecture, shopping mall, or that special place for which the city is renowned (lakefront, rural landscape, etc.). Many visiting clients, especially international clients, enjoy trips to a local shopping center, festival, arts and craft show, or museum. This activity is a wonderful opportunity for guests to experience firsthand the flavor of your community and its culture. Be sure to include these types of events on your list of options during your planning. Ask your clients to select their top three preferences; then select the one that works best with your planning. Consider completing the evening with dinner and the theater.

If you are planning a full, multi-event day for out-of-town clients, be sure to allow your clients time to freshen up at their hotel before dinner. This is a consideration that is too often overlooked. This ninety-minute to two-hour break is an important prelude to an evening dinner party or cocktail reception. If your guests are from another country, consider their dining preference in terms of time. While a 7:00 PM dinner is considered normal in the United States, most other countries serve dinner much later. This will also affect breakfast time. Therefore, you will need to find an agreeable time for everyone for all meals (e.g., the later the dinner, the later the breakfast. A breakfast compromise would be a light continental breakfast for the early risers, and a brunch at mid- or late morning for everyone.

Knowing that you are taking extra steps and considering everything is what makes for a successful event that builds a solid relationship. (More ideas are mentioned throughout this book)

Special touches go a long way.

③

TAKING THE GUESSWORK OUT OF BANQUET ROOM SETUP

If you are staging a formal dining event or simply an informal company banquet, you still need to be on top of everything, from selecting the appropriate-size table to choosing and positioning the centerpiece. Careful consideration should be given to the floor plan (table and chair selection) and cover (place settings). Otherwise, every movement becomes awkward.

The following recommended table accessory measurements are based on *traditional* guidelines. Realize that there are exceptions to every rule; therefore, consider the reason or logic behind the rule or suggestion before making adjustments.

Table and Chair Selection

 Tip: A general rule is to use round tables for a party of ten or less and a rectangular table for parties of more than ten.

Make sure that there is ample room between diners. This helps makes the service much smoother and more professional, because the staff does not have to pass plates or reach across guests unnecessarily and disruptively. There is nothing more frustrating than having twelve chairs squeezed in at a table designed for ten.

 Tip: The tabletop should measure twenty-eight to thirty inches from the floor for comfortable seating. The seat of the chair should be eighteen inches from the floor.

If these guidelines are not met, it presents a challenge for wheelchair diners and diners who are large in stature. Nor do you want the chair so high that a short person's feet do not touch the floor.

Everyone's challenges need to be considered. No one likes to feel squeezed into their chair or too small like a child sitting in a large chair. (If it is a family affair, booster seats and high chairs should be available.)

 Tip: Chairs should be one foot apart in order to allow diners adequate elbow room.

Plus, this spacing will accommodate left-handed diners when they are seated next to right-handed diners. If they are seated closer, you risk making diners uncomfortable by having their personal space violated and by having place settings so close together that the diners cannot distinguish which fork or water goblet is theirs.

There is a trend toward using cabaret tables and chairs (also referred to as "high-top" cocktail tables) for meals at casual events. In fact, you will see actual place settings at these tables. This works as long as there is a bar (also refer to as a *rung*) on the chair that can also act as a footrest. You do not want your diners' feet to dangle or to have them "hop up" in order to sit on their chair. High-top tables can also be used without chairs and are commonplace in cocktail settings so that guests do not have to balance their drinks and their hors d'oeuvres in their hands as they walk, meet, and greet.

> Be aware that people in some countries consider cabaret tables to be tables used for drinks and snacks only and never acceptable for an actual meal.
>
> –Amy Suess-Garcia, senior director of global customer service, Taylor Company

"Tablescaping" (or Table Cover): Place Settings and Utensils

A complete table setting is traditionally called a *cover*. Tablescapes, a more contemporary term, are creatively designed table arrangements that include centerpieces.

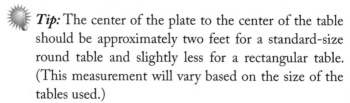 *Tip:* The center of the plate to the center of the table should be approximately two feet for a standard-size round table and slightly less for a rectangular table. (This measurement will vary based on the size of the tables used.)

The bread-and-butter plate is placed on the left just above the forks. In a tight place setting, you might find the bread-and-butter plate placed off-center (left) above the dinner plate.

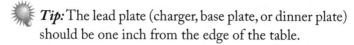 *Tip:* The lead plate (charger, base plate, or dinner plate) should be one inch from the edge of the table.

Utensils are arranged in the order in which they will be used (from the outside in), for efficiency and logic.

Tip: The utensil handles are one inch from the edge of the table. If the salad and dinner forks are the same size, the salad fork positioning is shifted slightly in order to appear shorter than the dinner fork.

If there is a dinner knife and a large, signature steak knife, the steak knife is often placed at the top of the plate. The dessert utensils will be brought with dessert or positioned as the last utensils on each side of the plate. Sometimes, the dessert utensils are placed at the top of the plate.

(For more on place settings, refer to *The Art of Professional Connections: Dining Strategies for Building and Sustaining Business Relationships*.)

Tablecloth and Placemats

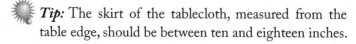 *Tip:* The skirt of the tablecloth, measured from the table edge, should be between ten and eighteen inches.

(This dimension is known as "lap length," as opposed to "floor length.")

If it is too long, it might interfere with a diner's feet or legs; however, at very formal events (e.g., weddings and black tie occasions) you will find tablecloths on small, round tables oftentimes touching (or draping) the floor. (This is not an issue with high tops because the tablecloth is tied around the pedestal as it drapes on the floor and does not interfere with the feet.)

The more elegant tablecloths are made of damask. Damask is a higher-quality and more expensive fabric with a luxurious feel. When placed on the table, the fold on the tablecloth should be aligned with the middle of the table.

 Tip: If placemats are used instead of a tablecloth, they should be one half inch from the edge of the table. (The edge of the plate would then be one inch from the edge of the table.)

Placemats are used when the tabletop is unique in design or the event is casual. If you are using small mats, utensils will go on the table. If you are using large mats, utensils will go on the mats. To personalize your event, customizable and stock mats are usually available at a small cost and can be ordered in small to large quantities.

Centerpiece

Your table setting and centerpiece are part of the room setup and should reflect the occasion. Make sure that your event decorators are given proper guidelines. Too often, decorators focus on the centerpiece design (or creativity) and not on how it might hamper eye contact at the table.

 Tip: The centerpiece should be between ten and fourteen inches high.

Be considerate of people who are 5'6" and shorter and of people in wheelchairs. You do not want to obstruct people's view of their table partners and hamper conversation opportunities.

A popular centerpiece has a very long stem (over the recommended fourteen inches), with the arrangement at the base and at the top. It is not as intrusive because the stem is very narrow and transparent; however, it distracts from the purpose of a beautiful arrangement. You have to look up to see it, and it creates a minor interference as you look beyond it to the person directly across from you.

If you are not responsible for the table setting or not involved in the selection process, assign a member of your staff or the restaurant staff to be mindful of centerpieces that obstruct eye contact and conversation. They should ask the event planner if they would like the centerpiece removed and, if so, have a special table set up for these centerpieces. Have them arranged on a table in a way that continues to add elegance to the room.

If you arrive at a table and feel that the centerpiece interferes with conversation, and no one has been assigned for centerpiece removal, never take it upon yourself to remove a centerpiece from a table. Too often people set them on the floor, which creates another kind of obstruction; plus, it signals disrespect. Instead, excuse yourself from the table and find the event chairperson (or responsible person). Explain the problem, and let the event chairperson take care of the situation.

When a centerpiece is removed from a table, the visual effect of the table will be disrupted; eye contact among your dinner partners, however, is more important. Typically, the centerpiece will be removed and placed in an attractive area. It is important to maintain the ambience of the room.

Candle and Flower Considerations

 Tip: If tall, slim candles (or a candelabrum) are used for the centerpiece, you should display one candle for every two people. (For example, a table of eight would have four candles.)

To avoid dripping, freeze candles ahead of time. Then light the candles just before your guests arrive or just before they are seated.

Be sensitive to guests with allergies by selecting unscented candles. Food that can be savored by all the senses stimulates the appetite. The scent of a candle could detract from or clash with the aroma of the meal. The same rule holds true for floral arrangements. Fresh flowers make a beautiful centerpiece; however, they are not recommended at winemaker dinners due to the aromas, which might interfere with the enjoyment and nuances of the fine wines. Also, seasonal allergies to fresh flowers can make a guest very uncomfortable, and flowers are therefore best avoided; however, there are many flowers that are visually attractive yet not overly pungent. It is important to always consider the strength of the scent.

> *I once attended an event where one of the guests suffered from asthma. The beautiful lilies on the table were attractive but highly aromatic. Consequently, the guest had a severe asthma attack and had to be taken to the hospital. At another event, the event planner brought arrangements of several tea-light candles on a mirrored surface to serve as centerpieces. The occasion took place during the holiday season, so the candles were pine scented. The chef was mortified because the pine scent overpowered the aroma from his culinary creations.*
>
> —Amy Suess-Garcia, senior director of global customer service, Taylor Company

Menu and Name Cards

 Tip: Use the name or menu card to note special orders (e.g., a vegetarian selection).

Banquets have predetermined menus, which means that the table should be already set with all of the tableware and utensils that will be needed to complete the course, from soup and salad to dessert. If something is not already set (for example, the sorbet spoon or coffee spoon), it should be brought at the appropriate time (with the sorbet course or coffee service). Be sure that the menu has been created with one or two alternative selections. This selection should be part of the reservation confirmation. The requests are then noted on the name or menu cards.

> *If there is a name place card, it is a good idea to add special selection options to that card (e.g., vegetarian, no salt, allergy to shellfish, Muslim/halal). If there are no name place cards, provide the guests some sort of card or indicator to ensure that they get the appropriate meals. Do not rely on the waitstaff to ensure proper delivery by memory. In even the best restaurants or banquet facilities, there are often variables that leave room for error (language barriers, guests who switch seats without telling the host, guests who are "no-shows"). Not only might a guest be offended that his dietary choice was not delivered, but also food allergies can be serious and life-threatening.*
>
> —Amy Suess-Garcia, senior director of global customer service,
> Taylor Company

There is more on name cards and seating charts in the next section. For more on table etiquette and protocol, read *The Art of Professional Connections: Dining Strategies for Building and Sustaining Business Relationships.*

Posture When Seated at the Table

 Tip: Good posture at the table dictates that you should be seated upright (not scrunched over) one hand's

width or one hand's length (preferred) from the edge
of the table.

Lean forward slightly when taking a bite, but do not lean into
the plate. Elbows should be off the table when food is present.
Good posture, when sitting and standing, exudes presence and
conveys confidence.

Ambience and comfort are everything!

HIRING CATERERS VERSUS CATERING YOURSELF

To eat is a necessity, but to eat intelligently is an art.
—La Rochefoucauld

All events include some type of food preparation and service. It is important to communicate how food and beverages will be handled. People need to know whether or not they should eat a hearty meal beforehand, because only light hors d'oeuvres will be offered, or come hungry because a buffet is planned.

The type of food service you are arranging should be made very clear.

 You have many choices:

- Evening hors d'oeuvres
- Butler passed hors d'oeuvres*
- Cocktail buffet
- Brunch buffet
- Lunch or dinner buffet
- Lunch or dinner service
- Outdoor buffet (e.g., an outdoor barbeque)

*A *butler pass* refers to a selection of food (or hors d'oeuvres) carried on a tray by the server (referred to as the butler). Each guest is offered a bite-size selection from the tray and either eats it immediately or places it on their cocktail plate. Typically there are several "butlers" circulating the reception room with different bite-size food selections.

The timing and coordination of the meal service needs to be discussed with the event planner and catering (or food) service personnel. Determine the food and beverages for breaks, as well as the number of courses for lunch or dinner, based on the amount of time you have for the meal. Your catering staff will take care of service. Here is an example:

- *Registration:* Thirty minutes to one hour before event begins
- *Between workshops:* Fifteen to twenty minutes
- *During workshops:* Ten to fifteen minutes
- *Luncheon:* Allow ninety minutes to two hours (three courses)
- *Dinner:* Allow two to three hours (four to five courses)

Selecting and Working with Catering Professionals

Larry P. Canepa is a certified culinary educator and the director of training and development, Dinner at Eight. Larry offers the following guidelines, considerations, and experiences when selecting and working with catering professionals.

Food and beverages at an event are best left to a professional catering staff. The trick is finding the right one for your needs. Caterers and their staff are part of the food service industry and must follow the same food and beverage laws.

Some refer to "caterers" as individuals who serve food with a waiting staff at dining tables or set up a self-serve buffet. The food may be prepared on site or delivered prepared; the caterers simply need to add the finishing touches once it arrives.

The trend for professional event caterers is to satisfy all the senses (taste, smell, sight, and possibly touch), with food being the focal point. This involves paying close attention to the atmosphere (decorations and ambience) and making the event special and memorable. Oftentimes this includes "action stations" for such customized services as pasta preparation, meat carving, specialty coffees, and flambé desserts.

Self-Catering Tips

If you are taking care of the food and beverage needs, the following tips will help you with your planning. When selecting appetizers before a meal, make sure the flavors of the appetizers do not conflict with the flavors of the meal. Replenish periodically. If hors d'oeuvres are passed (e.g., "butler pass" style), three or four passed items are appropriate for a one-hour period prior to a meal. When selecting servers, use the following as a guide:

> *Tip:* **Haydee Pampel**, professional meeting planner, recommends the following:
> - One server per thirty people for passed appetizers
> - One server per forty people for beverages

To keep people moving and interacting, make sure that the food and beverage offerings are located at different stations. This keeps people in motion, thereby facilitating better conversation. If the meal will be hosted in your home, realize that people will gravitate toward the food, so showcase your home and keep the guests in the socializing areas rather than the food preparation area.

Cold selections, hot selections, and desserts should be located at three different stations. The beverage stations should be on opposite sides of the room. You might consider having easy-pour selections such as wine, beer, and sodas at one station and mixed drinks at the other. This way the time it takes to prepare a mixed drink is not holding up the line for easy-pour selections.

Larry's "Catering Missteps" Scenarios for Home or Office Cafeteria Entertaining

Chef Larry Canepa has been a professional caterer for over thirty years and has endless stories to share. The following are his favorites. Whether you have hired a caterer or you are catering your own event or party, the following real-life examples illustrate how to ensure a successful event by derailing the same mistakes.

Issue: Momentous Minutiae: Missing Frill Picks

How It Happened: Little things can have a big impact, whether you are using a professional caterer or event planner or doing the majority of the work yourself. Candles, the choice of music, cocktail napkin quality, frill picks, and serving tongs and spoons can make a big difference. I remember a cocktail party when the hostess was providing the appetizers, and she was serving cocktail wieners in a grape-jelly sauce (yes, that dish!), and she forgot to buy frill picks. All she had was minted toothpicks in wrappers from her last takeaway dinner. Mint-flavored is okay for toothpaste but would have ruined the cocktail wieners. Fortunately, I had a container of frill picks in my van.

Moral of the Story: Keep a container of toothpicks as part of your party supplies (e.g., plates, utensils, glassware, frill picks).

Issue: Table Transgressions

How It Happened: What do you do if more guests arrive than you planned for? What happens if your best estimates for food (or worse, beverages) are not accurate and you run out of wine or food? It is a caterer's worst nightmare. The best advice that I have gained from years in the restaurant business is that code "86" (running out of an item) is *not* an option when you are catering. Do not under-prepare. The margins are high on catering, so plan ahead and always prepare 10 to 20 percent more than you expect or are guaranteed by the final guest count.

Moral of the Story: You may be eating leftover food for the next five days at home (or discarding a large amount of food), but it's unforgiveable to run out. Plus, it's just bad business and bad planning.

Issue: Ill-Mannered, Intoxicated, and Discourteous Guests

How It Happened: Guests occasionally have very definite opinions about food and wine and can inadvertently insult the host without even realizing what they are saying. I remember a situation when a customer wanted to serve a birthday cake from Costco, and the guests had nothing but bad comments about how inexpensive the cake was. If the hostess had hidden the cake box, no one would have known. Furthermore, there is no reason to apologize for a Costco cake. Good value, good taste.

Moral of the Story: Hide the store-bought cake box. It is your secret.

Issue: Environmental Apathy

How It Happened: Everything matters when hosting a party. My mantra is, "You never know what one detail will make the experience special." Check the outside surroundings, including walkways, plants, garden hoses, planter boxes, and outside lights. Inside, make sure that the lights, bath tissue, hand towels, and music are set for the party. And take out the garbage before the guests arrive. Good caterers will offer to take out the trash at the end of the party. It's unexpected, and it makes a good impression.

Moral of the Story: Leave the home cleaner than you found it when you arrived.

Issue: Menu Missteps

How It Happened: Food allergies, preferences, and restricted diets are all common today, and you should always plan for such an occasion. How? Stay flexible, communicate with the hostess, and be hospitable. Hiring staff that has knowledge of front-of-house operations and back-of-house cooking skills will definitely come in handy in a situation like this.

Moral of the Story: There will always be menu missteps, but communicating with the hostess long before the event can diminish the possibility of a menu misstep turning into a menu disaster.

Issue: Service Stumbles

How It Happened: Seamless service in a guest's home is a sign of a good caterer, but accidents will happen. How a caterer or host reacts is more important than the actual accident. Don't panic. It's just a glass of red wine. I remember one event when the hostess tried to open a bottle of red wine just fifteen minutes before the guests were scheduled to arrive, and the cork broke, and the bottle slipped and fell to the floor, splashing all over her newly cleaned white carpet. She was so proud of the new carpet that she nearly freaked out. She started sobbing and was going to really lose control. I quickly grabbed some soda water and towels, and in just five minutes the stain was removed from the carpet; no one was the wiser, and the event went off seamlessly and gracefully.

Moral of the Story: Always have soda water and extra dry towels available, stay calm, and act quickly.

Issue: Vacant Verbiage

How It Happened: "Elegant." "Local." "Natural." "Fresh." All these expressions carry a lot of baggage in today's food language. Once, a guest wanted to use her own china for a special event. It's rare that a person has a complete service for a hundred people, and besides, offering quality serving ware is just easier and adds value to the service. This time, the guest's "special china" was Corelle Ware that her grandmother left her in her will. It was plain, felt cheap, and included many mismatched pieces. There was not enough of any single pattern, and it made the event look cheap. Make sure that the language you use is clear to your guests and service personnel, and vice versa. Miscommunication can be disastrous in planning an event. Discuss all details, no matter how insignificant. It shows professionalism, adds value, and avoids mistakes.

Moral of the Story: If you are using your own china, whether it's heirloom, antique, or retro, let the caterer know and they will supplement or substitute with their own supplies. (I use quality china, silverware, and real glassware for my events, and I offer it to my clients at no charge.)

Issue: Outside Oversights

How It Happened: When planning a party outside, everything and anything can go wrong. And it's usually the wind that creates the worst disturbance. Trying to keep linen on the table, making sure the butane burners don't blow out, and even trying to keep candles lit can be an ordeal. Battery-operated votive candles or tapered candles can be a great investment, as can enclosed candles and a small preparation tent—but bring stakes to secure it. One good gust of wind and the tent can be airborne and gone.

Moral of the Story: In planning any catered event outside or on the patio, make sure to have a backup plan for inclement weather. Lots of party stores sell table clasps, heavy-duty disposable ware, and enclosed chafing dishes. Any good caterer will plan for seasonal weather, but depending on your geographic location, you should always expect the unexpected and plan for the unplanned.

Plan for the expected and for the unexpected!

⑤
LEARNING ENVIRONMENT SEATING OPTIONS

Seating will vary with the type of meeting or event. The ultimate goal is to be sure that the seating arrangements are conducive to both the purpose of the event and the number of attendees or guests. The comfort of all attendees should be respected, and the overall arrangements need to work within the constraints of the room. Based on the level of formality, there are a number of things to consider and specific protocols to honor when setting up a seating arrangement. Consider the following when determining whether to use rectangular, round, or square tables, and classroom, herringbone, or circular seating arrangements:

1. Is it a small meeting of two or three people?

2. Is it a speaker-led training seminar?

3. Is it a conference breakout session?

4. Is it a breakfast, lunch, or dinner program?

5. Will the dinner seating be preassigned with name cards, or will it require open seating?

6. What shape or size of table will be needed?

7. Will the event be held in an auditorium environment?

8. Are there special host or guest seating protocols to be honored?

9. What common nuances or distractions need to be discouraged?

To be effective, there should be a strategy behind every seating arrangement. This section discusses your options.

Interactive to Lecture Focused

A seating arrangement can affect interaction and dynamics. For interactive meetings and events, consider seating arrangements that are circular or has a circular feel. For example, when chairs are positioned in semicircles or chevrons, participants can see each other and experience each other's reactions. This arrangement works best for business meetings and banquet environments. Classroom seating can feel rigid; however, if classroom seating is unavoidable, make sure that you have interactive activities allowing the participants to connect periodically.

SEATING OPTIONS

Herringbone or Chevron

Tables and chairs are angled to create a feeling of a circle \\ //.

Audience-Centered Seating

The seating is curved to face the podium. If possible, avoid creating a center aisle. To accomplish this seating, flare aisles forty-five degrees off the end of the podium. Face each chair directly toward the podium.

Curved Seating (Half-Circle)

Typically the room is shaped in a half-circle and the room is auditorium style, with rows at different levels.

When possible, avoid classroom-seating arrangements (rectangular tables in straight rows) in an interactive learning environment. It limits interaction and is best used in an academic learning environment, such as a lecture, that does not require participant interaction. Participants face the wall or have to look at an angle rather than directly at the podium if they are not seated in the middle rows. Keep in mind that physical discomfort affects a great part of the participants' attention spans if they have to keep turning to listen. Also, make sure that accessing and exiting rows or aisles is not cumbersome or slow.

The use of oblong tables will vary. An oblong table is an extended square or rounded table. Oblong tables work well in formal board meetings or at meetings for a large number of people that only require one large table.

For meals, round table seating is best. However, if there is going to be a presentation during the meal, seat crescent-style. This will keep someone from having his or her back to the presenter's demonstration. Crescent seating means that a table of eight would have two chairs removed. The empty spaces could then be used to stack handouts so that place settings are not disturbed.

When setting up a business office meeting, the seating is more strategic. If there is a guest of honor (e.g., a client), the seating is based on deference. The host seats this individual to his or her right. For banquets, or when meals are served, one event diplomat (or table leader) may be assigned to each table to make sure that introductions are made and interaction takes place.

Keep in mind that participants want and expect to be engaged. This is best accomplished by creating a seating arrangement that is friendly, intimate, and conducive to audience participation. As a courtesy to those who arrive on time, designate the last row or table for late arrivals.

Open to Preassigned Seating and Tables

Upon arrival, check the seating arrangement. It will either be open seating, preassigned seating, or preassigned tables. All three come with their own challenges. Preassigned seating should never be changed, preassigned tables should be honored, and open seating requires certain courtesies to be respected.

For international occasions, try to keep language barriers to a minimum. I was once at an event planner international dinner with open seating. One of our guests arrived later than expected, and the only seat available was at a table where everyone else spoke German, and the latecomer was an English-speaking Canadian. This could have been avoided had we had prearranged seating, reserved a few seats for latecomers, or placed country flags on the tables as part of the centerpieces.

—Amy Suess-Garcia, senior director of global customer service,
Taylor Company

- *Open seating* allows you to sit wherever you select. However, it is to your advantage to be seated at a table of new people. Too often people stay within their comfort zones and sit with people they already know. Unfortunately, this can create a cliquish environment, because the conversation stays among familiar people.

If you are responsible for planning an open-seating event where several members of your company will be present, it is critical that you suggest that members of your company disperse themselves among the guests. It is awkward when host company members "flock" at one table because they are more comfortable sitting with their colleagues than they are networking with guests from other organizations. Not only will this dispersing of hosts make your guests feel more important, it will also create a hospitable image for the company and manifest an important networking atmosphere that will benefit everyone.

—Amy Suess-Garcia, senior director of global customer service,
Taylor Company

- *Preassigned seating* uses name cards and is typically utilized at formal events. Your seat and table assignment will be located at the greeting table in the lobby or at a designated table just outside the dining room, or your name card will already be on the table.

Do not alter the seating assignment. If you have a problem with your seat assignment, speak with the event coordinator. When you arrive at your table at a formal event, it is recommended that you stand behind the chair until the announcement to be seated has been made. Do not disturb the table setting, especially the napkin!

Hours of planning and coordination are spent creating seating arrangements. If you are seen disrupting the arrangement, you are creating a very poor impression for the company and the profession you represent. The seating arrangement is part of the event planning and is designed to bring people together and create new dinner partners.

I have witnessed with dismay a lack of respect or social savvy over seating arrangements. People who have no regard for preplanned seating will take the liberty of moving their dinner name card to another table or collect name cards and recreate the seating arrangement at a table to their liking. This is disruptive to the planning process, unprofessional, and rude to the planners.

—Haydee Pampel, president and CEO, MeetingLink, LLC

Pay attention to the seating arrangement and assignments; it can tell you how the host has arranged each company's hierarchies. You will learn who the VIPs are that you should get to know and who your table partners will be. Seek out people who will not be seated at your table during the mingling time to help you maximize your contacts.

- *Preassigned tables* are typically used for sponsors and VIPs; however, they are also used at general admissions. Always check your table assignment upon arrival, and then select your preferred seat. Never sit at a sponsor table or VIP table unless you are personally invited. This typically happens at sold-out events to fill in a canceled reservation.

When planning preassigned tables or sponsor tables, consider the following:

- If this is an opportunity to network and expand a sponsor's brand, consider having sponsors sit at a VIP seat at each table. Having signage on the table that announces that the table was "sponsored by ABC Company" and filling the table with a mix of attendees will give the sponsor visibility to a wider audience. The disadvantage of having the sponsor's staff sit at the same table is that it limits their networking opportunity with other professionals in the room.

- If this is an opportunity for the sponsor's staff to enjoy the event together, sitting at their designated sponsor table makes sense. This may be the only opportunity that staff members have to interact with each other, if they work at different locations or in different regions.

Careful planning and strategic seating will always add to the success of an event or business meal.

Seating Name Cards

Seating name cards are recommended when you are arranging to seat people who have never met. When creating the seating chart, avoid seating people together who know each other; instead make a strategic seating plan to create new introductions. If this is a business social affair (after five o'clock or on the weekend), avoid seating husbands and wives at the same table. Also, make sure that your arrangement alternates the men and the women.

Seating Charts

If your event is by invitation only or a prepaid event, there may be a seating chart with table and seating assignments. Check in at the seating chart table normally located in the foyer or just outside the dining room before you enter the dining room. Once you find your table, you will find your name card lying on the center of the charger or just above the plate. This is your seat assignment. Do not change the seating arrangement! If there is a problem with your seat selection, resolve it with the event host.

As previously mentioned, name cards are recommended when you are arranging seating for people who have never met. When creating the seating chart, make a strategic seating plan that helps create new relationship opportunities. This can be done by achieving the following:

- Avoid seating husbands and wives at the same table.
- Alternate men and women as much as possible.
- Alternate a young professional with a seasoned professional.
- Alternate domestic with international guests.
- Arrange each table with introverts and extroverts.

If you are creating a seating chart, not only should you consider rank, sponsorships, and other such details, but you should also consider wheelchair accessibility, the left-handed diner, and a large-size individual's comfort. Here are some examples:

Right-Handed/Left-Handed: When assigning seats, try to seat the left-handed diners at the end of the table so that there is no one on their left side. This is typically not an issue when eating continental style; however, it is a concern for diners eating American style.

> *If you are left-handed and the tables are oblong rather than round, it is appropriate to ask another guest who is the same gender and company rank as you to switch places after everyone has been seated. State the reason for your request, and ask if they don't mind. If there is not a guest who is the same rank and gender as you, speak with the event coordinator to see if there are other options. As a general rule, let the host know before the event that you are left-handed so that you may be seated accordingly.*
>
> —Amy Suess-Garcia, senior director of global customer service, Taylor Company

Wheelchair Guests: A guest using a wheelchair will need an open-ended spot or wider area at the table. Remove the chair (or placed a revised sign at the table setting) so that another diner does not mistakenly take this spot, and so that the diner in the wheelchair can find his or her spot quickly and discreetly.

Large-Size Guests: A large-size guest is also going to need special considerations. This is easy to do if the event has assigned seats; however, the host and serving staff will need to be alert when a large-size diner takes his or her seat. Very discreetly, remove the table setting and chair on the left or right side of the diner. Then center the place settings that remain on the left and right side.

Be prepared for last-minute changes. You will have guests who will disagree with the seating arrangement and want to be reseated. Be flexible; it is necessary for the comfort of the guests. For example, some people prefer aisle or end seats. Discreetly make the adjustment or kindly ask someone if they would mind changing seats.

Dietary: If you were handed a place card upon arrival that contains your dietary or religion-based special preparation, it needs to be placed in plain sight for the server. Typically, this is just above the fork on the left side of your plate. Keep in mind that you are served from the left. Having your menu preference card on the left makes it easier for the waitstaff.

Overall, seating should be conducive to the goal of the event or meeting, and it should respect the comfort level of the participants.

Social Events: Gender-Based Seating

In a social setting, especially at private clubs, dining partners typically alternate between men and women; this is known as the "gender rule." In a business setting, the seating arrangement has more to do with rank. However, in a business-related social, when spouses are present, the gender rule typically applies. If it is a formal evening event, be prepared for the seating arrangement to have husbands and wives at separate tables. This is proper protocol and is meant to encourage husbands and wives to meet new people.

In a social or business-related social setting, the men do seat the women. This is not necessary in a business setting. In fact, it can prove awkward for some women, although the intent is to extend a gender-related courtesy. When extended, the courtesy should be honored and accepted by the woman. Typically, this type of seating is the expectation at formal events such as black tie charities or corporate anniversary celebrations. It is also the expectation internationally. Therefore, knowing and practicing the seating protocol is to your social benefit.

In a formal social setting where spouses are present, the gentleman will follow the traditional (social and international) rule of etiquette and seat the woman as follows:

- Upon arrival at the table, everyone stands behind his or her chair until the signal to be seated is presented by the master of ceremonies.

- The gentleman seats the woman on his right.

- The woman walks to the right side of her chair and then in front of her chair.

- The man pulls out the chair, and when the woman feels the edge of the chair tap gently on the back of her leg, she is seated as the gentleman pushes the chair under her.

- Once settled into the chair, the woman can adjust it.

- The gentleman also seats the woman on his left if she does not have a gentleman to her left to seat her.

- He is responsible for the woman on his right and is only responsible for the woman on his left if needed.

- The captain will seat a woman who does not have a gentleman seated to her left to seat her. If the captain is not available, the woman seats herself.

- At the host table the male guest of honor seats the woman host, leaving the man on her left to walk around and seat the woman on the right of the guest of honor. If a woman arrives at the host table before anyone else, she may seat herself, or the captain will seat her.

- When the meal is over, the man will rise to pull out the woman's chair. The woman moves to the right of the chair and leaves the chair to the right. The man then pushes the chair back under the table before leaving the table.

This gesture adds an additional touch of elegance to the event. Remember to always take your seat by entering the space to the right of the chair and slide to your left. If you are responsible for your own seating, always push your chair back under the table.

(Private and small-group seating suggestions are covered in *The Art of Professional Connections: Dining Strategies for Building and Sustaining Business Relationships.*)

There are several software seating chart programs on the web. Find the one that best serves your needs.

REMOVING DISTRACTIONS AND POTENTIAL HAZARDS

Former Chicago Bears linebacker Mike Singletary was the key-note speaker at a suburban Chicago chamber of commerce banquet. Just as he was ready to deliver a key point to a personal story he was sharing and the room went silent in anticipation, a cell phone went off—loudly! He lost his train of thought. Being the professional that he is, he moved on, and when he mentally recaptured the point he was going to make, he backtracked slightly and finished the story. Clearly, it could have had a different outcome.

Such an interruption is inexcusable, because we all know better; however, it still happens. As a host or event coordinator, it is your responsibility to make sure that potential distractions are anticipated and eliminated. Consider the following:

Make an Electronic Protocol Announcement: The best time to make an electronic protocol announcement is during the opening ceremony or while introducing the event. This can be done by issuing a statement at the podium similar to the announcements made on airlines or by including a notice in the opening PowerPoint slide show similar to the slide announcement often shown at movie theaters.

Turn Off Cell Phones and Beepers: Cell phones and beepers should be turned off before you reach your event. An exception can be made if you are expecting an emergency call. In this case, make your apology and let your host or clients know that you are expecting an important call. If your beeper is on vibrate, excuse yourself to check the call, but avoid doing this more than once. It is very disruptive to conversations. Apologize and thank your host or clients for their patience when you return.

Handle Medications and Vitamins Privately: Do not open distracting bottles (vitamins or medicine). If you must take medicine or vitamins, do so in private. Bottled pills and vitamins will raise questions as to the status of your health.

Put Away Handheld Computer Devices: Do not interact with your handheld computer devices or cell phones when in the presence of others. This is a time for exercising your social talents; by putting your smartphone first, you risk appearing antisocial or discourteous, and you run the risk of losing a strong potential contact. When the urge to tweet something about the event occurs, be discreet, and do it privately!

Annoying Table Situations

A woman's handbag should be on her lap if it is small or beneath her chair if it is sizeable. Make sure that the strap is under the chair toward your feet and not in the path of the servers. It is also recommended that a woman avoid hanging her shoulder bag on the back of the chair. It could get in the way of other clients, plus it is an open invitation for theft. Protocol dictates that personal items (handbags, glasses, cell phones, gloves, etc.) should never be placed on the table.

While enjoying a cocktail hour with business associates, I placed my shoulder bag under my chair and did not realize that the strap was not completely under the chair. When I went to leave, my shoulder bag was gone! It had been stolen! According to the police, this is the oldest trick of all. The thief only has to slip his foot into the strap and drag it until he can pick it up. I received a ride home by the police and our grounds security had to be called to open my door. The next day the police contacted me that my handbag was found by a couple driving by a forest preserve. Since foul play was suspected, a search started until an officer found me at home ... safe! All because I put my handbag under my chair!

Challenges When Saving Seats

Have you ever attended a luncheon or dinner event only to find a woman's handbag—or an individual's computer tote bag—as your luncheon or dinner partner? To add to the dilemma, you also probably noticed last-minute arrivals walk past this chair looking for a seat and assuming that the handbag signified that the chair was being saved. Unfortunately, this happens at almost all events, business and social. A woman will put her handbag on the chair next to her, or a man will put his computer bag on the chair next to him, as if to create a makeshift desk.

One of the challenges of open seating is the manner in which seats are saved. If it is an open-seating event and someone has placed a personal belonging on a chair in an effort to "save" the seat, do not move the item to another chair. If you are unsure, ask if the chair is being saved. Oftentimes, it is not; it is simply being used for a personal item. (A chair should never be used for personal items!)

Unless there is ample seating, a woman should never use an entire seat for her purse, nor should she place a large purse on a table. As an event planner, I have often been short of seats because a lady needed one for her pocketbook. Women guests can help to avoid this. For an evening function, a woman can carry either an evening bag specifically designed to be small enough for her lap or use a portable metal "purse hanger"–these are becoming very popular. Otherwise, it is good to purchase a purse with "feet" (metal prongs positioned at the bottom of a purse so that it can be placed on the floor). When placing the purse on the floor, make sure that the straps are under the table so it does not trip a member of the waitstaff.

—Amy Suess-Garcia, senior director of global customer service,
Taylor Company

Personal items belong under the chair! When an item occupies a chair, it is assumed that the chair is being saved. In fact, the message you are sending is that your personal item is more important than a table guest. Worse yet, you are denying the person sitting next to the handbag a luncheon or dinner partner and the opportunity for networking. This practice makes the violating individual appear self-serving. Is that the message you want to send?

It is ironic. The individuals who should be careful about how they project themselves are the ones most likely to be annoying by how they go about reserving their positions at a function. The only time that it is acceptable to place a personal item on the chair next to you is at a private meal where you are certain the chair will not be occupied (e.g., dinner for two at a four-seated table.) Here are more ways to avoid creating a hazard or an unnecessary detour:

Do not prop up chairs. Another irritating situation is when people prop up their chairs as a way to save their seats. This is dangerous to the servers and other passers-by. Please do not prop up chairs! If you want to save a seat, place a personal item on the chair that you plan to occupy; then put your item under the seat when you are seated.

> *Yes, you guessed it—I have not only stumbled on the leg of a propped-up chair, but I have also snagged my hosiery in the process. I find that this practice occurs most often at conventions or conferences.*

Do not touch napkins or glassware. Do not take a sip of water and then leave the table to mingle with others.

> *At a business luncheon event, I occupied a seat that appeared available. Then a gentleman (or not) came by and let me know that it was his seat because he had taken a sip of the water. (There was no lip imprint on the glass or diminished level of water to serve as a clue.) This was awkward and embarrassing because he actually made me move instead of taking his used glass and asking a server to replace the glass, and then kindly taking another available seat. It is easy to see why this is a good way to lose a potential client. What if I were the potential client or a person of influence? Certainly others at the table noticed this behavior as well.*

All of these incidents lower your level of sophistication in the eyes of other diners, regardless of whether you are attending a high-profile formal event or just a casual gathering.

Other incidents are noted throughout this book and are covered in *The Art of Professional Connections: Dining Strategies for Building and Sustaining Relationships.*

> By removing distractions and potential hazards, you are assuring a successful event.

Chapter 3

INVITATION
FUNDAMENTALS

> If you're invited, *respond.*
>
> If you accept the invitation, *show up.*
>
> Once you arrive, *greet the host, stay, and mingle.*

You have set the foundation and arranged the logistics for your event, whether large or small. Now it is time to take care of the invitations, determine the dress code, and prepare the name tags. It is also important to respect an invitation with a response.

 The objectives of this chapter are . . .

1. To understand the need to carefully determine the guest list and to send out well-conceived invitations;

2. To unravel the confusion around the various dress codes we encounter and distinguish between business casual, formal and black tie; and

3. To create name tags that accurately reflects people's names and titles.

A successful event depends on everyone's consideration, regardless of the type of event or party. Realize that any lack of consideration is remembered and shared. It is in poor taste and extremely inconsiderate not to respond to an invitation. In some situations, records are kept of those who do not respond and then show up or those who respond in the affirmative and then do not attend. Because the caterer's fee is based on the number of responses, the final count is normally given three days to five days before the event. This is why you must respond and, if your plans change and you cannot attend, it is your duty to notify the hosts or planner immediately.

A division of a large Fortune 500 international trucking company decided to move forward with its annual holiday dinner during a time of huge budget cuts. They felt that their employees still

> needed to feel appreciated. They sent out eighty invitations to employees and a few area customers. The invitation stated "Regrets Only."
>
> Since only a few sent in their regrets, the division event planners moved forward with seventy-five meals. Then only around twenty-five people showed up! This was not only an embarrassment for the company, but also a huge cost. They were responsible for paying for all seventy-five meals ordered—most of which were wasted and had to be discarded. Clearly, the employees who did not send their regrets and failed to show up showed very little respect or appreciation for their employer. Furthermore, the company planners have their names on file. Not responding could influence a management decision or career opportunity.

Perhaps each person simply thought "what is one less person?" It is never about one less person when fifty people are thinking the same way. Not showing up may have been an employee's way of messaging discontent with a company decision. Thinking this way is definitely a career-breaker!

Job Hopping to Party Hopping

Too many people not only "job hop," they also "party hop." Perhaps this is why companies are discouraged from putting time, money, and energy into planning an appreciation party or sponsor an event.

Because people's personal life and professional agenda are heavily scheduled, invitations are just not taken as seriously anymore. It is almost as if people are awaiting a better offer—this is especially true around the holidays. Sometimes they wait and do not respond, or they forget to respond, and then they show up anyway, assuming that the host knows they are coming or that it is okay. This is rude and inconsiderate by anyone's standards.

Needless to say, the following attitudes or habits ruin things for others:

- Ignore the invitation because you are unhappy about a company or management decision or because you have an issue with someone.

- Wait to confirm until the morning of the event—afraid to commit because something better might come up.

- Just show up after not responding to an invitation.

- Call to confirm your attendance and then not show up.

- Bring uninvited guests.

- Arrive at the end of a party or event and then stay beyond the designated time.

- Only attend for a brief moment because you are trying to cram several events into one evening, or call to say you are busy but will "stop by" for a minute.

If you are one of these people, you are noticed, and your career could suffer as a consequence. In fact, rudeness also gets posted on social media. It is just not worth the damage it causes, and it is almost impossible to reverse when it goes viral.

Invitation Considerations

Sending an invitation has never been more challenging. The variety of invitations seems endless, and the styles range from very casual to extremely formal. It is easy to make a formal invitation too casual and a casual invitation too formal. Furthermore, it is very difficult to offer a step-by-step guide for preparing a guest list, handling invitations, determining the dress code, and taking care of arrival details (e.g., name tags) when there are so many variations.

When planning your invitation, adjust the language of your announcements and invitations, and their sequence, to the type of party or event that you are organizing. By paying attention to the detail involved in developing the invitation and also demonstrating a high level of respect for other people's time and effort, you communicate an impressive work ethic and strong people skills.

 Frequently Asked Questions

- Should the invitation be sent by postal mail, e-mail, or fax, or verbally extended?
- Should I state how to dress and assume that everyone will know?
- What if there is a personality conflict among some of the invitees?
- How are invitations addressed to couples who do not share the same last name?
- Plans change. Can I attend at the last minute or cancel at the last minute?
- Is it rude not to accept or reciprocate an invitation?
- As guest, how do I find out the dress expectation?
- Should name badges have first and last names?

These questions will be addressed throughout this chapter. The suggestions in this chapter are designed to serve as guidelines, but realize that the more formal the event, the more protocol is involved and the more respect they should be given. Just follow the guidelines set forth and then relax, knowing that you are covering all the details and considering every option.

> Don't overlook asking for additional advice or insight from experienced planners.

EXTENDING AND RESPONDING TO INVITATIONS

"Eighty percent of success is showing up."
–Woody Allen, Actor

An invitation can blend both business and social agendas, and responses are necessary and expected for any type of event. When you are extended an invitation, the host wants you to be a part of the celebration or event. Sometimes an invitation represents an expression of thanks for your business and friendship. Whichever the case, consider the invitation an honor. As the guest, honor the invitation with a response.

Host and Guest Invitation Responsibilities	
1. Determine the Type of Invitations	5. Check Your Calendar and Respond
2. Components of the Invitation	6. Declining the Invitation
3. Note the Dress Code and Type of Event	7. Cancellation Obligation
	8. When Plans Change
4. Determining the Guest List and Personality Mix	9. Respecting Deadlines
	10. Reciprocating an Invitation

1. *Determine the Type of Invitation (Postal/Evite/Verbal)*
You can send (or receive) an invitation in several forms. Much depends on your budget, your need to control the list, and your time commitment.

Postal Mail:
If you need to keep your invitation list private, then postal mailed invitations are recommended. A mailed invitation

can be as simple as a store-bought invitation with card and envelope and the basic information (e.g., type of event, date, time, place). Or it can be an engraved invitation to a formal event. The upside is that a postal mailed invitation is more reliable than an emailed invite. The downside is the postage cost and the time it takes to create, address, and send. However, for a more formal or private affair this extra expense of time and money is well worth it. (There is more in the next section covering formal events.)

Online Invitations:
Busy times and schedules create the need to take shortcuts with invitations. There are numerous ways to extend an invitation online, from social media announcements (e.g., Facebook, LinkedIn, Twitter) to Evite templates. While a traditional invitation stamped and mailed in an envelope is more personal, online invitations from sites like Evite.com have become an accepted alternative for casual invitations.

Online invitations are used heavily for product line announcements or grand openings; more and more charities are using them because they are cost-friendly. As the recipient, do not ignore an online invitation. Make sure that you understand the event and whether or not it involves an important business connection or charity that you support.

An Evite invitation will appear on your computer screen in an envelope that you click on to open. One of the wonderful advantages of some electronic invitations is that they are so sophisticated; they often allow you to see an updated invitation list daily, along with comments made by the invitees. Once you sign in, your name is added as a yes, no, or maybe on the attendance list. The host can see which recipients have not opened the e-mail and can then follow up with another e-mail message or even a phone call. An Evite invitation also allows the guests to view which essential items need to be brought to the party.

Sometimes, perhaps because of the casualness of a mass-mailing online invitation and the volume of people on the list, it is not necessary to respond. In these cases the sender is more concerned with "accept" responses, for the benefit of others. If the event will be held at a food establishment, the organizer may have arranged for menus and an open bar; then a food and beverage count is not a concern. Everyone takes care of his or her own food and beverage desires.

The downsides of mass-mailing online invitations are that the guest list might deter someone from attending, if there is a personality conflict, or that people may show up who did not respond to the invitation. Plus, the invitation can be forwarded to people you did not invite. It can get totally out of control!

An invitation sent to a business e-mail address should be just that—a business activity! If the event is casual, online invitations are often appropriate. While online invitations and thank-you notes have become more acceptable lately, they still should not be used in formal situations. While they are appropriate for coworkers or casual acquaintances, online invitations are not the most impressive option for a corporate list of high-ranking individuals.

More and more company-sponsored events are using online invitations because of budget and time concerns. While electronic invitations have been viewed as an answer to this dilemma, they are not 100 percent reliable. Because of the continuing problem with spam and other unwanted e-mail, companies are setting up stronger and stronger blocks and filters. Your invitation may simply not get through; it may get deleted as non-business e-mail or automatically filtered to the spam file. If it is an important event, postal mail invitations are much more reliable and appreciated.

Some hosts use websites such as MyRSVPLive. com (popular with weddings and anniversary parties) so guests can reply from a telephone or computer. This style of response initially was only used for casual invitations; however, formal events are now offering online options to make it easier for their guests to respond. Guests can select meal choices, see the number of guests attending, and leave personal responses that can be saved on a CD.

Verbal:

Verbal invitations are typically used when the event is a gathering of business associates, coworkers, or a select group of business and social friends. You still need to include who, what, when, where, and why, as well as dress code. For example, you might say this:

> The *(who)* marketing department is meeting for a *(what)* game of foosball at *(when)* 6:30 PM next Wednesday the second at the *(where)* Continental Club on State Street to *(why)* unwind, relax, and enjoy. Dress is casual. Box lunches available for $5.00 or bring your own brown-bag lunch.

In this instance, you are relying on everyone's memory. It is always a good idea, however, to follow up a verbal invitation with an e-mailed or faxed reminder the day before the lunch or activity. Simply say, "Just a note to let you know our reservations are for (indicate date, location, and time). If reservations and directions are needed, ask."

Never verbally invite or confirm an invitation to someone in the presence of someone you are not inviting (or who was not invited); even if you know that his or her schedule would not allow attendance. This is rude and creates a very awkward moment.

2. *Components of the Invitation*

Your invitation needs to include the following basic seven things:

1. Host or sponsor

2. Type of party or event

3. Date

4. Time*

5. Location/address

6. Response instructions

7. Attire (casual or formal)

(Also refer to the "Five W's" in chapter 1.)

*Invitations typically have specified time frames (7:00 PM to 11:00 PM) unless you make them open-ended (e.g., 7:00 PM to?). If you want your event to conclude at a specific time, it needs to be noted. If you have a wet bar (open bar), give instructions for a "last call" thirty minutes before the evening concludes. This gives individuals with beverages time to finish; otherwise, you may have people lingering beyond the ending time because they wish to finish their drinks.

The length of time mentioned in a reception invitation is usually based on a flexible time frame and the fact that guests will come and go (e.g., an open house). If the invitation states 4:30 PM to 7:30 PM, it means that you must arrive no earlier than 4:30 and stay no later than 7:30. It also means to plan a stay of one hour to one and a half hours. It does not necessarily mean to arrive at 4:30 and stay until 7:30. The exception to this rule is a reception that precedes a dinner or theater event. (More on receptions is covered in *The Art of Professional Connections: Dining Strategies for Building and Sustaining Business Relationships.*)

3. *Note the Dress Code and Type of Event*

As you prepare your invitation, be certain to define the dress code. This is probably the one area that causes the most confusion, because everyone's interpretation varies. If your invitation states formal or semiformal, specify business suits or black tie. If your invitation states business casual, be prepared to describe business casual when asked. For example, do you mean jeans and a T-shirt or a golf shirt and khakis? Avoid making up new names for casual dress. It just confuses everyone. (For guidance, refer to *"Unraveling the What to Wear Dilemma"* in this chapter.)

When extending an invitation, be clear. Will it be for cocktails, a cocktail buffet, dinner buffet, sit-down dinner, outdoor barbecue, or casual or formal luncheon, for instance? People need to know if they should eat a hearty meal beforehand or come hungry.

4. *Determining the Guest List and Personality Mix*

How well does everyone know each other? The personality mix is crucial to the success of any gathering. It is your responsibility to ensure that your guests are getting to know each other. It is the guests' responsibility to make an effort to mix and mingle. This is not an easy task for shy or introverted people. Always assume that someone is looking for someone to talk to, and be that person. It is so much easier when you take the pressure off yourself by focusing on the comfort of others.

You will have both introverts and extroverts. You might want to assign a "people connector" to help those who are not comfortable mixing and meeting people to become engaged in conversation. (Refer to chapter 1 in *The Art of Professional Connections: Success Strategies for Networking in Person and Online* on how to identify or become a people connector.)

Whenever I create my guest list, I give a great deal of attention to personalities as well as to purpose. If I feel there might be difficulty getting my guests to mix, I invite an individual who is especially good at making people feel at ease and keeps them mingling. I brief this individual on my purpose and intent. And I reward him or her with a special thank-you gift after the party.

If you feel there might be a conflict in personalities or that one person may be upset because a certain other individual was invited, let both parties know that they both have been invited. Avoid surprises! Allow each person an opportunity to decline the invitation or make the adjustment. Do not avoid offering an invitation because of a personality conflict. This could be the perfect opportunity to mend an issue.

5. *Check Your Calendar and Respond*

On the day the invitation is received, check your calendar. Make up your mind, reply promptly, and stick to it. If you have to give a tentative yes or no, ask the host or planner if you can confirm at least one week before the event.

Most importantly, do not ignore the invitation. Decide whether or not *you want* to attend. Your calendar might be open; however, the event might not appeal to you, or you might be uncertain. You still need to offer a professional response. Check to see if the invitation has an RSVP or *Respond by* notation.

RSVP stands for a French phrase, "répondez, s'il vous plaît," which means "please reply." The term is rarely used today, because it is not understood. "Respond By (*date*)" or "Regrets Only" are preferred.

"RSVP" or "Respond By" does **not** imply "optional." Much to the dismay of many, responding to an invitation is considered optional and no longer a priority. Some think that the fading RSVP signifies a new etiquette of freedom. For the event organizer, it is considered a nightmare. From casual get-togethers to catered affairs, the once-common act of replying to invitations seems to have become a lost cause; however, the response remains critical for a food and beverage count, and sometimes a minimum count is needed to reserve a private room.

Reply in the same manner in which the invitation was sent (e.g., verbal, e-mail, or postal mail). This is a professional and personal courtesy. Is there a "reply by" date noted on the invitation? If so, respond by that date with a yes or no. Or does it say "regrets only"?

If the invitation reads, "Regrets only," you should notify the host or event planner if you are *not* attending. This is an important responsibility and demonstrates your professionalism and consideration. It does not mean that you do not have to respond.

Furthermore, technology is changing our culture and the way we communicate, which means it is changing the way we connect and disconnect. Why not make life easy for everyone and take the time to respond? Who knows—you might one day be the event planner who is depending on these responses.

Bottom line: Do not leave your host in suspense because you want to wait and see if something more interesting comes up or because you just want to keep your calendar open.

The host needs confirmations not only to determine the food and beverage count but to plan logistics as well. Therefore, your response or your lack of response to an invitation has a direct bearing on the event's success and will have a direct influence on future invitations.

If you are unsure, call and say that you would like to

attend, but you have a conflict. You do not have to give a detailed reason. This courtesy lets the host know that you did receive the invitation, and that you are not simply ignoring it.

 Suggested Scripts

- "I am calling to accept your invitation."
- "I'm sorry, but I will not be able to attend because of a conflict; however, if my commitment changes, I will immediately let you know."
- "Thank you. I will (or will not) be attending."

Respect the invitation if it is addressed only to you or to you and one friend. If you want to bring extra people, make sure that it is okay with the host. Be specific, and do not bring friends at the last minute, even you think if will be okay. Always check!

6. *Declining the Invitation*

If you have to decline an invitation at the last minute, call immediately. This allows the host an opportunity to call someone who may be on a waiting list or to suggest that you send someone in your place, if it is appropriate.

If you are the host and your invitation is declined, do not take it personally. Realize that each individual invitation is in competition with a potentially busy lifestyle.

7. *Cancellation Obligation*

If you accept and something unexpected comes up that causes you to cancel, simply call your host immediately and apologize. Do not just fail to show up. This is rude. If there is a waiting list, your regrets allow someone else to attend.

The acceptable reasons for canceling typically include family emergency, illness, or car problems; however, more often people cite reasons such as not wanting to drive, feeling tired, or having to prepare for an early morning meeting.

Even those who call for directions an hour before the event never appear. Then there are the individuals who arrive after the party has ended, expecting the host to accommodate them. This is rude by anyone's standards but unfortunately has become commonplace. A confirmation that you will be attending, or notice that you cannot attend, demonstrates consideration and is just good business.

If a last-minute problem arises (i.e., on the day of the event) and forces you to cancel or to be delayed, call your host's cell phone or contact his or her office immediately. Make every effort to reach your host. If you are unable to reach your host, call the establishment or restaurant and request that your cancellation or delay is relayed to your host. Apologize briefly upon arrival for being delayed. It is not necessary to go into a lot of detail. If you inconvenienced your host with a long delay or if you were unable to attend, be sure to send a written apology when you return to your office.

If you are canceling a theater engagement, call your host's cell phone or contact the ticket office immediately. If you do arrive late, expect to be instructed to take a back-row seat that has been reserved for late arrivals; then locate your party during the break. Depending on the situation, you may or may not be able to sit with your group.

8. *When Plans Change*
If you declined but your plans have changed and you can now attend, call and ask the host if you may still attend. It is best to communicate your change in plans at least a week before the event. Do not be offended if the host offers his or her regrets and cannot accept your late acceptance; it has to do with seating and food and beverage count. You can, however, ask to be placed on a waiting list.

9. *Respect Deadlines*
Realize that invitations with limited seating have a definite cutoff point. If you have hesitated until the last minute, your

seat may have been filled with someone on a waiting list. If the time to respond has expired and invitations are closed, be courteous and understanding. Request to be put on a waiting list or to be called if a seat does open up, even at the last minute.

If you are the host or event planner, be diplomatic. If you show signs of being abrupt and inflexible to a closed-seat situation, you could ignite a difficult situation. When checking the registration list, ask the food service director (or person in charge) if another seat or plate can be added. If there is a waiting list, ask to be notified if there is a cancellation once the waiting list has been exhausted.

 Be Diplomatic

- **Do not say** the invitation is closed when someone tries to attend at the last minute.
- **Do say** that you will check to see if there was a mistake, or if the invitation was overlooked, or if there might be a last-minute cancellation.

You do not want someone to feel unwanted. Everyone wants to feel important. Your number-one objective should be to make sure that they do feel important. If for some reason they were not invited and they call and ask why they were not included in the invitation list (and some people can be bold), you want them to feel like there was a mistake or that there was an oversight. This does not mean that you have to extend an invitation to them; kindly apologize for the oversight and state that the invitation list is unfortunately closed. Should an opening occur, they will be notified.

10. *Reciprocating an Invitation*
When appropriate, reciprocate an invitation. This does not mean that you have to have a party. An invitation to breakfast, lunch, or dinner for the host is another way of reciprocating. If it was an elaborate party, the invitation should be

to a very nice restaurant. Of course, the best reciprocation is an invitation to a similar event. You do not have to reciprocate every invitation; just the ones that qualify (e.g., you were the guest of your client). Reciprocating an invitation is extending good will and showing appreciation.

If you meet an interesting individual or couple at a friend's or business associate's party and want to invite them to an upcoming party you will be hosting, it is good etiquette to also invite the original host to the same party as a way of showing appreciation. Once that invitation has been honored, it is not necessary to always invite the original host to every party you have. (Reciprocate in kind for one invitation.)

In Summary:
Offer a Courtesy Confirmation

Both host and guest should consider a *courtesy confirmation:* For the host, call or e-mail your guests a few days (three days is appropriate) before the event to confirm the time, location, and other specifics. (If you use e-mail, consider using the *read receipt* in your computer options toolbar to confirm that the message was received.) If you do not get a response, call! For the guest, send a note or make a phone call confirming your attendance within three days of the event. This gesture is a win-win for everyone because it demonstrates follow-through, shows consideration, and expresses appreciation.

> Invitations should be a win-win effort
> between host and guest.

②

PROTOCOL FOR
FORMAL INVITATIONS

Formal affairs require months of planning, and every step in creating the invitation has a defined protocol, because the invitations are very carefully selected, composed, and mailed. Depending on the size of the event, the amount of lead time will vary. The larger the event, the more lead time is required.

Many inconsistent rules or new rules are creating confusion around formal affair invitations, especially with the use of a woman's title (Ms., Miss, or Mrs.) or when an individual has a Ph.D. title (Mr. or Dr.). Taking the time to learn how an invitee prefers to be addressed eliminates offending your invitee. When unsure or unable to learn an invitee's preference, rules always work.

> When a former administration made a large White House guest list for a state dinner, there were many inconsistencies. Most of the confusion resulted from two-career couples, celebrities accompanied by other celebrities, the use of "Ms." versus "Mrs.," and married couples with different last names. Several were offended by these missteps. In part to avoid such confusion, other administrations have kept guest lists small and intimate, which limits the opportunities for social and diplomatic blunders or ego-related guest displeasures.

Whenever possible, avoid using preprinted labels. Also, affix the stamp by hand instead of using a postage meter; this gives it a more personal touch. There are several books on the market that will show you how to address a formal invitation.

Addressing the Invitations

In some situations, it is advisable to include the invitee's profession or position and company. It gets tricky when it comes to married couples with different last names, because "Ms." implies a business professional (or it can also imply a divorced woman). Mrs. implies a married woman and is traditionally attached to the husband's last name.

Married: Traditional Style (spouse's name is put in parenthesis)

> Mr. and Mrs. Jose Smith (Meredith)
> Vice President, ABC Company

Married: Modern Style (spouse's name is listed second)

> Mr. Jose Smith
> Vice President, ABC Company

> Ms. Meredith Smith *(or Mrs. Meredith Smith)*
> Sales Director, XYZ Company

Or (married with different last names)

> Mr. Jose Smith
> Vice President, ABC Company

> Ms. Meredith Sandquist
> Sales Director, XYZ Company

Here are more examples when addressing invitations to couples:

1. When a woman has kept her maiden name, her title is "Ms." The husband's name appears first. Although you will see deviations (e.g., Mrs. Karen Smith), you need to be very careful because the interpretation could be different from what you planned. (For example, in traditional etiquette, the title "Mrs." Karen Smith could imply divorced and continuing to use her previous married name. This is why "Ms." is often preferred.)

   > Mr. John Doe and Ms. Karen Smith

2. If a couple is not married and living together, their names are on separate lines with the invitee's name first, or if both were invited, they are listed alphabetically.

Ms. Karen Anderson *(invitee)*

Mr. William Jones *(guest)*

Formal invitations should include the person's title (i.e., Ms., Mrs., Mr., or Dr.). Casual invitations may use just first name and last name or just the first name.

There is an excellent book, *Protocol: The Complete Handbook of Diplomatic, Official and Social Usage* by Pauline B. Innis which serves as an excellent resource.

Designated Titles

All correspondence should be addressed with an honorific or professional title, but not both. This can be very confusing because there are so many variables. The envelope should be addressed with the designation at the end of the name, which eliminates the title, and the salutation should be addressed with the title. If an individual has a Ph.D., he or she is always addressed with the title "Dr." If the woman has the Ph.D. and the husband does not, they should be addressed as Dr. Jill Jones and Mr. Tim Jones. If both have doctoral degrees, address them as "The Doctors Jones" or "Dr. Tim Jones and Dr. Jill Jones."

 Addressing with Titles

Envelope:	Jose Valdez, MD
Salutation:	Dear Dr. Valdez
Name Card:	Dr. Jose Valdez
Introductions:	Dr. Valdez

If you do not know the title or honorific, address as Jose Valdez.

Addressing other Titles

Accountants:	John Doe, CPA

Lawyers:	John Doe, Esquire
Clergyperson:	The Reverend John Doe
High-Ranking Officials:	The Honorable John Doe

Never put more than three designations after a name.

For example, avoid "Joe Smith, CPA, CMP, CPP, CSP."

"Joe Smith, CPA, CMP, CSP" is sufficient.

(Use the designations that are understood by the industry that you represent.)

Unisex or Androgynous Names

To add to the confusion, we have names that are unisex or androgynous in nature (e.g., "Chris" can be the name of a woman or a man), and international names in which the gender is not understood. If you are unsure, you will need to ask. Make sure that you know the gender of a person, especially if the name is unfamiliar (or unusual), along with the correct pronunciation. This helps with both the invitation and with greeting in person at the event. If you have never met and your only dialogue has been online, imagine your surprise when you actually meet and find that the individual is not the gender you expected.

If you have a non-gendered name, it would be a wonderful courtesy to have your name listed as (Ms.) Chris Jones or (Mr.) Chris Jones This would be an appropriate listing on your business card as well. (The parenthesis is used to offer clarification.)

I know of one young male executive in sales with a non-gendered name, Unri Babb. Before recognizing the need to have his name prefixed with Mr. in his correspondence, he can attest to missing many a business opportunity. Several telephone calls directed to Ms. or Mrs. Babb fell through the cracks, owing to some rather clueless employees taking the calls and indicating that there was "no one in the company by that name.

> *" However, good business sense eventually prevailed. Mr. Babb realized the error of his ways and the importance of this critical etiquette tip to his career (and financial!) success.*
>
> —Lisa James, managing director, Lisa James and Associates

If you are uncertain as to how to address a correspondence because you do not know the gender of the addressee, address the correspondence using the first and last name (e.g., Attention Chris Jones or Dear Chris Jones).

Refer to step 3 in *The Art of Professional Connections: Seven Steps to Impressive Greetings and Confident Interactions* for more tips on titles and unique names.

Sampling of Invitation Styles

The style of the invitation should reflect your theme. All formal invitations should be sent by mail on high-quality business stationery at least six weeks ahead of the event. A reminder card should be sent two to three weeks prior to the event. In some cases, it is recommended to call those who have not responded. Unfortunately, this step has become necessary to ensure a good turnout and an accurate food and beverage count.

Making follow-up calls is extremely time-consuming; therefore, use *reply cards*. If your invitation includes a reply card, respond!

Sample Invitations

RESERVE THE DATE CARD

Please reserve this date

(Date)

For a dinner in honor of

Mr. and Mrs. _____

(Invitation forthcoming)

(Name of Company)

THE INVITATION

(Corporate logo/symbol)
(Name of host)
(Phrasing the invitation) "request the
pleasure of your company"
(Type of party) "Dinner"
(Purpose of party) "To honor ____"
(Date) "Day of the week, Month, Date, Year"
(Time) "Seven o'clock PM CST
(Place)
*(Indicate the following in the
left or right-hand-corner:)*
Respond by: or RSVP: *(phone number)*
Dress Code
Special Instructions *(e.g., parking)*

REMINDER CARD

(Company)
(Address)
(City/State)
(Name, Company, President)
To Remind
Dinner in Honor of ____
Mr. and Mrs.
(Date)
(Time)
(Location)
(Address)
(City/State)
(Telephone)

Sample Invitation for Dignitary or International Guest

(Seal or Logo)

On the occasion of the Birthday Anniversary of

His Majesty King *(complete name)*

The Consul-General of *(country)*

and Mrs. *(wife)*

request the honor of the company of

Dr. (title plus first name and last name)

at a reception

on Saturday, October *(day)*, *(year)*, from *(time)* PM

at the *(name of ballroom)*

(name of hotel or private club)

(street, city/state address)

Dress: Black Tie   Regrets only: *(telephone number)*

It is necessary to follow up written invitations with a phone reminder to guarantee good attendance. As mentioned in the previous section, always put "Please respond" or "RSVP" on the invitation.

For more examples, seek out an invitation print house and ask for samples of their Business Event Invitations and Company Announcements, Invitations and Cards. This should be a company that specializes in business announcements and not wedding announcements.

> **An invitation is a gift.**
> **Always respond and honor your response.**

③
UNRAVELING THE
"WHAT TO WEAR" DILEMMA

There was a time when an invitation was straightforward and stated exactly what to wear, and we understood. Today there is a wide range of casual and formal dress instructions. It is enough to make one decline the invitation! There seems to be a strong need to be as different (or creative) with the dress code as one is with the event theme.

> *As a former personal shopper for Nordstrom, I often encountered these dilemmas when helping a customer put together an ensemble for an event, and I was supposed to know the interpretation of various event dress codes. I found that keeping it simple and within certain parameters worked no matter how different or creative the invitation's dress code.*

Confusion can deter participants or guests. In a time when people are extremely busy making more decisions than they care to ponder, trying to interpret a creative dress invitation may prompt them to avoid your event. Keep it simple and easily understood.

The following guidelines are for business events where your reputation and the reputation of your company are paramount. (Nonbusiness social events will have a different interpretation as to appropriateness.)

Dressing for the Occasion

Noting and interpreting the "dress code" on an invitation used to be simple. It was formal or semiformal. We all knew what each meant. However, with the advent of "business casual" and the desire to be different or creative, new descriptions have emerged.

What exactly do "vintage black tie," "casual chic," or "casual glamor attire" mean? Furthermore, the more relaxed dress code has created a rule-less attitude. If you are an invitee and unsure, just ask, "What does it mean?" or "What should I wear?"

The best advice is to dress to complement the event and to look and feel at ease. Your overall appearance sends a very strong message; it conveys how you feel about your profession and that you feel the event you are attending is important. If you are unsure about what to wear, inquire about the event's dress code; then select attire that will best represent you and your organization.

If you are attending with your spouse or date, be sure that you dress to complement each other. Couples should dress as a team. One wearing cocktail attire or a business suit and the other in khakis (or jeans) and a casual blouse or shirt does not work. You will look like the odd couple.

The host should always include a description of the dress expectation on the invitation (e.g., business casual, sport casual or formal). The dress expectation you select will set the tone for the event. Be prepared to describe what you will be wearing, should the guests inquire.

Do not dress below the level set by the invitation. It is very important to appear in clothing that is appropriate for the occasion. It is insulting if you arrive dressed very casually (e.g., blue jeans or shorts) and the host is dressed formally and has set a very formal tone. Unfortunately, with the advent of casual dress, we are seeing a range of every possible outfit at parties—from jeans to sequins, or jeans with sequined tops—and it has become the norm.

It never ceases to amaze me when I attend a semiformal event or celebration banquet and there is a mixture of jeans with dressy tops (for women) or polo shirts (for men) among cocktail dresses and tuxedos. It definitely confirms the confusion that exists in the interpretation of dress. Therefore, it is important to take the invitation that extra step by defining the dress expectation so that your guests easily understand it.

If you unknowingly arrive underdressed, briefly apologize, and handle yourself confidently. Let your confident posture, positive attitude, and impeccable manners override your casual attire. If you arrive overdressed, briefly comment that you did not realize the event was casual, and focus on being approachable. To avoid appearing stuffy or unapproachable, a gentleman can always remove his jacket and tie to fit in. A woman should make an extra effort to be approachable. (If unsure, and as a precaution, you might put an extra set of clothes in the car just in case you misinterpreted the dress code.)

Deciphering Casual-Dress Confusion

When invitation dress codes get creative, guests get confused; therefore, good judgment is necessary! Depending on the region, season, and theme, you will see a full array of casual dress descriptions; therefore, dressing for casual events requires more thought. As previously mentioned, if you are not sure what is appropriate, ask. Business casual can range from blue jeans and a T-shirt to microfiber trousers and a tab-front shirt with a jacket. What one event considers appropriate attire, another event might consider inappropriate. What is fashionable may not be stylish or appropriate. Again, use good judgment.

If an outdoor activity is planned, carry a refresher kit and a change of clothing. A refresher kit contains travel-size deodorant, mouthwash, and moist hand wipes.

Overall, casual dress should not look sloppy, revealing, or sexy. It should look well thought out and appropriate. Be sure your clothing is pressed, neat, and clean and fits properly. Also, pay attention to your grooming and hygiene. Active, sport, or resort wear implies an outdoor theme or retreat. A spare shirt (or top) is also a good idea. Consider the following popular invitation *dress codes*:

Business Casual or Daytime: For men, business casual implies a sport coat with an open-collar shirt, not a suit and tie. For women, business casual implies slacks, trousers, or casual skirt. Tops are typically tab-front, sleeved, collared T-shirts, classic sweaters, or blouses.

Activewear: This would include any outfit that is a uniform for an activity in which you are participating (e.g., golf or tennis attire). If you are a spectator, wear comfortable outdoor clothing that is not distracting. Walking shorts, jeans, polo shirts, and T-shirts are appropriate, as are jogging clothes.

Sweatsuits are not appropriate. For example, if the invitation reads "jogging apparel," this does not mean sweatsuits. Jogging apparel is a three-piece coordinated outfit normally in a shiny nylon-type fabric. A sweatsuit is a two-piece, long-sleeved sweatshirt with pants in a cotton fabric and commonly worn to the gym.

Sportswear: This is anything that you would typically find in the sportswear department of a store. Tab-front shirts, T-shirts, jeans, slacks, khakis, Capri pants, split skirts, culottes, walking shorts, and sandals or canvas shoes are the norm. Avoid short shorts and bare-midriff styles.

> *Wrong clothes! I have had people show up at the box for an NHL hockey game in short sleeves—we were at an ice rink! At other events, I have been asked for such things as golf shoes or a tie. I do not carry these items in my handbag! It is unfair to expect your host to supply the "extras."*
>
> —Tania Carrière, Advivum, Canada

Upscale Sport: This means designer or "bridge" clothing in coordinated styles. High-quality fabrics, creative design, flawless construction (e.g., the patterns match), and designer labels are very important. This also includes silk turtlenecks or tab-front shirts for men.

Resort Wear: Resort wear gets tricky because it also implies shorts and swimwear. Walking shorts, culottes, sundresses, and Capri pants are the norm. Anything poolside should also include a cover-up or beach jacket, which should be worn poolside when mingling with colleagues and guests. Avoid any swimwear that is too revealing or skimpy (e.g., thong swimwear for women or Speedo swimsuits for men).

To help take the guessing game out of the interpretation, consider the following.

Styles to *avoid* remain the same for all categories:

- T-shirts with offensive artwork or words
- Tops that show cleavage
- Short shorts
- Skimpy, revealing clothing and fabrics
- Hip pants or skirts worn with crop tops (bare midriff or exposed belly button)
- Distracting clothing that is too tight or sexy
- Battered shoes

These are *appropriate* styles for all categories:

- Khaki trousers
- Polo or tab-front shirts
- T-shirts
- Walking shorts, culottes, or skort (mid-thigh or longer)
- Capri pants
- Sarong skirts

Above all, remember that what you wear reflects on your reputation as well as the reputation of your company. This is a business-related event, and you should look approachable, not threatening. Moreover, be aware that this is not a time to show off your body! Mature or conservative clients and guests are very uncomfortable when women wear clothing that is extremely revealing or overly sexy, or when men unbutton their shirts and reveal chest hair.

Dressing for the Opera or Live Theater

The time of the performance has a great influence on the degree of formality in dress. For example, the dressiest occasion at the opera is opening night. Often, formal clothing is required, including gowns for the ladies and dinner jackets for the gentlemen. Saturday night performances normally call for dark suits for men and cocktail dresses or suits for women. For performances on weekday nights, the attire can range from upscale casual (e.g., in New York) to jeans (e.g., in Phoenix). For matinées, the apparel is typically casual.

One's attire should reflect the formality of the environment; for example, jeans do take away from the elegance of the opera. If you want to impress, do not wear jeans when entertaining clients!

Dressing for a Game of Golf

Golf clothing continues to retain a sense of formality that is not the norm in today's casual society. Most clubs maintain a consistent dress code for both the golf course and the clubhouse. If you are uncertain, always check with the golf club where you will be playing.

The polo shirt is the traditional golf shirt and is just as cool and comfortable as a T-shirt, except it has a collar. The general rule here is that men must wear a shirt that has a collar. When wearing long trousers, socks need to match your pants; however, when you wear shorts, the shoe and sock combination should be the same (light shoes with light socks and dark shoes with dark socks). Shorts and slacks should have belt loops.

In women's golf clothing, a sleeveless golf shirt must have a collar, but a sleeved golf shirt does not have to have a collar. Shorts should come down to just above the knee (e.g., walking shorts). Culottes are a popular short option for women.

Apparel to avoid includes T-shirts, jeans, khakis, cut-off shorts, shorts that are too short or too tight, and slacks with cuffs. Overall, common sense is the rule. Visit golf shops for ideas, and talk to the staff for direction on clothing choices and appropriate shoes. Golf clubs can vary somewhat in their rules. Individuality is important, and it needs to be represented in good taste.

Open Dress Code

If the invitation is not clear or makes no mention of attire, always call and ask the host or hostess the level of formality (casual, semiformal, or formal). When in doubt, wear a nice shirt and trousers (for men), or a blouse and a skirt or pants (for women). These ensembles will always fit in. The casualness of blue jeans is appropriate only for very relaxed events.

Posture, Accessories, and Grooming Count!

Proper attire and appearance is the total package. Whatever the event, make sure that you have double-checked every detail.

Posture: Your overall posture should be relaxed, approachable, and confident. Walking and sitting with good posture communicates high self-esteem.

Accessories: Jewelry should be appropriate for the ensemble. Avoid jewelry that makes a lot of noise (bangle bracelets) and over-accessorizing. Over-accessorizing will distract from you.

Shoes: Shoes should be polished and well cared for! If the invitation suggests sport shoes, they should be in good shape. If you plan to wear open-toe shoes or sandals, be sure to have a pedicure.

Grooming: Your impeccable grooming (hair, face, and hands) should be a reflection of the quality person that you are and project your attention to detail. This means that your hair has a fresh style; a woman's makeup has a polished look; men's faces are well shaven or beards are well groomed; and your nails are manicured. Keep fragrances mild so that they do not make someone who is allergic to fragrances uncomfortable.

If you have the habit of brushing your teeth after a meal, use mouthwash instead. It is more dignified when out of the house. Carry a travel-size mouthwash in your handbag or breath strips in your pocket. Your client and colleagues will not be impressed washing his or her hands next to you as you brush your teeth and dispose of your toothpaste.

Be mindful of nose, chin, and ear hair. These little things can be overlooked but should merit a quick check.

Tattoos and Piercings: If the affair is formal and you have tattoos or piercings, try to wear something that covers your tattoos, and eliminate the piercings. You do not want to distract from your elegant apparel. This is very important if you are attending an event on behalf of your company. Image is an important part of a company's reputation.

No matter what creative description the host designates, know how to select the appropriate attire and be well groomed. Business attire will vary from a rural area to a metropolitan city. Realize that a formal event has a higher level of expectation and the rules of formal attire should be honored.

> Wear appropriate attire,
> and remove the risk of feeling
> uncomfortably conspicuous.

INTERPRETING BUSINESS DRESS AND FORMAL ATTIRE

If it's a gala, you have to put on a formal gown.
−Letitia Baldrige, etiquette expert and author

Business dress is most commonly identified for formal events (e.g., live opera) on weeknights. If the invitation says "informal dress," it still implies a coat and tie for men and a tailored suit or a dress for women. After five o'clock PM (or, more formally, six o'clock PM), the woman should wear a very dressy dress or cocktail suit and the man a dark suit and tie.

For men, business or informal dress includes a jacket; however, you will see a deviation from the tie with a silk turtleneck sweater, which is considered an appropriate alternative to the shirt-and-tie combination.

Cocktail attire should include a jacket and tie for men. Women typically wear a dressy-skirted suit (cocktail suit), dressy pantsuit, or knee-length party dress; however, it should be festive, not sexy (avoid low-cut or extremely short clothing).

For women, evening accessories (and possibly a silk or satin blouse) can dress up a daytime tailored suit and take it into the evening. The shoe is a dressy boot or pump, preferably with a closed toe and a heel that is no higher than two and a half inches. Slingbacks are appropriate. Mules and sandaled shoes (open toes) are appropriate as long as they are not too casual looking. Although you will see a trend away from hosiery for women, hosiery is strongly recommended for a more polished look.

The Look of Elegance

It is easy for men: when an invitation calls for "black tie," it means he should wear a tuxedo. But women have many more options. Is a long gown a must, or is a shorter cocktail dress an option? Much will depend on the formality of the invitation and the venue.

The look of elegance in formal attire is never sexy or risqué. It is tasteful and has the look of royalty. "Formal" means that the man wears a suit or tuxedo and the woman wears a gown, cocktail dress, or cocktail suit. This is not the time for a costume (e.g., top hat and cane). Keep it simple, and make it elegant.

> *In the last ten years or so, it has become acceptable for a man to wear a vest as an alternative to the cummerbund. If it is black tie, it is definitely best to wear black, although for holiday events sometimes a little color adds an impressive touch.*
>
> —Patricia Leupp, co-owner, Savvi by Mr. Formal, Phoenix, Arizona

Let the time of the event be your guide to the degree of formality. The dressiest occasion is typically at an evening event, especially on a Friday or Saturday.

Formal Attire Tips

If it is a gala or when in doubt, opt for a gown; however, most fashion experts will advise that a cocktail dress will do just fine. Fabric is key! Consider velvet, lace, and brocade or sparkle with beading, embroidery, or sequins. Although black is the most popular color choice, color (e.g., metallic shades, rich jewel tones, bold fashion colors) shows individuality.

Formalwear is all about elegance. Fabric, fit, and the right design for your personality and body type are critical. Once your dress is selected, your accessories should enhance the dress and not distract or compete with each other. For example, if you select one or two dazzling accessories, then your other pieces should be more understated.

Cocktail Attire: Cocktail attire means suits and ties for men, and street-length (to the knee) or tea-length (to the calf) dresses for women. This now includes dressy pant-suits for women. The fabric complements the occasion. Dresses or pantsuits should be made of silk, satin, or sequined or other dressy fabric. Shoes for women can be open-toe or strappy with a heel.

Black Tie/Tuxedo: This designation is most commonly used for official dinners and evening affairs taking place at six o'clock PM. Black tie for men means a tuxedo. The tuxedo can be accented with a white, colored, or print handkerchief and/or a cummerbund. Military person-nel wear an equivalent uniform. A white dinner jacket is worn in the summer only. Women wear long evening dresses or ball gowns. Gloves for women are optional. Tuxedos can be worn to the theater, opera, ballet, or even an elegant restaurant (four-star or above) as well as black-tie events.

Black Tie Optional: If your invitation reads "black tie optional," this means that you can select between business suit and a tuxedo.

White Tie: This designation is for formal affairs such as balls, dinners, and receptions that take place after 6:00 PM. White tie denotes the wearing of "tails" for men. The man wears a long tailcoat and bow tie. The woman wears a long evening gown (preferably a ball gown). If the gown is strapless, long gloves and/or a shawl add an elegant touch.

Checklist: Formalwear for Men

For men it is easy. To personalize their tuxedos, they only need to change the color scheme of their accessories (e.g., cummerbund, bow tie, braces, handkerchief, vest).

- Tuxedo or all-black dinner suit
- White (plain or pleated) dress shirt
- Black bow tie
- Black braces that button into the waistband (not suspenders that clip onto the waistband)
- Highly polished lace-up black leather shoes or shiny black loafers
- Thin black dress socks
- Cufflinks, no larger than a quarter; the smaller the cufflink, the more elegant the look
- Studs for a tuxedo

Checklist: Formalwear for Women

A good rule of thumb:
The simpler the dress design, the more ornate the accessories.
The more ornate the dress, the simpler the accessories.

- Gown is tea length or floor length
- If appropriate, formal pantsuit with tuxedo styling made of evening fabrics (e.g., satin, crepe, finely woven wool); or palazzo pants in crepe or chiffon
- High heels or pumps that are in excellent shape
- Gloves (optional; see description)
- Shawl (optional; see description)
- Expensive (real gold or gemstones) jewelry or designer costume jewelry

Hosiery

There is much debate on hosiery for women. Fashion dictates

that hosiery is not needed, and you will see runway models and celebrities alike wearing beautiful gowns without hosiery. Hosiery gives the gown a "finished" and elegant look. Most women do not have beautifully tanned legs or varicose-free legs. Hosiery creates the illusion of well-maintained legs and keeps the attention on you instead of your legs. For a pulled-together, elegant look, wear hosiery that matches your skin tone or blends in with the color of your hemline.

Hosiery for men is easier to define. The over the calf sock should blend with the shoe and trouser to create an uninterrupted flow of color (e.g., black hose, block sock, black trouser).

Formalwear Gloves

Gloves with gowns are optional; however, they do add a touch of elegance. Gloves are worn more frequently outside the United States (e.g., European and Latin American countries), so expect them with international guests.

The rule of thumb is the shorter the sleeve, the longer the glove. The idea is to establish the relationship between the sleeve and the glove. If the gown is strapless or sleeveless, the glove is long, to cover the bare arm. For mid-length sleeves, the mid-length glove is used; for long sleeves, the short glove is used. (The eighteen-button glove does not refer to eighteen buttons; it refers to a French measurement.)

Tradition dictates that the glove is always white, but fashion has put a different twist on this with a more modern look that is color-coordinated with the gown or black with dark-colored gowns.

> Rings are worn inside the glove;
> bracelets are worn on the outside.

The right-hand glove should be removed when shaking hands at receiving lines. Gloves are kept on while dancing. Always remove gloves while eating or drinking. While eating, place the gloves on your lap and fold your napkin on top and around the gloves to form a small, soft package. If you are only using the right or left hand when drinking, remove only that glove; or open the buttons on an eighteen-button glove and tuck the hand part of the glove into the back of the glove to form a pouch (this was the original intended purpose and style). This allows the glove to remain on while eating.

To remove gloves, start by slowly tugging gently at the fingers to loosen them one at a time. Then push the glove along the arm, first from the wrist, and then below the elbow. The removal should involve a slow, dramatic touch.

Shawl

A shawl offers a look of pure luxury for a radiant presence; a shawl creates a sophisticated impression and adds a touch of class to a strapless gown. It is an elegant wrap worn around the shoulders and sometimes the head for added style. The fabric is typically lace, velveteen, or satin. The popular pashmina is made of cashmere or a cashmere blend, which is known for its unmistakable softness and elegance. There are many varieties of shawls.

A shawl is a must for a strapless gown, especially when seated at a formal dining-room table. You do not want to appear "naked." This is especially a concern if you are a short woman. Shawls also add comfort in air-conditioned rooms.

> A *triangular* shawl can rest on the shoulders or wrap around the forearms. A *rectangular* shawl typically rests on the forearms. Both loop around to the front and are anchored next to the side of the body, just above the elbows.

A large, square scarf can be worn as a shawl simply by folding it into a triangle and resting it across the back of the shoulders and neck, wearing it around the shoulders in a symmetrical fashion, with the pointed ends draping down the front of the gown; or it can be worn in an asymmetrical fashion, centered and draped down one shoulder of the gown with the ends draped around the other shoulder.

Elegance Deserves Elegance

⑤

CREATING NAME TAGS, BADGES, AND SECURITY PASSES

Your invitation list has been completed, invitations have been mailed or circulated, and you have received your responses, now it is time to determine whether or not you will be using name tags or name tents, and the type of security that will be needed. This is also a time to be sure names have been spelled correctly and titles have been confirmed.

Whenever you bring people together who have not met, it is very helpful to have name badges or name tents. Name tags or badges can be color-coded to distinguish attendees, exhibitors, or members of the media. High-level sponsors may also be provided with a special form of visibility on name tags or lanyards. This color or design coding will help you to identify different classifications of people or groups at a large event such as a conference or convention.

Take your cue from the invitation when making out the name tags or badges. If the invitation is to a casual gathering, first names will probably be the norm. If the invitation is formal, first and last names will be important on the name badge.

Personal Identification: Name Tags and Badges

Name tags help initiate an immediate conversation. The most effective way to do this is to attach the name tag or badge to the upper right shoulder area so that you can discreetly see the individual's name as you shake hands. Make sure that you are wearing a jacket or a garment made of a fabric than can handle the pin or clip without damaging the fabric (avoid silk and other delicate fabrics). Magnetic name tags are another option because they do not pierce the fabric; however, the fabric cannot be thick or the magnets will not make contact.

> *Wearing a customized name tag rather than the paper one that is supplied at some events is more impressive. Why? It will look more professional, and you will be assured that your first and last name and your company name will be legible on the tag. If you do bring your own name tag, make sure you pick up your tag from the registration desk too so you do not look like a no-show; then discard it.*
>
> *–Diane Roundy, director of business development, Schenck*

Do not remove the name tag and insert your business card into the name card holder; business cards are very difficult to read as name tags, and you will risk coming across like a self-serving billboard.

If you are required to write your own name tag, place first and last name on separate lines. If the event is casual, place the first name in large, bold letters on the first line and the last name in smaller letters on the second line. If the event is formal, reverse the sequence by having your last name (on the second line) larger and bolder. The name of the company can be placed at the bottom.

For computer-generated name tags or badges, consider using different font sizes. Place the first and last names on separate lines. If it is a casual event, make the first name bold, or put it in all caps; but if it is a formal event, make the last name bold, and put it in all caps. This lets everyone know how you prefer to be addressed and communicates the level of formality. Adding the company name and department or title in small print under the name is also very helpful, especially if the event includes people from various states, regions, or countries.

Casual: Refer to as "John"

JOHN

Smith

Account Executive

ABC Company

Formal: Refer to as "Mr. Smith"

John

SMITH

Account Executive

ABC Company

If the event includes international guests, find out which part of the name is the family name and put it in all capital letters, bold or underlined. In some countries, the family name comes first or is the middle name, unlike American names in which the family name is always last. For example:

Spanish

Paulo VALDEZ Martinez
Referred to as Mr. Valdez

Portuguese

Juan Mendes GARCIA
Referred to as Mr. Garcia

For a business social event with spouses present, use the following "two line name tag" example as a guide. This will help people make the connection, especially if a married couple has different last names.

Two Line Name Tags

	Same last name	Different last name
Spouse:	**Jane Smith**	**David Smith**
Employee:	(John)	(Mary Cohen)

Employee:	**John Smith**	**Mary Cohen**
Spouse:	(Jane)	(David Smith)

(Bold or make the first line name slightly larger)

Name tags or badges can be tacky-looking on formal attire. You may want to consider eliminating name tags. In this case, consider making a copy of the guest list available so that guests can familiarize themselves with everyone's name. Then, when you or your guests meet someone new, the name is already in your memory. You are simply putting a face to the name. This will make it easier to remember the individual throughout the event.

If you are a speaker, remove your name tag before going to the podium. Also remove your name tag during a photo session. It looks tacky!

> *An image that has never left me is one of Jacqueline Kennedy on the cover of a leading business magazine back in the 1980s. She had a name tag on and I thought "how ridiculous." Who asked this woman of distinction to wear a name tag? And why didn't the photographer ask her to remove it for the photo? This was many years ago, but the visual and the name of the magazine stuck!*

Famous people do not need name tags! If you have a speaker or guest who is well known, it is not necessary to identify him or her with a name tag.

Name Tents

Name tents are typically used at meetings. Be sure to put the first and last name of each person on both sides of the name tent. This will avoid someone inadvertently turning his or her name tent to face him or herself. (Best practice is to have your first and last names on separate lines.) It is important that the name tents face outward. They are for the purpose of helping others remember you. If the seating arrangement changes, be sure to take your name tent with you.

ID Lanyard

ID lanyards serve as security identification tags and event passes. These ID name tags are hung like a necklace on a long rope made from a tightly woven polyester ribbon, rope cord, or polyester tube, or they are clipped to your jacket or shirt pocket.

If your ID lanyard is also to serve as your name tag, consider shortening the strap so your name tag sits just below the collarbone to avoid the awkwardness of having to look down to catch someone's name as you make your introduction. Having to look "down" is awkward because you do not want to risk a misinterpretation of the gesture!

Events Without Name Tags

If name tags are not going to be used, arrange for "introducers" or "mixers." These are people whose primary function is to make sure that people are meeting and mixing comfortably. They are excellent with names and remembering people. They can also serve as a resource if you forget the name of someone you have met earlier in the evening.

> Name tags make it easy for people to connect!
> They should be easy to read, and they should be appropriate.

Chapter 4
ENGAGING ASSISTANCE AND IDENTIFYING DUTIES

> ### Experienced People + Special Touches = A Memorable Experience

The planner (or host) of a business event is often a jack of all trades; however, this can be mindboggling when planning large events. Sometimes it is best not to take on all the responsibilities yourself, but instead to assign the positions of concierge, introducer, master of ceremonies, and receiving line organizer to someone within your team or to a professional of that capacity or experience. And the larger the event, the greater the need to have an experienced team of specialty positions on your side.

 The objectives of this chapter are . . .

1. To introduce you to the need for specialty positions at large events and show you how to fill those positions and perform their functions;

2. To provide you with a blueprint for becoming a gracious host or an impeccable guest by avoiding common faux pas; and

3. To offer tips for accommodating participants such as spouses and individuals with special needs.

Whether the event is small or large, the host and guest are partners; both are responsible for the success of any party or other event. Just as the host has distinct responsibilities to be sure a party or event runs smoothly, the guest is responsible for complimenting the host's effort. People love to be invited for a good time, to be pampered and to feel the rewarding and encouraging side of doing business. A lot of time and money is spent on planning, offering, and debriefing events. It needs to be a win-win situation for everyone involved.

This section will outline specific duties of everyone from concierge and master of ceremonies to host and guest.

HOW TO BE A CORPORATE OR PERSONAL CONCIERGE

Concierge (con-cierge) is a word that evolved from a French term meaning "keeper of the candles." During the Middle Ages, this person catered to the whims of visiting nobles, was in charge of a building, and was the owner's representative or caretaker.

Concierges are problem solvers. Their motto is to say *no* with a *yes*, and that is exactly what gives a concierge value. This "aim to please" attitude enhances the enjoyment of any visit.

Not all companies have event-planning departments, yet planning events is still an important part of a company's image. Therefore, as a public relations gesture, it is advantageous to assign an individual to serve as a corporate (or personal) concierge.

 Attributes of an Exceptional Concierge

☑ Is detailed-oriented.

☑ Has an in-depth knowledge of a city (and company).

☑ Has well-cultivated contacts for acquiring restaurant reservations and booking theater tickets.

☑ Is a good listener and never second-guesses a request.

☑ Asks questions to learn needs.

☑ Specializes in being a problem solver.

☑ Handles unusual requests, providing they are ethical and legal.

☑ Demonstrates great people skills.

☑ Has a great deal of patience.

☑ Maintains a friendly smile.

☑ Excels at pronouncing and remembering names and titles.

☑ Knows the community and company personnel.

Although concierges are typically associated with hotels, they are certainly not limited to positions at hotels. Today, the average person has access to much the same information as a concierge, through the Internet, newspapers, and local magazines; however, it takes in-depth knowledge of a city and well-cultivated contacts to truly serve as a concierge. If you have ever utilized the services of a hotel concierge, you understand how they work.

Take your cues from the hotel industry. Hotel concierges handle every special need that a guest may have, from room reservations to securing tickets to events, and from making restaurant reservations to serving as tour guides. A concierge can also be described as a travel agent, personal assistant, or counselor. Their goal is to make an experience as pleasant and memorable as possible. If a room, restaurant, or theater reservation is an issue, the concierge will provide the guest an alternative option. A concierge always has a can-do attitude.

> *Visitors and business people love having a place to go while in town. With the assistance of a concierge, I got a pair of tickets for a show in San Diego and was open to going to it by myself. It was a nice outing for me and was totally unexpected.*
> —Neelum Aggarwal, associate professor of neurology, Rush University Medical Center

Offer or serve as a personal concierge to your guests or clients by helping them with details that are outside your planned activities. Everything you do to make their visit memorable will be profitable for you.

A designated concierge should be accessible to help guests with theater tickets and dinner reservations, find special services like the cleaners, shoe repair, and emergency information, answer questions, and generally help clients have a good time.

You can also access personal or corporate concierge companies as an outside resource if you do not have a staff member to assign this responsibility.

Concierges Add That Personal Touch

Since they know the area merchants, a personal concierge can help alleviate the meeting planner's tight schedule by preparing the welcome packet or arranging for goody bags at the banquet table or as gifts upon leaving.

Prepare a *welcome packet* and have a basket of fruit or wine and cheese put in each guest's hotel room as part of the *welcome*. It is always impressive to offer this personal touch of a concierge from your company. This is handled by either a concierge or the event planner. (Also refer to "Selecting Introducers and the Master of Ceremonies" section of this chapter.)

When tickets for an event are required, obtain the tickets ahead of time and include them in your guest's welcome packet or distribute them upon arrival. Call the venue and determine the best time to arrive. This is especially important if your group is large.

 Welcome Packet Suggestions

☑ A brochure about the company.

☑ Listing of company personnel that they will be visiting or meeting.

☑ A map of the city with transportation options.

☑ Tourism information.

☑ Shopping locations.

☑ A list of banks and the locations of ATMs.

☑ A list of restaurants and menus that you recommend, with tips on the food, atmosphere, and price range at each.

☑ Hospital and medical information with physician and dentist contact information.

☑ A visitor pass to a local exercise club.

☑ A set of complimentary tickets to a cultural event (e.g., the symphony).

A *goody bag* is a bag of samples from local merchants. Although they are nicer to have as a separate item in its own bag, the samples can be included with your welcome packet literature. Contact local merchants who offer their services or products as samples or gifts, and in return provide them with honorable mentions that include their website addresses. Consider also putting the merchant's name in the next edition of your company newsletter as a thank-you acknowledgment. Sometimes these goody bags are placed at each place setting as part of a meeting takeaway. It is a win-win situation because the participants receive gifts and the merchant receives free advertising.

In summary

To learn more about the role of a concierge, contact the National Concierge Association (ncakey.org). They originated in Chicago and now have chapters throughout the United States

> It is all about special touches and going above and beyond to serve.

②

SELECTING THE INTRODUCER AND THE MASTER OF CEREMONIES

There are many components to a banquet or conference. Determine which are most important to the overall success of your event. The more formal the event, the more protocol will be required. Begin by preparing the *introducer* and selecting the right *master of ceremonies (or more commonly called "emcee")* to set the tone.

Paul A. Logli, former state's attorney for Winnebago County, Rockford, Illinois, and current president and CEO of the United Way of Rock River Valley, has long been sought after as master of ceremonies because of his wit, humor, and ability to connect instantly with the audience. The following section contains Paul's advice for the introducer and master of ceremonies.

The Introducer

An effective introduction contributes to the speaker's authority by making it clear that he or she speaks from special preparation, knowledge, or experience. (Examples of effective ways to introduce a speaker can be found in books such as Dale Carnegie's *Effective Speaking*.)

> *I believe it works well if the introducer is someone already known within the host organization, someone who has credibility and is perceived to have special familiarity with the speaker. For this reason the introducer should have an opportunity to visit with the speaker prior to the presentation. If the visit cannot happen prior to the day of the event in person or by phone, then consider simply having the two sit together at the event, or have a brief visit an hour or two before the program begins, or perhaps even share a ride to the site.*
>
> –Paul A. Logli, president and CEO, United Way of Rock River Valley

If possible, select an introducer who has a public speaking background, who is charismatic, and who smiles! Make sure that the introducer is well rehearsed and enthusiastic. The introducer will set the tone for the entire program. When the person introducing a speaker reads the introduction with a flat, dull voice, it diminishes the impact of the audience's first impression. "Well-rehearsed" means that the introducer is given the speaker's bio in advance. He or she needs time to practice so that the introduction flows flawlessly and there is no stumbling over words.

Also, the introducer must pronounce names, titles, and company names correctly and with the correct protocol. Never say, "Here's Judy." Instead say, "It is an honor to introduce Judith Smith."

 Tips for the Introducer

☑ Know the correct pronunciation of the speaker's name.

☑ Know the speaker's title and company name.

☑ Adapt to the overall personality of the topic. If it is light and lively, be witty and fun. If it is more serious or technical, be graceful and factual.

The introduction should not take more than thirty to forty-five seconds. Keep it short, and make it count! If you feel the written version is too dry or cumbersome, go over it with the speaker. He or she will appreciate the effort and concern. It is all about you making them look good!

Master of Ceremonies

The master of ceremonies introduces the speakers and the entertainment for the event. The master of ceremonies and the dinner speakers are typically representatives of the host company and may include a hired professional speaker.

It helps not only the MC but also everyone involved in the program to have a blueprint of the event in the form of an agenda or script. The document should include a time-specific and reasonably planned schedule. For instance, do not allot twelve minutes for dinner for two hundred and fifty people. Include the names of persons responsible for particular elements of the program as well as the speakers. As for particular remarks, some masters of ceremonies will do well with a script, while others may simply need a series of bullet points.

To keep the event on schedule, it helps to keep the number of speakers or presenters the lowest number possible. The greater the number of people who are given the microphone, the greater the chance that someone will abuse the opportunity by carrying on too long. It helps the master of ceremonies do his or her job by having one person do many things rather than many people each doing one thing.

–Paul A. Logli, president and CEO,
United Way of Rock River Valley, Rockford, Ill

When selecting your master of ceremonies, consider the following qualities and responsibilities:

 Qualities

☑ Has a sense of humor and is inoffensive.

☑ Has the ability to think quickly on his or her feet.

☑ Projects his or her voice in a clear and articulate manner.

☑ Reacts quickly and calmly to an emergency.

☑ Does not ramble, and is not self-serving.

☑ Knows how to keep the event moving.

Responsibilities

☑ Introduces the event and speaker(s).

☑ Announces the protocol (e.g., turning off beepers and cell phones).

☑ Keeps the event flowing and the audience involved.

☑ Sets up cues for the speaker so the speaker also stays within the event time frame.

☑ Handles the closing comments.

Handling a Dual Role

There will be times when the introducer and the emcee are the same person. Make sure that there is a distinction made between the two roles. The *master of ceremony* sets the tone for the entire event by making sure that his or her comments support the main event and keep the program on schedule. The *introducer* prepares the audience for the speaker.

If your role is to serve as master of ceremony, consider personalizing your script by interviewing people beforehand. You can accomplish this by asking for a list of key individuals to call or e-mail. Or, walk around at the event's cocktail hour and ask questions. Look for humorous anecdotes or stories to share. Then share your script with the introducer and event planner to make sure that it does not cause confusion or make someone uncomfortable.

> In both scenarios, keep your script short and concise.
>
> If the introducer or emcee takes too long, it takes the focus away from the event.

③

RECEIVING-LINE PROTOCOL FOR FORMAL EVENTS

A receiving line is typically arranged for a large formal banquet. The purpose of a receiving line is to provide each guest the opportunity to greet the host or hosts and honored guests. Receiving lines are typically utilized at formal events (e.g., retirement celebrations) when dignitaries or high-level executives will be present and to honor very important people within the community. Most commonly, receiving lines are associated with the military and diplomatic circles; however, they are an important part of any formal event.

A receiving line can be as simple or complex as the event dictates. Therefore, there will be deviations; however, it is important to maintain proper rank protocol. If your staff has never participated in a receiving line or attended an event with that level of formality, schedule a practice session.

Preparation Tips

Send a receiving-line protocol memo to your staff beforehand so that they are prepared in case they have never before participated in a receiving line. This provides added confidence and comfort.

Know the dress code. Receiving-line attire is formal or semi-formal. Casual dress (e.g., jeans, khakis) is not appropriate and will detract from the ambience of the room and formality of the event.

If the gathering is *less* than thirty people, informally receive guests by positioning the host or hostess and guest of honor near the entrance. Allow them to greet people casually as they enter, always ensuring that the guest of honor and his or her spouse are properly introduced.

If the gathering is *larger* than thirty people, a formal receiving line is recommended. When setting up your receiving line, select a member of your staff who is excellent at pronouncing names and remembering titles to serve as the "introducer." He or she should receive the guest list several days in advance so that there is time to rehearse names and titles. Include photos of the guests if they are available.

At an informal business function, the person who holds the more important position precedes—regardless of gender. At a social function, the woman precedes the man. However, you will find that the rule for the woman preceding the man will often be honored at business functions as well when a more traditional rule of etiquette is observed.

If drinks have been served prior to the receiving-line procession, place the drinks on a nearby table. It is improper to greet guests with a drink in one's hand.

Receiving Guests

A receiving line will depend on the level of formality and type of event. In preparing to receive the guests, the minimum acceptable number of people in a receiving line is four. They include the following:

1. Company host or hostess
2. Guest of honor
3. Spouse of the host or next in rank
4. Spouse of the guest of honor or next in rank

If the list is longer, the additional people are lined up in descending order by rank and seniority. If the event is strictly social, spouses stand next to each other. (Furthermore, the woman precedes the man if she is the primary invited guest.) Here is an example:

1. The designated introducer will greet each guest with a handshake.

2. The guest supplies his or her name and company name.

3. The introducer repeats the guest of honor's name to the first person in the receiving line:

> "Mr. Cohen, may I present Ms. Shelley Wu, vice president of ABC Company." "Ms. Wu, this is Larry Cohen, executive director of the Charity Foundation."

4. Mr. Cohen and Ms. Wu shake hands while the introducer turns to the next person.

5. Mr. Cohen then turns to the person next to him and introduces Ms. Wu:

> "John, this is Shelley Wu, our guest from ABC Company."

6. John shakes her hand and gives his full name.

7. Shelley Wu passes on to the next person in line to shake his or her hand and gives her full name. They in turn give their name, and so forth down the line.

The guests do not shake hands with the introducer. Guests simply state their name and title to the introducer. The introducer will then present the guests to the host or hostess. The host will then introduce this person to the guest of honor. Beyond the host and guest of honor, the guests simply proceed down the line and greet any remaining people by shaking hands and saying, "How do you do?" "Good evening," et cetera.

For more on receiving lines, visit www.ediplomat.com/nd/ protocol/entertaining.htm and *New Manners for New Times* by Letitia Baldrige.

> Receiving lines are a form of courtesy and add an element of formality and class.

"MUST KNOWS" FOR BEING A GRACIOUS HOST OR AN IMPECCABLE GUEST

> *A host is like a general; calamities often reveal his genius.*
>
> —Horace, Roman poet, born 65 BC

A *gracious host* knows how to create an atmosphere that is considerate and comfortable for everyone. As a host, it is your responsibility to be sure that your company is represented in the best fashion and that everyone's needs are being met. An *impeccable guest* knows how to behave appropriately and to be appreciative. As a guest, your responsibility is to make sure that your behavior and attitude reflect positively on your company.

Study the Guest List Prior to the Event

If you are the *host,* prepare in advance by doing your homework and carefully reviewing the guest list. This allows you to better prepare your topics of conversation, become familiar with everyone's names, and practice the correct pronunciation of challenging names. This is a real moment saver when you read an individual's name tag and are able to pronounce the name correctly.

If you are a *guest* and the invitation is an online one, the guest list is part of the invitation. If it is a postal-mailed invitation, however, you may have to make a special request to see the guest list. Assure the host that the list will not be circulated or posted; it is for your private use only. Do not be offended if, for whatever reason, the list is not made available to you. Confidentiality may be a concern.

Here is a suggested script:
"I want to represent my company in the highest professional manner. Knowing the guest list in advance will help me learn names and identify clients and key guests so I can greet them appropriately."

The following are reminders and additional strategies for hosts and for guests. In some cases, the tip or suggestion can apply to either the host or the guest. The breakdown is designed to give you a guideline. (Also, there is some overlap with the "Invitation" section. This cannot be avoided.)

How to Be a Gracious Host

Whether you are the guest or the host, it is important to know that someone took the time to think of how best to please you.

–Maripat Quinn, Ph.D., public relations director at Heritage Trust, Mt. Sinai, New York

The first rule to remember when entertaining is that *you* are the host. This means that you are in charge of all of the arrangements, from selecting the venue and handling the logistics to working with the staff and making introductions. It is the host's duty to maintain complete control of the event.

It is the host's responsibility to see to the comfort of all of the clients or guests. If this is overwhelming because of the number of clients or the size of the venue, the host should assign helpers, often referred to as "minglers" or "people movers," to assist with introductions and helping the guests circulate. You might have your mingler wear a special name tag or hat to differentiate him or her from the guests. This person could be a staff member or a hired professional mingler. In either case, they should have a great smile and excellent people skills, and they should be good at remembering people and names.

Hosting Tips

1. Arrive early to be sure that the reservation or arrangements are correct, that everything is set up correctly, and that logistics are in order.

2. Greet your guests upon arrival. Make sure that your guests receive an introduction, especially if there is a guest of honor.

3. For formal or large events, ask your event coordinators, people movers, or hired minglers to assist in greeting guests. They should make sure that introductions are being made, people are circulating, and everyone feels welcome. In fact, this is good advice for any event, small or large.

4. Keep your radar live. As you greet and interact, be observant of your guests and the environment. Maintain complete control of the event.

5. Do not occupy yourself with "other duties" or stay with the same group of guests for extended periods of time.

6. The host should acknowledge guests when they leave and thank them for coming.

7. The host should give a "Thank you for coming" signal when the event or meal should end. This signal can be as simple as standing and offering a closing toast at the close of a meal or standing at the doorway making closing remarks.

8. If possible, call all of the guests within the next few days and thank them for coming. This is an excellent way to demonstrate your follow-through to your guests and receive important feedback. If the guest list is large, engage the help of your planning team.

Certainly, there is more to being a host than the above nine points. Every phase of event planning has its unique hosting responsibilities and they are covered throughout this book.

How to Be an Impeccable Guest

Attend – Behave – Circulate
It is your duty to be an appreciative guest.

Executives pay special attention to how their employees handle themselves at business and business-related social functions. Your organizational skills and social behavior will have a direct effect on your career path and your company. Make sure that you are mingling with everyone and *not* just staying with people you know or off to the side, texting, because you feel shy or bored. In fact, it would be wise to leave your smartphone in your car to avoid the temptation.

Accepting or declining an invitation will require a certain level of sensitivity and gratefulness. It is important to always be a guest in good standing. As previously mentioned, respond to all invitations that include an RSVP (or Respond By) that you "will attend" or "will not attend," or as instructed by the invitation. It is not necessary to respond to a mass-mailed invitation, such as those introducing a new product line. When responding to the invitation, ask for the dress code if it is not specified, especially if it is an evening or weekend invitation.

You are responsible for you! Upon arrival, greet your host or event coordinators. If they are busy, make it your duty to introduce yourself. It is important to notify the host or hostess of your arrival. This gesture allows them to know who you are, especially if your previous contact has only been by phone or e-mail. How you handle yourself and how you treat the event staff communicates a lot about your social ability and how you interact with people. This is a valuable soft-skill trait.

Upon departure, let the host or event coordinators know that you are leaving by thanking them and commenting on the event.

Everyone likes to hear that his or her efforts were appreciated. It is your feedback that makes the next event even better. Also, you will be remembered for taking the time to comment. Although this book is primarily about hosting, being a considerate and responsible guest is just as important. Some of the following points were covered in the previous chapter on invitations, but they are worth mentioning again in this context.

Guest Dos and Don'ts

1. Confirm your invitation upon receipt. Never ignore an invitation. Accept or decline within three to five days. Do not wait to confirm until the morning of the event or hesitate because something better might come up. Declining or accepting should be done within at least two weeks of the event and never less than five days before the event.

2. Never accept an invitation by saying you will "stop by for a minute." Quality people deserve quality time.

3. Never make your confirmation and then not show up. This is rude, and you will be remembered for your lack of consideration!

4. If you confirm and your plans change, contact your host immediately with your apologies. Unexpected conflicts do arise. Respect your host's efforts to make sure that enough food and beverages are ordered.

5. If your invitation includes a guest, be sure to respond that you will be attending with or without a guest. If the event includes couples and your invitation only has your name, call and ask if you may bring a guest. Your host may have overlooked adding "guest" to your invitation. Never bring an uninvited guest!

6. Do not hedge by asking who else will be attending the event; however, it is appropriate to inquire about or request a guest list after you have confirmed that you will be attending. If the invitation was sent by electronic means, such as through

Evite.com, you may have automatically been given this information.

7. Do take a gift if it is appropriate. A bottle of wine, a bouquet of flowers, or a box of candy is appropriate for a home dinner party. If you bring wine or candy, do not insist that it be opened and served. This is the host's decision. The host has already planned the wine pairings and dessert and might prefer to keep the bottle or candy for another event or dinner party.

8. Respect the time frame and be on time. Do not arrive at the end of the event or party and stay beyond the designated time. Your host or event planners have much to do following an event.

9. Dress appropriately and with good taste. Even is the event is casual, do not take liberties and wear sloppy, racy, or revealing attire. You will risk changing the image your coworkers and clients have of you.

10. Do not stick with your date or friends during the entire event. Take every opportunity to meet new people and circulate.

11. Do not let a casual party or invitation tempt you into becoming careless or lull you into a false sense of security whereby you feel comfortable sharing confidential information or discussing sensitive topics.

12. Engage in conversation with people you do not know, and help others to interact. Do not just stay with familiar people. By helping others interact, you will get to know coworkers' personalities and interests on a more personal level. This helps improve communication at work as well.

13. Seek out the host or event planners and thank them for an enjoyable time before you leave.

14. Mail or e-mail a thank-you note within three days following the event. A verbal thank-you followed by a written thank-you is the best way to show sincere appreciation for the time, effort, and expense that was involved.

15. Do reciprocate the invitation if it is appropriate. This will depend on the circumstances.

A good host will not leave until all the guests have left; therefore, it is up to you, the guest, to know when to call it an evening. This does not mean you have to be one of the first to leave; just do not linger after all the other guests have left. If the event concludes at a meal, pushing your chair in when you leave the table signals that you are taking your leave.

Behavior Accountability for Hosts and Guests

This is not a time to vent or complain, no matter how angry or disappointed you are with work, management, or a client. These feelings must be put aside. To broaden your horizons and gain confidence, make every effort to meet people with whom you have not had a face-to-face encounter.

Keep alcohol consumption to a minimum. A two-drink limit is recommended. Be sure to alternate with a glass of water and eat food; otherwise you risk saying and doing something embarrassing or inappropriate. It will be remembered!

No one works with the perfect people or necessarily has the perfect boss or client or enjoys perfect workdays. That is life! More important, it is what you decide to make it.

 Avoid the following temptations:

- Flirting
- Complaining
- Entertaining gloom-and-doom topics
- Expressing political, religious, or cultural biases
- Asking for favors
- Gossiping or sharing office grapevine information
- Showing off
- Discussing confidential information

- Talking on your cell phone, texting, or checking your e-mail
- Being loud and obnoxious
- Engaging in insulting humor or humor at someone's expense
- Being rude
- Telling inappropriate jokes or jokes at the expense of others
- Talking too much about work
- Do not take photos and post on the Internet without "everyone's" permission. There should be no surprises! And, if you have permission, seriously consider sharing them by email for final approval before posting.

Remember, your behavior is on display; reputations are hard earned. Whether you are the host or a guest, it is your responsibility to circulate, establish mutual comfort, and socialize. Keep the conversations balanced; do not monopolize.

Make yourself as memorable and accessible as the best host or the best guest you can be by creating a partnership between the host and the guest.

> Whether host or guest,
> always handle yourself like a diplomat.

⑤

TIPS FOR BRINGING A SPOUSE OR ATTENDING AN EVENT SOLO

> Spouses and dates have a very important impact on your image.

Spouses influence a decision. A spouse (or significant other) is just as much your guest as a business guest. Treat the spouse with the same respect and level of importance. Similarly, your spouse or significant other should be allowed to participate in as many social events as possible. This allows spouses (yours or the guest's) to have a better understanding of the company's business and leadership.

Understanding the importance of business entertaining to corporate success and the key role that spouses play in this process, a major international corporation recognized the value of making a significant financial investment not only in its executives who handle their high-end corporate guests, but also in the spouses of those executives. This they accomplished by commissioning a comprehensive program consisting of training and executive coaching in image management, etiquette, and protocol for their entire executive management team and their spouses.

While not all the executives were initially in agreement, it soon became evident that this was a non-negotiable item according to the company's executive chairman, who was quoted as saying, "It brings you little financial return if you place all your investment in the executive, only to find that it can quickly amount to naught due to one single inappropriate act by that

> *person's partner." Needless to say, the initiative was a resounding success, both for the company and for the participants. This example serves to reinforce the point made by British image consultant Lesley Everett that "if you're not investing in the personal brand and image impact of your staff (and by extension the spouses of those staff), you're not maximizing your investment in the brand awareness of your products and services"* (Lesley Everett, *Walking Tall: Keys to Image Impact*).
>
> —Lisa James, managing director, Lisa James & Associates

Prepare a personal briefing by prepping your spouse or your date for an event on the people, their titles, and the purpose of the event. Inform him or her as if he or she were a member of your staff. The more they know about your work and the corporate culture, the easier it is for them to blend in and complement you. Brief them on everyone you work with, from management to coworkers, and practice saying challenging names correctly. Avoid sharing negative feelings toward a coworker or a member of the management team. A guest will often make a decision based on the interaction with your guest or spouse. Keep it positive.

If your spouse or guest is well prepared, you increase his or her confidence. It is important that your spouse or guest be able to discuss business-related topics with intelligence and enthusiasm. The background information allows them to listen and speak confidently whether the conversation is business or social. Also, if you are entertaining a client accompanied by his or her spouse, make sure that someone from your team is available to chat amiably with the spouse while you are chatting with your client (or make sure that your conversation is also directed to the spouse so the spouse does not feel left out).

Be mindful of your spouse's or guest's alcohol intake to be sure that he or she is conducting himself or herself appropriately. Your spouse's or guest's behavior is your responsibility. If your spouse does not mingle well or tends to drink too much and you know he or she would be uncomfortable (or act inappropriately), it is best that he or she not attend. Your reputation is connected to the actions of your spouse or guest.

One of the biggest faux pas you can commit is to ask what a guest's spouse does for a living or where he or she works. If it involves taking care of the home and children, this comment may create some uneasiness. Be sure to respond with a comment that implies that taking care of the home and children is the hardest job of all—without sounding patronizing.

> **Caution:** Never ask a spouse or a date personal questions or pry into anyone's personal life.

If the spouse works for a competing company, he or she needs to understand that his or her presence might make management uncomfortable; and he or she might become privileged to conversations that should not be shared outside the event. Use your best judgment in this type of situation.

Socializing Solo at a Predominantly Couples Event

You are invited to a casual party or formal dinner, and you do not have a date or escort. You can decline the invitation or decide not to attend. The smarter thing to do, however, is to go alone and enjoy the event!

A woman alone at a formal event stands out more than a man attending alone. One's first inclination typically is to feel bad for her or to think that she could not get a date; however, a woman alone at a corporate social event has a unique opportunity to call attention to how poised she is, how secure, and how smart. Dress in your favorite cocktail dress or ball gown, valet park, and walk in with confidence. Others will appreciate your confidence; this is a great time to shine!

Simply come prepared with lots of upbeat conversation starters, go easy on the alcohol, and even ask a man to dance if appropriate. If he is married, ask the wife's permission. It is most important when interacting with couples to focus on the wife or girlfriend to establish a non-threatening presence and then converse with the gentleman.

I have attended numerous gala dinners without a date. I will wear cocktail attire that is not revealing (avoiding low necklines and transparent fabrics), valet park, and walk proudly into the private club or formal venue. Of course, I am always hoping to be seated at a table with other singles without dates; however, when I am seated with all couples (single couples and married), I always start a conversation with the women and let it evolve with the men. The conversation is typically comfortable and engaging, and everyone is gracious.

When music starts, I have a very difficult time sitting still, and this is noticed; however, I will not ask a woman's husband or date for a dance. Eventually one of the wives or dates will say, "My husband loves to dance, and I really do not. Would you like to dance with him?" By the end of the evening, I am dancing and having a great time! It is important to keep it non-threatening.

Probably the most uncomfortable situation occurs when there is personal attraction. In this instance, it is extremely important that the conversation stays focused on business and not to allow any personal conversation of a dating nature to take place. How you dress and present yourself is going to determine the outcome. Keep conversation and appearance on a professional level. Allowing a business engagement to turn into a date is extremely risky! Once a reputation has been compromised, it is almost impossible to reverse it. (If there is personal interest, suggest meeting "socially" on a separate day or time for coffee or cocktail.)

When it is time to leave, walk alongside one of the couples from your table to the door, say good night, and wait for your valet-parked car. Do not let the fact that you are single, divorced, or widowed stop you from having a great time. Go!

> **You are responsible for You!**

ACCOMMODATING GUESTS WITH DISABILITIES

—by Jennifer Longdon

Jennifer Longdon is a writer, speaker and policy advocate on issues impacting people with disabilities. Jennifer contributed the following guidelines and considerations for accommodating guests with disabilities.

The most important point to remember about guests with disabilities is that they are *people* first; they are not their disability. People with disabilities do not have *special* needs, they have exactly the same needs as every other person; safe, dignified, autonomous access. Do not allow the accommodation to impair any interaction. That a person is disabled should not mean that he or she cannot enjoy an event or participate fully in a business discussion. Always focus on people's interests and abilities, not on their disabilities.

Avoid overly patronizing language and behavior; this implies that the individual with a disability is somehow fragile or unable to cope. Assistance is all about context. Treat a person with a disability the same as you would any other individual. As with every point of etiquette, your efforts should be invisible and should be designed to make the individual with whom you are interacting comfortable and maintain their sense of dignity.

Especially in a business setting, individuals with disabilities are prepared to find their own solutions to most issues and will be comfortable finding the appropriate individual to speak to for accommodation. Also, never initiate discussion of people's disabilities. This is not the attribute to use as an icebreaker; the nature of one's disability, how the individual came to be disabled, or whom you know that may have a similar disability are inappropriate topics of conversation. Speak directly to the person rather than through a companion who may be along to provide assistance. If you want to offer help, wait until the offer is accepted, and then listen to instructions, or ask for them.

Most individuals prefer the word "disabled" when broadly discussing disability issues. In general, people-first language is most suitable (i.e., "woman using a wheelchair" or "person with epilepsy"). Never use the word "handicap" to refer to people. For example, stairs handicap a person who has paralysis and uses a wheelchair. Other words that tend to have a negative connotation include "deformed," "lame," "limp," and even the word "senior" because it implies old age. (However, when inferring rank, "senior" is appropriate.) Context will indicate when the use of these words is appropriate and not demeaning.

Disabilities can strike anyone regardless of age, gender, or income level. It is naive to think that a disability is solely birth-related or that it could never happen to you. Once it happens, your ability to provide for your family, to function normally, and to work in your chosen field may be hampered.

Every day, disabled soldiers return to resume the lives they left behind. It is very important that you treat the individual with a disability the way you would want to be treated if an unfortunate incident happened to you. Bear in mind that while there are instances where a tragedy has happened to an individual and left its mark, but that person is not forever tragic as a result.

Adaptive Technology

Technological advances are making it easier for disabled individuals to travel, worship, and work. Take into consideration special equipment, chairs, or aids that will be needed. Ask the individual if you are unsure of their need for accommodation.

Wheelchair-users

First, note that it is still common to hear "wheelchair-bound" or "confined to a wheelchair." However, individuals with mobility challenges find these terms pejorative. Wheelchairs do not confine people, they liberate them.

Do not over-assist. For example, before being overly helpful and opening a door, ask if he or she needs assistance with the door. Do not create awkward spaces by rushing for a door or holding it way too long for either of you to be comfortable.

> *Following my presentation as a speaker for a disabilities conference, I approached a gentleman in a wheelchair. He gave me positive feedback—until I attempted to open the door for him. Then I was scolded: "How dare you assume that I need assistance." Stunned and realizing that others were watching for my response—clearly I had violated a point of etiquette—I apologized and asked the gentleman what I had done wrong, so that I could learn from the incident. He calmed down and told me politely that he had been in a wheelchair only a short while and it was very important to his sense of independence to open doors for himself. If he needed assistance, he would ask. He suggested that I emphasize the importance of asking before assuming someone needs assistance.* —Gloria Petersen

The same applies to squatting to reach eye level with someone in a wheelchair. While some will appreciate this gesture because it makes conversation less awkward, others might find it degrading or insulting because people squat to talk to children. If the conversation is going to be short, remain standing but take a step back so the person in the wheelchair does not need to hold their neck at an awkward angle. If it is going to be long, suggest getting a chair.

When planning seating and considering wheelchair users, position them where table legs and other obstacles will not be an issue. Ensure there is ample clearance for the individual to navigate into the spot and be able to move freely once others are seated. Many wheelchair users are less able to turn around in their seats so they should not have their backs to a program. When planning the seating, remove the two chairs from that post and replace two place settings with one place setting. This allows room for the width of the wheelchair. Furthermore, along with the missing chair, it will signal that this space is for a diner who uses a wheelchair.

Visually-Impaired or Blind

As with most disabilities, vision impairment takes place on a scale; some individuals have a greater or lesser level of vision. When greeting individuals who are visually impaired, they will often extend their own hand early so that you can take it. If not, say, "I would like to shake your hand." This allows them the opportunity to extend a hand. You are also letting them know that you are in front of them. Also, use their names when addressing them, and speak directly to them, not to their companions.

> *While working as a personal shopper for Nordstrom, I encountered my first sight-impaired customer. I kept speaking to her companion about her sizing and preferred styles, and she quickly and angrily snapped at me, "Quit talking like I am not here!" Her response taught me a lesson that I never forgot, and it was an awareness that I needed.* —Gloria Petersen

Do not be embarrassed if you happen to use words that seem to be in conflict with their physical challenge, such as "walk this way." Your meaning will be understood.

Hard of Hearing or Deaf

When interacting with someone with an auditory disability, do not change your speech patterns; but do avoid chewing or placing your hands in front of your face. If a sign language interpreter is present, look at and speak to the person with the hearing impairment, not the interpreter. The interpreter should be invisible. Be patient if the hearing-impaired person is using a hearing aid and there is not a person signing. However, do not speak so loudly that you draw undue attention and create humiliation. Speak distinctly and clearly but do not over-enunciate.

The challenge is to realize that one tends to look and speak in the direction of the voice. It takes a moment of focus to overcome this tendency and redirect one's attention toward the proper individual. It is a skill worth having. If you did not understand something that was said, do not pretend that you did. Paraphrase what you think was said, and allow the correction. Even if signing is used, your eyes should remain on the hearing-impaired person and your ears directed to the companion who is interpreting for you. It is dual communication and worth the effort.

> Note that individuals with hearing impairments will not be able to hear emergency alert sounds. Make special arrangements to have them personally alerted if there is an emergency.

People with Cognitive Disabilities

Treat individuals with cognitive disabilities with the same respect and familiarity as you would any other attendee. Shake hands, etc., as you would with anyone else. Be patient, be clear, be concise, and avoid distractions.

Amputations/Immobile Limbs

Handshakes are an important business greeting, but they can create awkward moments for individuals who do not have the use of their right hand. If the person wears a prosthesis on the right hand, the handshake acknowledgment can be extended with the left hand or simply place your hand on their forearm or upper arm while saying hello. The acknowledgment is so important.

Senator Robert Dole shakes with his left hand because his right hand was injured during his military experience. Typically, and when possible, he will carry a pen in his right hand to avoid having someone extend a right-handed handshake.

Depending on the circumstances, let the person with the disability take the lead. Sometimes they need a moment to turn their hand around (or position it) for a right-handed handshake. In this instance, one's handshake grip should match their grip. If the injury does not allow for a handshake, a simple but noticeable nod of acceptance and acknowledgment (or a touch on the shoulder or wrist) is appropriate.

When it comes to mealtime, a person with an amputation or immobile limb should make the same adjustments a left-handed diner (who eats American style) would naturally make. If the table is round, try to sit next to an empty chair; if rectangular, select a seat at the end of the table. (For examples on different eating styles, refer to *The Art of Professional Connections: Dining Strategies for Building and Sustaining Business Relationships*.)

The Presence of Service Animals

Individuals with disabilities are sometimes accompanied by service dogs. These animals are trained to perform a number of tasks based upon an individual's disability. These animals may or may not wear vests denoting their service work. There is no official agency that "certifies" service animals, so asking for such a certification is not only inaccurate, it is a violation of the person's civil rights. You may tell a person that you do not welcome pets but as soon as the individual identifies the dog as a service animal and themself as a person with a disability, the animal in almost every circumstance must be admitted.

Do not touch, talk to, or pet the dog; the dog is working. This could cause the dog to become distracted enough that it cannot follow its handler's commands. The same dining consideration should be taken for someone who has a service dog. Replace two chairs with one chair. This allows room for the dog to lie next to the handler without creating a disturbance. Do not offer treats; but it is acceptable to ask the handler if they would like water for their service animal. The handler should always be prepared to personally provide for the needs of the animal and most likely will decline. The gesture, however, is generally appreciated.

> *During breakfast at a convention, I sat at a crowded, round table. It was obvious that the gentleman to my left was sight-impaired. His aide was sitting to his left, and I thought nothing more of the situation. As I was speaking to the gentleman on my right, who had recently left the military, I noticed that he suddenly became very rigid and gave me a very uncomfortable look before directing his conversation to the sight-impaired gentleman.*
>
> *I could not imagine what I could have said. Suddenly, I felt something furry hitting my leg and gave him a strange look. Then it dawned on me as I lifted the skirt of the tablecloth and saw the sight-impaired gentleman's dog. Because I was wearing hosiery, I could feel the dog's hair. Since the military gentleman was wearing trousers, he could not feel the dog's hair and thought I was getting friendly under the table. We all had a good laugh.* —Gloria Petersen

Ideally, a chair with a "reserved" sign should be positioned on the left or right side of the individual with a disability for his or her dog to rest without being in the way of a diner's feet.

Equal Opportunity

Disability is not a determination of an individual's ability to excel professionally. Do not assume that a person does not work because they have a disability. People with disabilities are more likely than others to start businesses and you will find people with disabilities in all walks of life.

On July 26, 1990, the Americans with Disabilities Act was signed into law, eliminating discrimination in employment, transportation, and public accommodations for the nation's fifty million disabled adults and children. For more information, visit www.ada.gov or call the ADA Information Line at 1-800-514-0301.

Additional information and guidelines are available from the National Easter Seal Society, which makes it their mission to help focus on a person's ability rather than his or her disability.

A person with a disability should be given the same respect you would extend to any individual. Put challenges aside and enjoy the gathering.

 Helpful websites:

- ada.gov *(Americans with Disabilities Act)*
- nfb.org *(National Federation for the Blind)*
- rid.org *(Registry of Interpreters for the Deaf)*
- nad.org *(National Association of the Deaf)*
- amcin.org *(Association for the Mentally Challenged)*

> The person with the disability
> is in command of his or her situation.
> Only assist when asked.

Chapter 5

CULTURAL EVENTS AND AT-HOME ENTERTAINING

> *I want to give the audience a hint of a scene. No more than that. Give them too much and they won't contribute anything themselves. Give them just a suggestion and you get them working with you. That's what gives the theater meaning: when it becomes a social act.*
>
> —Orson Welles, 1915-1985

The arts add a special *touch of class* to any occasion. To be successful entertaining at a cultural event, there are specific behavior rules and expectations to honor once all the planning is in place. Rock concerts are an entirely different breed of entertainment and require a different protocol; however, they are still all about music, and music is a cultural event.

 The objectives of this chapter are . . .

1. To cover the rules and expectations and proper etiquette for attending cultural venues, review the policies and practicalities of attending the theater, and what to do or avoid in disruptive situations;

2. To understand that rock concerts are not out of the question for client entertainment but that there are cautions and caveats; and

3. To introduce home entertainment as an art within itself. For some, the greatest honor (especially for international guests) is to be invited to your home.

Cultural events can include community events that are celebrated around a holiday or a historical date, ethnic festivals, exhibits at museums, and much more. They can be a great way to entertain without involving a huge investment.

My tip on business entertaining would be to consider public venues for various business entertaining functions. Museums make for great locations. They are already decorated with a theme, so you can save time and money there. You can easily tie in your business theme to the location. In fact you can weave in various or even different sub-themes, as each gallery usually has a specific focus or theme. It's also a great way to support institutions that need funding.

As the former associate dean of the University of Toyota, I had many opportunities to utilize public venues. For example, Toyota would often use the Petersen Automotive Museum in Los Angeles for many events. The Nixon Presidential Library is also one of my favorite venues, as it has presidential elegance as well as exhibits that are sure to start a conversation. A variation on this theme is using a university as a site. Cal Poly Pomona has a hospitality management program, and we often held events there. Many schools have hospitality management programs. The students do a good job, and they get credit for working the event. Most colleges will also have some upscale facilities that are appropriate for even executive-level meetings. Decorations are also easy, as the school has its mascot, school colors, shirts, hats, etc.

–David Medrano, training manager for a major
Southern California utility company

Maripat Quinn, Ph.D., the public relations director at Heritage Trust, Mt. Sinai, New York, and nondenominational and nondiscriminatory wedding minister for over twenty-five years suggests that if you select a featured artist, do your homework and learn something that not everyone may already know about the artist, so you can entertain your client and show your sophistication.

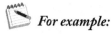 *For example:*

- What is their most important work?
- Who influenced their work?
- Does the artist work by theme, subject matter, or media?

Also, consider gallery openings, book signings of a favorite author, antique or craft auctions, food tastings, boat shows, or touring a naval vessel. Another possibility is going to an observatory and letting them see the night sky from a different perspective.

Lastly, Maripat suggests that you may even want to consider taking your client on a city tour. There are so many different types of tour that might be suitable. For instance, history buffs may enjoy visiting local historical sites; architecture aficionados may enjoy learning about the construction styles of local buildings or homes. Depending on the city, some tours are conducted by bus or by boat, and others are walking tours. Again, take into consideration your clients' abilities and interests.

The beauty of these types of entertaining is that the theme and the decorating are taken care of for you, and everyone enjoys new experiences. There is probably an online city guide to entertainment that will provide a full list of opportunities, complete with location, date, time, and cost.

At-home entertaining truly embodies another type of cultural experience because it captures the essence of that person by exposing their personal interests and lifestyle. For many international visitors, it is considered the highest honor. While some CEOs and corporate officers like to showcase their homes, which are filled with art collections, conversation pieces, or landscape art, others prefer to demonstrate their laid-back lifestyle of simple pleasures, cozy atmosphere, and at-ease hospitality. Whichever the case, there are rules and guidelines for both guest and host to make at-home entertaining a most pleasurable experience.

While the options are endless, this chapter will focus on the theater and on concerts, because the guidelines for these can be applied to any cultural event. Then we will turn to perhaps the most personal form of business social event: home entertainment.

> The arts add that special touch of class.

THEATER ETIQUETTE AND AUDITORIUM SEATING

Imagine this: You grew up in small-town USA, secured your bachelor's or master's degree, and have been hired by a Fortune 500 company in a large metropolitan city. Your job description includes entertaining elite clients and their spouses (or dates) at the theater or symphony. You, however, have never been to a symphony or the theater! Now what?

> *This is a scenario that I have encountered many times when presenting business entertaining seminars. It can be daunting for a graduate eager to make a good impression, as well as for someone who has made a career change and is faced with a similar scenario.*

That is exactly what this chapter is designed to do! By familiarizing you with the etiquettes, protocols, and expectations involved you will overcome unnecessary awkwardness.

Handling Tickets for the Theater

Purchase the best seats possible when entertaining clients; avoid the "cheap seats." Make sure that everyone receives his or her ticket in advance. If this is not possible, let your guests know that you will greet them at the ticket counter. In this instance, you should keep your cell phone on in case one of your guests needs to reach you. Once everyone has arrived, your cell phone should be turned off. An alternative would be to tell your guest that you will arrange for a *will call* box pickup.

> "Will call" is a term for a box office where you can pick up pre-purchased tickets either just before the event or in advance.

Box office rules and hours vary; always check. Some may not be open until an hour prior to event time, while others may be open during regular business hours. Most venues will not let you pick up your tickets from *will call* until the day of the event.

The box office will not release tickets if the name on the ID and credit card does not match the name used to purchase on-line tickets or if the photo on the ID does not match the photo of the person retrieving the tickets. In order to pick up your tickets, you might be required to present identification:

- Your driver's license or passport
- The credit card you used to purchase the tickets
- Your confirmation number

If your host purchased the tickets, ask your host about the required ID or procedure for picking up your tickets at the will call box. To find out what other types of photo ID are acceptable at the venue's will call, contact the venue directly.

Arrival and Seating

Arrive on time so you do not distract the performers. In some situations, you will not be allowed to enter until the intermission if you are late. If this happens, accept responsibility and be pleasant and apologetic.

Generally, you should arrive at a theater about half an hour before the show to give yourselves enough time to get through the ticket line and be escorted to your seats. The usher who shows you to your seat will also give you the program.

The host generally tips the usher a small gratuity, depending on how many people are seated. For a group of four people, one to two dollars is sufficient.

–Maripat Quinn, Ph.D., public relations director, Heritage Trust, Mt. Sinai, New York

If all but one of your guests has arrived, instruct the guests who have arrived to take their seats and say you will join them shortly. If the event is starting, it is not necessary for you to miss the opening if a guest has not arrived. You can always notify the usher or the ticket office that you are missing a guest, and have them escort the late arrival to your party.

As host, you will want to make sure that all of your guests can see the stage. If there are any seating problems, be sure to ask the theater's house manager if you can make any changes before the show begins. When asking for special treatment of any kind, be sure to take care of it quietly and unobtrusively so that no one is made to feel uncomfortable. If the theater is able to accommodate your request, be sure to have your company send them a thank-you note. (Also review "Auditorium Seating and Policing Challenges" in this chapter.)

Theater Etiquette and Behavior Cautions

If you have very little or no experience attending the theater, observing the following policies and etiquette will help make it a comfortable and successful experience; especially if you are asked to entertain a client who prefers the theater:

1. *Recording Devices:* Cameras and recording devices are normally prohibited. Most events now post a "Please turn off your cell phone" notice on the theater screen as well as make the announcement. Unfortunately, people forget! How many times were you certain that your phone was off, when, to your shock, it rang in the middle of a performance? In this moment of panic, you cannot locate your phone quickly or easily enough. This effort conjures up even more noise and creates embarrassment for you.

   Electronic beepers, cell phones, and alarm watches should be turned off upon entering the lobby, hall, or auditorium. If your cell phone was not checked by security upon entering the building, be sure you double-check to make sure your cell phone is in silent mode. Do not think the phone's "vibrate" or "light alert" options are an appropriate alternative. Sometimes the vibrations and lights are more disruptive than a tonal alert. Put away all handheld electronic devices. This is entertainment, not work. Focus on the event and on your guests.

> For those who do not think that anyone can see the glow of a cell phone, you are wrong. My son and I were at the Adler Planetarium, in the dome theater, looking at the stars above, and among all the twinkling of the simulated stars, there was a pale blue flicker coming from across the room. Furthermore, the attendant had no problem locating the man with his BlackBerry.
>
> —Neelum Aggarwal, MD, associate professor of neurology, Rush University Medical Center

Also, do not pull out your mobile device and start texting or tweeting. The glowing screen and your rapid thumbing will be a distraction. If you are expecting an urgent message or call, check your phone during the intermission. Your emergency should not disrupt anyone else. If you feel a need to tweet, tweet during the intermission.

2. *Late Arrivals:* All shows will start promptly at the time indicated on your ticket. Anyone who arrives late or leaves the auditorium during the performance will be seated at the discretion of theater management. Nor should you leave early. Everyone is urged to remain seated while the performance is in progress. Often a section is roped off for late arrivals (typically, it is the last row). You should occupy this seat even if it is not your ticket-assigned seat. You can locate your correct seat (and friends) at intermission. Furthermore, it is unfair to your party, to the artists, and to other ticket holders to arrive late or leave early. Respect the performance schedule and performers.

3. *Seating Signal:* When the lights flash, you have just a few minutes to dispose of your refreshments and take your seat. It is standard operating procedure that theaters will flash the house lights fifteen minutes before the start of the performance. This serves to notify people to dispose of their refreshments, gather their theater companions, and quietly show their tickets to the usher and take their seats.

4. *Taking your Seat:* Face the stage as you enter your row. Do not remove your coat while moving to your seat; take it off before you enter your row. Then hold your coat close to your body so it does not brush up against someone already seated; this applies to handbags too. Nor should you remove any of your clothing while in a row moving towards your seat (e.g., a sweater).

> We went to the Dorothy Chandler Pavilion (in Fullerton, California), to see La bohème, which was excellent. Having "student" tickets, we were at the very top of the theater, and it was warm. During the intermission, a man in his mid-twenties stood, unbuttoned his shirt, and took it off! Standing in his V-neck T-shirt, he stretched and sat down. I was so stunned. It is these experiences that bring etiquette to life!
>
> –Jackie Sanborn, instructor, Fullerton College

5. *Hats Off:* Gentlemen typically remove their hats, while ladies are permitted to leave their hats on. This is can be considered unfair because a woman's hat is larger and more obtrusive to the patron behind her. It is best to not wear a hat, whether you are a man or a woman, during the performance. This also applies to baseball caps, which should not be worn to the theater under any circumstances. If a woman prefers to wear a hat, it should be small so that it does not block the view of those behind her.

6. *Clapping:* Prior to a musical score, the orchestra conductor is applauded when he or she enters (before the curtain goes up). When the conductor steps up on the platform and raises his or her baton (or the curtain rises), all clapping ceases and the audience becomes silent. Clapping is then withheld until the end of each act (or performance). Watch the performers carefully for signals as to when they are ready to begin or when it is appropriate to clap. You can also clap (and cheer) during the *appropriate* times during a performance and at the final curtain. To determine the appropriate time, follow the lead of the audience. Once the performers have taken their final bow, clapping stops and it is time to take an orderly leave.

7. *Behavior:* Your ticket makes you a member of the audience, not a member of the cast. Do not approach the stage during breaks or stand during the performance unless everyone is applauding an encore performance.

   When you attend an event and display inappropriate behavior, whether it is out of deliberate rudeness or innocent response to the music, you are noticed and remembered. Your paths may cross again. Furthermore, the theater reserves the right, without refund of any portion of the ticket purchase price, to refuse admission to or remove any person whose conduct is deemed disorderly or who fails to comply with theater policies.

   Overall, audiences are well-behaved; however, it only takes a few to disrupt a live performance. These disruptions are sometimes simply oversights or innocent faux pas.

8. *Refreshments and Cough Drops:* Refreshments are offered during intermission. The policy regarding taking food or beverage into the auditorium may vary from theater to theater or show to show. Typically it is not allowed, but in some cases bottled water is allowed in the auditorium. Ask the usher about this policy.

Most theaters have signs that prohibit bringing food such as candy bars, chips, or beverages into the auditorium. Resist the temptation to hide food in your handbag or pocket. Others will hear you unwrapping or tearing paper and chewing. Do not let a piece of hard candy roll around your teeth, making a clanking sound, or make smacking noises chewing gum. It can be heard.

Wait until intermission to enjoy a beverage and a snack. If you believe you will need cough lozenges, unwrap a couple prior to entering the auditorium, and wrap them in a paper tissue to avoid disruption during the performance. If you do begin to cough during the performance and you cannot control it quickly, excuse yourself immediately.

> *If you have to unwrap a cough drop, do it while the orchestra or musicians are warming up. People do not realize how annoying the sound of wrappers is to both their companion and to those around them. I have been at a performance where a full-blown argument has occurred because of a Halls wrapper moment.*
>
> —Neelum Aggarwal, MD, associate professor of neurology, Rush University Medical Center

9. *Conversation:* Do not have sidebar conversations during the performance or dig through your handbag because you are restless. Your full attention should be given to the performance, even if you are not enjoying a particular segment.

10. *Box Seat Courtesy:* If you have a box seat and are seated in the first row, *offer* to change seats during the intermission. This etiquette is appreciated. It gives others in the box seat an opportunity to have a front-row view of the orchestra or play.

11. *Remain Seated:* Do not stand during the performance, even if

the musical score gets you excited and you feel like jumping up and dancing. This is not a rock concert.

> *During several episodes of a contagious musical score at the popular musical "Mamma Mia," groups of people in the audience kept standing, clapping, and expressing isolated dance moves. This blocked those of us behind them from seeing the stage performance. A theater is not set up like a rock concert with an elevated stage. It is meant for sitting and enjoying. Standing should only take place as part of the ending applause. My client and I were appalled at the lack of respect for the audience.*

12. *Proper Time to Stand:* Only stand and applaud at the encore. Pay attention to the applause moments; they are specifically timed. As mentioned previously, the timing for applause can vary from one theater or production to another. A lull in action does not necessarily mean it is time to applaud. A little hesitation may save you embarrassment. Observe what the seasoned theatergoers are doing, and follow their lead.

> *Following the lead can be especially important in classical music venues. Often all applause is held until the whole piece is played. Applause in between movements can be very distracting to the orchestra members and conductor.*
>
> —Neelum Aggarwal, MD, associate professor of neurology,
> Rush University Medical Center

13. *Noise Control:* If you can hear it, everyone can hear it. Common noises include zipping and unzipping your coat, fumbling through your handbag, releasing Velcro, and (as previously mentioned) opening paper-wrapped candy.

Extenuating Circumstances and Special Requests

There are always extenuating circumstances for any event and other extra things that are helpful to know.

1. *Illness:* If you have a fever, cough, or constant sneezing, please stay home. Your coughing and sneezing will be disruptive to others. Explain your illness to the theater management, and they might allow you to reschedule. They do not want their audiences infected.

2. *Special Requests:* Phone ahead of time to inquire about special seating needs or other special needs. In some theaters, infrared hearing devices are available at no charge and may be secured from the coat check on a first-come, first-served basis upon presentation of a driver's license and major credit card for security. If you anticipate a need to be contacted during the performance (e.g., an anticipated emergency), advise the theater's house manager of your seat location (and situation) prior to the performance.

3. *Lost and Found:* If you lose something or misplace an item, visit the coat check in the lobby. This is where lost and found items are kept during the play or performance.

4. *Fragrances:* Allergies are on the rise. Avoid fragrances, or wear a fragrance that has a very light scent. You will be seated in close proximity to others. If you sit next to someone with an allergy, your fragrance will start a sneezing streak. This will be disruptive to you as well.

5. *Smoking:* The law in most states prohibits smoking. You may smoke outside the theater during intermission; however, retain your ticket stub so you can return to the building.

Auditorium Seating and Policing Challenges

Most events have preassigned seating indicated on the tickets. As host, you might need to arrange for escorts to assist people in finding their seat numbers. If there is an usher, the usher takes the ticket stubs and handles the seating. The usher will then return the stubs and hand out the programs. Respect the usher's seating direction. Outside seats are needed for the elderly and those with special needs. The back rows should be sectioned off for late arrivals.

An open seating policing challenge for ushers is how to get people to fill the middle seats after they have assumed an end seat. One way is to make an announcement asking for everyone's cooperation in filling the middle seats first as they arrive. Repeat the announcement, thanking those who have complied with the request. This will encourage others to do the same. Obviously, not everyone will or can cooperate. There are extenuating circumstances that make aisle seats necessary.

I have experienced many situations where people have an underlying reason for needing an aisle seat (e.g., an unseen medical condition such as a bladder control problem, a doctor who may need to leave for emergency pagers, or a person who feels sick to his stomach). As an event planner, I have handled this by having assigned seating in auditoriums or by placing signs at the doors stating that patrons requiring an aisle seat should notify the ushers prior to being seated or prior to seating themselves.

–Amy Suess-Garcia, senior director of global customer service, Taylor Company

If seating is not preassigned on your ticket, respect the escort's (or usher's) efforts to try and fill in the middle seats first and the aisle seats last. It is very difficult and awkward to work your way to the available middle seats if all of the aisle seats fill up first. This avoids the constant interruption of passing by people who are already seated. No one likes a constant parade of people in front of him while seated. Face the stage as you enter your row. If you are saving a seat and your companion has not arrived when the show opens, you should relinquish the seat to someone else.

In a business context, the protocol of a seating arrangement starts with the guests entering the row first and the host being seated last along the aisle. In a social context, the usher will direct the woman to enter the row first. It is still considered proper for the man to sit "aisle-side," just as traditional etiquette dictates that the man should walk curbside when escorting a woman in a social setting. Traditional rules of etiquette are best observed in social settings and almost always observed abroad. In other words, a woman should never interpret these gestures of courtesy as preferential treatment. Although this gesture is rarely practiced or expected in the business arena, it is important in social circles and at business-related social events.

Another reason for the host to take the aisle seat is in case he or she has to get up and make any last-minute changes to accommodate a guest. However, if someone in your group has extra-long legs, he or she may appreciate having the aisle seat to stretch out a bit. (Share this need with the usher.)

Set the right example for others to follow by demonstrating courtesy when using the armrest. Limit yourself to one armrest! Select the one on your right or left. When you use an armrest, do not overlap; you risk invading someone's space. If everyone used one armrest, everyone would still have the comfort of one arm resting elevated during a long program.

Security

Be sure that your guests have the phone number of the theater. Realize that several theaters, art institutes, and museums now have security staff check your cell phone to be sure it is turned off before entering the building. If you are unable to reach your party because your cell phone is off, check with the desk periodically for messages.

Make sure that your guests know the theater's policy on holding tickets. Most theaters will hold tickets until fifteen to twenty minutes before the show begins or curtain time and then, if they are not claimed, will sell them on a first-come, first-served basis. As previously mentioned, be sure that your guests are aware of any security protocol they may encounter when entering the building. In most cases, a picture ID will be required.

Backstage Opportunity

In some cities the opera house (e.g., Lyric Opera of Chicago) will sponsor an annual backstage tour. If you are new to opera, this is an excellent opportunity to learn about the opera house and opera. Plus, the experience and education will serve as a great conversation starter when attending an opera with your client (or guests). These tours include the building and company history, property room, catwalk, wardrobe and costumes, sewing room, wigs and makeup, chorus, armory, rehearsal center, orchestra pit, scenery handling facility, lighting, and main stage. Taking a tour will also give you an even greater appreciation of the opera.

A Note on Movie Theaters

A movie theater is more relaxed than a live performance; however, courtesy to others is still paramount. The things that are disturbing to a live performance are not an issue in theaters (e.g., eating, opening wrappers, whispering), however, loud conversation, yelling, and a constant getting up and down are distractions. Because you are allowed to eat in the theater, be sure to dispose of your disposable containers and napkins in the trash receptacle.

If someone is causing problems or being rude, excuse yourself from your guest, find the movie theater manager, and alert him or her to the behavior. Let them take care of the behavior; you should not be involved!

> Respect the rules of the theater.

ROCK CONCERTS AND MUSIC IN THE PARK

The phrase "rock concert etiquette" might sound like the ultimate oxymoron, since concertgoers are an eclectic lot. The bands not only attract fans across the generations, but they also attract behavior and dress that one would never see in a traditional theater.

> *Depending on the preferences of your client, you may do better by opting for a single performing artist like a jazz musician or a pop music concert rather than a loud and raucous rock concert. It is difficult to talk when music is so very loud.*
>
> –Maripat Quinn, Ph.D., public relations director, Heritage Trust, Mt. Sinai, New York

If you opt for a single performing artist, you will need to take into consideration that artist's current popularity, along with generational music preferences. This could be challenging if your or your client's staff or overall event has an age mix from the twenties to the sixties.

Many of our new leaders and executives come from a rock concert generation; therefore, it should also be an option when entertaining. Just be certain that it is a concert your guests will enjoy and that they know what to expect. Unless you are able to secure bleacher seats, make sure your guests wear comfortable shoes and clothing. In most cases, attendance is standing room only.

> *Rock concerts are known for "anything goes," so the conditions and seating may change. You need to be able to move easily without a lot of stuff. Also, limit the amount of jewelry you wear to a concert, as you are probably going to lose that favorite earring if you get up and move around or get moved around. Trust me; no one is going to get on the floor to look for your lost jewelry piece.*
>
> —Neelum Aggarwal, MD, associate professor of neurology,
> Rush University Medical Center

When selecting a rock concert venue, check the band or artist's website for "tour" or "live" information. Also check local publications (e.g., newspapers or magazines) for familiar favorites.

When you are ready to buy tickets, consider the following:

1. Decide *whom* your guests would like to see (some consultation might be appropriate).
2. Where is the show going to be held? Is the location convenient for your guests? Will they need transportation?
3. Double-check the time and date of the show.
5. Find out when the tickets officially go on sale, and watch for pre-sale options. Check ticket provider websites (e.g., Ticketmaster) for concert dates and pricing.
6. Are the tickets sold strictly online, or do you have the option of a local business establishment (e.g., a retail store)?

Seating Options

Rock concerts typically have either assigned seating or free-for-all seating (or both). Unfortunately, unruly seems to be the rule in areas that do not require seating or quiet behavior. They are all about expressing oneself with the energy that comes from the band. Fans wrestle for limited standing room space, squirm to see around taller fans, or weasel their way through the crowd to front and center. Those who indulge in boorish behavior usually are the ones that make the headlines. In rare situations, such mob behavior has cost fans their lives.

Aggressive Behavior and Flexibility

> *If you have a client who is completely into rock, then that desire is the one you fulfill. Just schedule another time to talk about business or to get the information you need. Whichever venue works best, the same rules apply: your conduct must be above reproach, and you look after the needs of your client. While you may certainly enjoy some alcohol, you must be available and levelheaded enough to usher your client home safely in case he overindulges.*
>
> —Maripat Quinn, Ph.D., public relations director, Heritage Trust, Mt. Sinai, New York

Unlike the symphony or a theater musical, audience participation is part of the rock concert program. Although the vast majority of the audience is civil and courteous, there are those who have a strong need to cut loose. Therefore, crowd control and safety should always be a top priority with rock concerts because too often audience members expect it to be a rowdy time and behave accordingly. It is as if their ticket is a license to do whatever they want and be as obnoxious as they want. Even mosh pits have security teams to monitor bizarre behavior tendencies.

> "Moshing" is an aggressive, self-expressive style of dance in which the audience pushes or slams into each other, and it is especially stimulated by hard rock music. There are many variations.

A mosh pit is an area in front of a stage where people stand, slam dance, and body surf. It is not an area recommended for your guests, although you may have enjoyed the experience at your last rock concert. Although fans do get their share of bruises and scars, serious injuries are rare. The good news is that an unwritten code of behavior is encouraged and enforced.

Because mosh pits have a dangerous nature and a reputation for injuries, they are not as common today; however, a generation that grew up with it may be inclined to invite a client or guest to this type of entertainment. Attend the concert but do not participate in the mosh pit.

To challenge things further, people have short fuses today and find rock concerts to be a form of release, so expect to be flexible in the range of behaviors you might encounter, and enjoy the event; otherwise, aggressive behavior will only escalate. The good news is that there is an unwritten etiquette that even rock entertainers try to encourage and fans usually abide by. Consider the following concert complaints and possible solutions.

> *Complaint:*   Offensive comment or slogan by those around you.
>
> Solution: Ignore it and consider the source.
>
> *Complaint:*   People who force themselves in line ahead of you.
>
> Solution: Stand your ground, but be polite. You do not want to ignite a confrontation!
>
> *Complaint:*   Loud whistling and yelling.
>
> Solution: It is out of your control. Bring a good pair of musician's earplugs! Musicians actually do wear them as a way to allow their music to come through while screening out shrill noises.
>
> *Complaint:*   Incessant talkers—they talk through the ballads, the quiet numbers, and the stage banter.
>
> Solution: Try a subtle "Shhhhh" with a pleasant expression. We learned "Shhhhh" as children and tend

to automatically respond to the suggestion. The offending party may have momentarily forgotten his manners. Then say, "Thank you."

Complaint: Out-of-control dancing—good music inspires happy feet and active bodies.

Solution: Try to shuffle out of range, or you will surely be hip-bumped and elbow-jabbed. If the fan resorts to chair dancing, ushers typically will remove that person.

Complaint: It's standing room only, and the view is blocked by a taller fan.

Remedy: Try to stand between the two people in front of you, or, in a very courteous manner, ask the tall person in front to change positions with you. Most fans understand and will respond to a courteous request.

Displaying courteous concert behavior is critical to the enjoyment of the show for everyone. It is too easy to get caught up in the moment or the excitement and forget that your behavior is on display and will be remembered or captured for YouTube usage.

Music in the Park: The Sacred Rite of Summer

The "music in the park" concept took off in the mid-1960s as a Mother's Day concert, and its popularity increased, all the way to the infamous 1969 Woodstock. Rock concerts and classical music concerts have enjoyed their spot in the park ever since. Most often they take place in a band shell or pavilion where there are chairs and open grass areas for picnicking on blankets.

When you are beyond a season of weather that is too cold or too hot, people will flock to outdoor concerts. It is a wonderful way to enjoy nature and the outdoors; however, concerts should be equally enjoyable for everyone.

Etiquette for Picnicking on the Lawn

1. Do not place your blankets so close to others that people cannot walk around you. Leave a walkway.

2. Keep your conversations low, just as you would at an indoor concert, so that your neighboring picnickers can hear and enjoy the music. In other words, no yelling, whistling (or use of ear-popping whistles), catcalls (a shrill sound expressing disapproval), or screaming.

3. Keep your picnic basket on your blanket or have a low-to-the-ground portable picnic table to hold food and beverages. Chairs should also be unobtrusive to people behind you. At some outdoor concerts there are bleachers. If sitting for a long period of time on the ground is uncomfortable, set up near or at a bleacher area.

> *If you can't sit on the blanket or you have a loved one who can't sit on the blanket because of frailty, hip issues, or bad knees, consider bringing a folding chair (one that is just off the ground) and positioning it to the side of the grass or concrete area. This way the view is not obstructed as much as it would be otherwise.*
>
> *I have seen nasty situations in which elderly persons have brought lawn chairs to Ravinia (outside Chicago) and had those sitting behind them upset because they obstructed a view. Yes, this was a musical concert, but the lawn people also wanted to see the conductor.*
>
> —Neelum Aggarwal, MD, associate professor of neurology,
> Rush University Medical Center

4. Do not bring liquor unless the park allows alcohol consumption. If liquor is not allowed, do not sneak it in.

5. If you bring children, make sure that they understand the need to stay seated and are respectful of others and not running all over the grounds and making a game out of the picnic aisles. Also, contain your pets so that they are not barking or attacking someone's blanket for food.

6. Do not walk on other people's blankets. Their blanket is an extension of their home.

7. Be courteous about smoking. You are outside and smoking may be permitted; however, smoke away from the crowd.

8. Lastly, clean up. Do not leave a mess for the grounds people to clear. Demonstrate respect for the property.

Whether the music is inside or outside, be respectful and considerate so that everyone can enjoy the music and the people.

Keep behavior "in check".

③

AT-HOME ENTERTAINING:
From the Patio to the Dining Room

> *To be honest, I'd be more nervous having a dinner party than I am entertaining fifteen thousand people a night.*
>
> —Shania Twain, singer

The small, at-home dinner party is a time-honored way to entertain, but it has gone to the wayside with more women working and with hectic family schedules. Dining out offers a lower-pressure alternative that allows you to concentrate on your party instead of worrying about meal details in the kitchen. An invitation to a home dinner party, however, is perceived as an honor with international guests and offers a very valuable extension of yourself. It is a great way to share your art collection or backyard artistic landscaping from your patio. Certainly, single-family homes offer more space; however, an apartment or condo can offer an amazing view from the balcony.

To be invited to someone's home should be treated with the utmost respect. Home entertaining can range from simple coffee gatherings or casual outdoor cookouts to formal sit-down dinners in the dining room.

How you choose to entertain reflects a personal signature of your lifestyle and tastes in the same way that we find styles of dress, décor, and daily routine that suit our personalities.

If you opt to have your soirée at home, think about the flow of the party. Which rooms will be used and for what purposes? How can you rearrange furniture to help with the flow of the event? Should a caterer be hired to free you for mingling?

When extending an invitation to your home, the invitation should read "to dinner" at your home not "for dinner" at your home. If some of your guests smoke, be sure to have a designated smoking area, even if it is outside. Also, be sure that your invitation includes a map to your home, with parking instructions. Do not just assume that they will find your home because it is "easy." If your home is in a gated community, include your cell phone number and instructions on how to proceed when they arrive at the gate (e.g., gate code). Also advise if your gated community has a separate entrance and exit.

The traditional image of a dinner party includes a well-planned menu, crisply ironed tablecloth and napkins, heirloom silverware perfectly aligned, exquisite-looking china, and a breathtaking centerpiece.

A partner in a New York engineering firm invited thirty colleagues and clients to a dinner party. The guests included physicians, lawyers, authors, and government officials. Invitations were sent six weeks before the party, with a follow-up phone call three weeks before the event. Four days before the dinner party, less than ten had responded. After phone calls were made, a few more confirmed their attendance.

The invitation stated that cocktails and hors d'oeuvres would be served from 5:30 PM to 6:30 PM, with dinner starting at 7:00 PM. Many of the guests did not arrive until 8:00 PM and stayed beyond the designated time!

A designated smoking area with ashtrays was provided. Only two ashtrays were used! Several smokers stubbed out their cigarettes on their cocktail plates.

Despite requests to stay out of the kitchen where the caterers were working, guests persisted in congregating in the kitchen, making it difficult for the caterer to prepare and serve the food and clear the dishes.

> Of the guests who attended, only a few sent thank-you notes. The partner was devastated at the general lack of social skills and the professional ignorance. He never offered a dinner party again. In fact, he eventually left the firm, and key clients followed him.

Whether entertaining at a restaurant or in the home, a host can do all the right things, only to have the guests create a domino effect that ruins careful planning. Unfortunately, scenarios similar to this one have become all too common.

Today, for the most part, home entertaining has been turned over to caterers. Rarely will you find a formal dining room in today's newer homes. The eating area is typically made up of a breakfast bar and a small dinette, and food is arranged buffet style. Seating arrangements for the overflow of guests are handled in various areas of the family room.

The thought of entertaining guests or your boss at your home can be both exciting and stressful. Not only are your hosting skills on display, but also your skills at organization, cooking, housekeeping, and in some cases childrearing and animal care. Your ability to organize at home translates to the office. If you have been unsuccessful in proving your organizational skills, an "at home" event might be the answer; however, if you are doing the cooking, this is not the time to try out a new recipe.

Do not entertain in the garage unless it is an outside barbeque and it is raining. Otherwise, you take the risk of sending a message to your guests that they are not valued enough to be in your home; this consideration applies even if you have white carpeting! If the patio is the gathering place, have a backup plan in the event of inclement weather, or if bugs become a nuisance.

Be sure that your home is conducive to business entertaining and can accommodate the number of people you are inviting, and parking must be available. Some communities have very limited parking, if any. In addition, there is a gradual decrease in eating space in newer residences, especially condominiums and townhomes. Kitchen areas are designed smaller to accommodate quick meals instead of elaborate meals. People who once dined at the family table are eating off coffee tables and lap trays. As a result, "grazing" is a growing habit, which means that instant meals are eaten in transit from the kitchen to another room or from the coffee table or lap tray.

If you are conducting a meeting, juggling food and beverage can make handling business paperwork, laptops, and meals awkward; therefore, any business that needs to be transacted is best accomplished after the meal, not during it.

Home Preparation Suggestions

Depending on your theme, preparing your home can be simple or involved. There are things that need to be considered that you would not encounter when planning a gathering at a restaurant or event hall. The more formal the gathering or dinner, the more steps will be needed to make your home conducive to entertaining guests. Use the following as a guide and select what is appropriate for your party:

1. *Invitations and Theme:* Send a "save the date" notice by e-mail or postal mail. Determine whom you want to invite. Send out invitations at least two weeks out, preferably longer. Make your dinner party memorable by giving it a theme. The theme could be centered on a season of the year, a popular sports team, a particular holiday or special celebration, etc.

2. *Guest List.* Always try to invite a diverse group of guests. Varying the ages, professions, and ethnic backgrounds will help make the evening livelier. Make sure that you invite someone who is great at helping people mix, to prevent people from staying isolated. Consider inviting a surprise

guest, someone your guests have not seen for a very long time or perhaps a popular public figure.

3. *Attire.* Dress for comfort, ease, and elegance. Make sure that your invitation states the dress code if your dinner is formal. Another way to set the tone for attire is with the invitation. If you want formal dress, send an invitation that is formal in design. If the dress is casual, send a fun invitation that might include animated clip art.

4. *Parking and Entertainment.* The host is responsible for every detail, including directions to his or her home, where to park, and the type of entertainment.

5. *Children:* If your children will be home during the gathering, they should be kept occupied by a sitter once everyone has arrived. Guests and colleagues do like to meet children; however, the children should not be intrusive or distracting. If your children will be at home and a sitter has not been arranged, make sure that you instruct your children on proper behavior—instruct them to play elsewhere and not to disturb your guests, no matter how well-mannered and cute they are, and even if your guests say it is okay for them to be present. Brief your children on good behavior and reward them afterwards. Never put your guests in the position of entertaining your children! (If at all possible, have your children stay with a friend or relative.)

6. *Pets.* If you have pets, you need to be sure that your guests are not allergic to them. It would be a great courtesy to your guests to put your pet in a separate room that has food and water and in an area whereby barking or other animal noises cannot be heard. Do not expect your guests to fall in love with your pet; however, guests who are pet lovers will welcome your pet. Vacuum your furniture and carpet to eliminate as much pet hair and dander as possible that morning. Be sensitive to your guests' clothing; keep sitting areas free of pet hair. Sometimes vacuuming is not enough and a guest who has severe allergies to pet dander will have to decline.

Guests who are allergic to animals or birds should ask the host if he or she has a pet. If they do, take an allergy pill before you go, or decline the invitation. Do not expect the host to send his or her pet to a friend's or to the kennel (although this would be a wonderful courtesy).

7. *Housekeeping and Bathroom Etiquette:* The home is clean and tidy, and the kitchen is well organized and sanitary. Bedroom doors are closed! Lighting is appropriate (not too dim). Have plenty of toilet paper, hand towels, and soap accessible in the bathroom. Make sure that the hand towels look like they should be used! Sometimes the décor in the bathroom looks like a "showroom" and a guest does not want to soil beautifully arranged towels so they try and air dry their hands. Also, please flush the toilet after usage and wash hands. Your bathroom etiquette will be noticed!

8. *Coats and Personal Items:* Have a space for guests to put their coats and personal items. Better yet, designate someone to take them as they arrive and retrieve them when they leave.

9. *Ambience.* Create a mood with candlelight and music. Make sure the music is soft so that it does not compete with conversation. When dispersing candles around the room, group them in odd numbers. This is the same concept that is used in flower arranging.

10. *Eating Areas, Seating, and Catering:* The caterer has been arranged or special help in the kitchen provided. Get all the preparations done at least a half hour in advance so you have time to relax and ready to receive your guests without being rushed. Eating areas are well planned. This is especially important for smaller homes or apartments. If your guests will need to sit on the sofa and there is not enough room on the coffee table for food and beverages, provide lap trays or TV trays. If you are having a dinner party for more than six, devise a seating arrangement to maximize guest enjoyment and interaction. (Place cards are a nice touch.)

11. *Cooking Tip*: Cook the meal yourself if it would not be too disruptive. It is a chance to demonstrate your creative cooking skills. However, catered or "order-out" meals give you control over the conversation and eliminate any confusion about your role in the business proceedings. It is important to minimize the disruption of going back and forth to the kitchen or the awkwardness of doing dishes. Your focus should be on the guests, not the meal preparations or cleanup. If you decide to cook, designate someone to keep the guests mingling and conversation flowing so that your presence is not missed when in the kitchen.

12. *Dinner Table and Centerpiece.* Vibrant colors and unusual dishware shapes attract attention and add character to your table setting. Select a centerpiece that reflects (or establishes) a mood and compliments the table setting. It can be as simple as displaying votive cups in colorful glassware or a sprinkling of the season's foliage. You might also consider individual centerpieces. Make mini-arrangements of flowers in small juice glasses or plastic tubes on a stand. Place one at each setting, or set them in a cluster in the center of the table. Let each guest take one home as a token of the experience.

13. *Place Cards.* If your gathering is large, arrange place cards identifying each guest's place at the table. Names can be written in calligraphy to add a touch of elegance or put in a variety of photo frames. If your hobby is scrapbooking, this is an excellent opportunity to share your talent with creative menu and place card designs. If you don't scrapbook and one of your teenagers does, allow them this wonderful opportunity. Involve your family!

14. *Greeting:* The host should greet all guests and make sure that everyone is properly accommodated and introduced. "Work the room"! Make sure that your guests are mingling. Use commonalities to bring strangers together. Be on the lookout for guests who seem isolated or uncomfortable. Be aware when guests are leaving, and thank them for coming.

15. *Conversation.* To start the conversation around the table, consider using gimmicks. For example, tie tags onto the stems of glassware that identify popular movies, books, or movie stars. Have people look at their tags and discuss what they have read or seen or what they plan to read or see.

16. *Toast.* Do not forget to make a toast. The toast can signal the beginning of the meal, it can honor someone special, or it can be silly by toasting something new you learned about a guest.

17. *Smoking.* There are guests who like to smoke, especially at social events. Even if you are a nonsmoker, designate an outdoor area (or an indoor smoking room). Never make a smoker feel uncomfortable because he or she needs to leave to have a cigarette.

18. *Keepsakes.* Take photographs, arrange them in a collage and mail or e-mail them to your guests. You might even include your menu at the bottom of the collage. (Again, this is where a scrapbooking talent can be shared.)

19. *Thank You Note.* Thank each guest for coming as they leave. Extend a thank-you to your planning team and family members who helped.

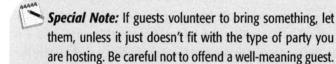

Special Note: If guests volunteer to bring something, let them, unless it just doesn't fit with the type of party you are hosting. Be careful not to offend a well-meaning guest.

Guest Responsibilities

A guest can make or break a host's efforts. Respect the invitation, and do not become your host's horror story! It is still business. As a guest, you are responsible for responding to the invitation within three days of receipt and honoring the invitation. If your invitation is addressed to you and a friend, be sure to inform the host if you will be bringing a friend or state that you will be coming alone. If your invitation does not include a friend, call and ask if you may bring a friend. Do not be disappointed if the answer is no. The host invited the number of people his or her home can accommodate.

Keep your shoes on at the door of someone's home unless you are asked to remove them. Too often, people feel that a party is an opportunity for them to get comfortable by removing their shoes, putting their feet on the seat of a chair or sofa, or sitting on countertops. Don't disrespect the furniture or host!

To become the guest who is always invited back, follow these tips:

1. *Attend:* Never say you are coming and then not show up.

2. *Children:* Never assume that you can bring your children, even if you allow guests to bring their children to your home. If you call and ask to bring your children, you will put the host in a very awkward position. If the invitation does not imply that children are invited, do not bring your children, or call and ask if children are allowed. If the host replies that no children are allowed, respect his or her wishes. Even when at someone's home, the gathering is for the purpose of building relationships.

3. *BYOB:* If the invitation states BYOB (bring your own bottle), do not take the bottle home, opened or unopened, when you leave. Casual gatherings often include this option as a way to defer alcohol expense. It is very difficult and expensive to provide enough alcohol options to meet everyone's preference. Or, you can limit it to a simple beer and wine choice.

4. *Hostess Gifts:* If the hosts are celebrating an event or promotion, consider bringing a token gift. This gift could be a bottle of wine, a box of gourmet candies, or fresh flowers. If the gift is a bottle of wine or champagne, however, do not expect that it be opened. The host has already selected the wines that best complement the meal. Your wine will be enjoyed on another occasion. If the invitation is a house-

warming, bring a gift that complements the home decor (e.g., a decorative candle, a set of four balloon wine glasses, or unique napkin holders).

5. *Dress appropriately:* Be careful that you do not dress too casually. The quality of the invitation should give you a clue as to the type of attire that is appropriate.

6. *Participation:* If the party has a theme, come prepared to participate, even if it seems silly. You want to add to the enjoyment of the party, not to distract from it.

7. *Arrival and Departure:* Always introduce or announce yourself to the host upon arrival and departure. It is your responsibility to introduce yourself to other guests. Never overindulge in your host's generosity or behave in an unprofessional manner.

8. *Business Cards:* Do not try to sell your product or service. This is not the appropriate time to exchange business cards or conduct business unless the host offers you the opportunity. This is a social event. If you do want to discuss business with another guest, arrange a coffee or lunch meeting for another day.

9. *Manners:* Plan to use your best table manners and conversational skills and appear to be enjoying yourself, even if you are having a bad day. You do not want to put a damper on the host's efforts or the other guests' enjoyment.

10. *Dietary Restriction:* If you are a vegetarian or eat kosher, do not expect the host to accommodate your needs by preparing a special dish. A home is not a restaurant. Nor should you mention dietary restrictions to the host at dinner when it is too late to make adjustments. If you only eat kosher, call the host and offer bring a side dish if the host will be unable to accommodate a kosher meal; this should be done discreetly. Otherwise, focus on food selections you can tolerate.

11. *Offering to Help:* It is commendable to offer help in the kitchen, but not if there is a catering service or hired help.

12. *Respect Private Property:* Do not snoop through or help yourself to food in the cupboards or refrigerator unless instructed to do so. Nor should you help yourself to food as it is being prepared. If cupboard doors are shut, they stay shut. It is a personal home, not an office. The hosts have shown trust by inviting you into their home. This also applies to bedroom doors. Unless the bedroom is being used for coats, the door stays shut.

13. *Smoking:* If you do not see an ashtray, do not ask to smoke. If you must smoke, go outside.

14. *Food is Served:* Follow the lead of the host when it comes to serving oneself. The host will announce that it is time to eat.

15. *When to Depart:* Do not overextend your stay. A good rule of thumb is to leave approximately one hour after dessert and coffee have been served. Certainly, there are extenuating circumstances regarding your departure.

16. *Thank You:* Say thank you to the host before departing and follow up with a handwritten thank you note or e-mail message, whichever is more appropriate and memorable.

17. *Reciprocate:* Plan to return the invitation to your host within three months. This gesture will let your host know that you were grateful for the invitation.

On a final note, guests should never ask to take extra food home, even if everyone brought a dish to pass, unless the host makes the offer. Although it seems appropriate to take the extra food home that you brought in your dish, it is a courtesy to ask the host if he or she would like to keep it. The host would then transfer the food to another dish so your dish can be washed.

Buffet and Open Seating

A buffet approach is much easier to undertake than a sit-down, formal dining room setting. It provides a more relaxed atmosphere, as your guests serve themselves and select their preferred seating. Meals can be cooked at home or catered, or everyone can be asked to bring a dish to pass. Make sure that everyone has a place to put his or her dish. Never expect guests to balance their plates on their laps! It is very difficult to handle food and beverage on your lap, so be sure that there are TV trays or lap tables so diners can set down their plates and beverages when relaxing.

Advantages of At-Home (or At-Office) Buffets

- Guests serve themselves the food selections and portions that they prefer.
- Seating is open.
- Eating is at one's leisure.
- Unexpected arrivals can be accommodated.

When it comes to serving buffet style (or potluck) at home, there is no need to prepare every dish, or to set the table perfectly. With everyone pitching in, the event is informal and economical. However, you still need to plan and prepare. You have to make sure that there are chairs throughout your rooms to accommodate everyone. The table has to have an attractive, cohesive look, and each dish needs to be displayed in the correct order (cold dishes to hot dishes) and attractively.

> **Tip:** Consider placing a "Start here and proceed ➔" signage on the table. This will keep guests from colliding and remove buffet table confusion!

Make sure the courses are replenished at different intervals if extra servings are planned or if you are utilizing an open-house format and people will be coming and going at different intervals. Have your hot dishes separate from your cold dishes. If placed on a long table, your sequence should be as follows:

- Place settings (dish and utensils)

- Cold dishes
- Hot dishes
- Desserts
- Beverages (It would be best to have the beverages on a table in a different area of the room.)

Dinner should be planned for one hour after the invitation's stated time. This gives everyone time to arrive and get settled. Have beverages available upon arrival.

Upon departure, guests should take their dishes and glasses to the kitchen. An offer to help is always appreciated; however, do not be offended if the host or hostess declines your offer. Make sure that trash containers are easily accessible if guests will be disposing of their own paper plates and plastic utensils.

At Home Casual Coffee Meetings

The boom in telecommuting and home-based entrepreneurship has made the home a logical place for business transactions. This allows for an exchange of ideas in a relaxed, unguarded manner.

When the home is the office, your kitchen becomes the lounge. It is cozy and very relaxed. People who run businesses from their homes have special considerations. Keep in mind that just the thought of conducting business over a casual coffee at someone's kitchen table can make some guests or colleagues feel less professional or uncomfortable. Make sure that your arrangement is agreeable for everyone, and that it is professional. This means you should dress as if you are going to a public building—no shorts or unkempt clothes!

Inviting one guest or colleague to your home or apartment can be awkward if he or she is of the opposite gender. You run the risk of causing misinterpretations or discomfort. It is always best to conduct business with at least three people to avoid any awkwardness, unless you know the other individual well and there is no chance for misinterpretation of intentions. If alcohol is to be served, it should follow the meeting when it is time to relax and socialize over a cocktail. This allows an individual who is not comfortable drinking alcohol to leave or to stay and enjoy a soda.

Formal Dinner Party

A small evening dinner party at someone's home is a gracious gesture. A dinner party is more personal than a cocktail party, but it can also be more confining. If your goal is to unite one small group of guests, then the formal dinner party does it best; however, if your goal is to get people mingling, a cocktail buffet is a better choice.

Follow the traditional rules of etiquette when you are unsure of yourself or if this is a first-time dinner party. Once you become comfortable with the formality, demonstrate your more creative talents. If you are inviting guests for a dinner party at home, try to limit your courses to between three and five if your guests are being served. If you have several food options for your guests to enjoy, a buffet setting might be more suitable.

Create an eclectic setting. It is not necessary for a formal home dinner party to use china and silver. A mix of stoneware, a ceramic serving platter, and mismatching glasses can be a gorgeous statement of your creative talents and eclectic spirit. In addition to the tips already covered, here are five eclectic ideas:

1. Mix your patterns of china, flatware, and glassware. Use a different kind of plate for each course. If your meal is being catered, check with the catering company regarding the dinnerware. As mentioned in chapter two, caterers often bring back-up dishes, glassware, and utensils just in case the host runs out. You want to be sure that everything works together attractively.

2. Use white wine glasses for water instead of water goblets or

glasses. In fact, if you do not have an assortment of wine-glasses, the white wine glass is the most commonly used substitute.

3. Serve from a cart, deep windowsill, or kitchen counter, or peasant-style from pots on the stove.

4. Your table arrangement can be simple, such as candles arranged on a square glass mirror, a vase full of seashells, or a colorful potpourri.

5. Choose a color theme for dishes and linen; mix designs and patterns. For example, use a salad plate in one design and dinner plates in a different design. Be careful that they do not clash; you would be creating a patchwork effect.

Set your table an hour before your guests arrive. This will allow time to see if anything is missing and give you a chance to relax. The table should be set with filled water glasses before guests arrive. Do not put ice in the water glasses. This causes them to sweat and make a puddle on the tablecloth. If ice is preferred, fill the glass halfway and add the ice with an ice bucket tong just before everyone is seated.

If you find that no one is leaving and you want to conclude the evening, simply stand, walk toward the door, comment on the evening, and then start thanking everyone for coming. This must be done in a pleasant tone and with a friendly smile. The guests should recognize this gesture, take the hint graciously, and thank the host for the invitation and the great food. (In business, protocol dictates that a meeting concludes when the chairperson or host stands.)

It Is Not Your Home!

The familiar saying "my home is your home" does have its limits. When you are at someone else's home, it is easy to get too comfortable and revert to your own "at home" behavior. This can include sitting on counters, taking off your shoes and putting your feet on the sofa, double dipping, or helping yourself to the refrigerator. Certainly, there are situations when the host is a close friend with a "my home is your home" motto; however, when other guests are present, you need to temper these tendencies.

A marketing consultant invited guests and neighbors to her home for a holiday meal. One of the male guests came into the kitchen where the food was covered with foil while the remaining food was being prepared. He lifted the foil and started picking at the turkey with his fingers. Appalled, she asked if he would please wait until everything could be served at once. He replied, "In my house, the guest is king, and can do whatever he wants!" He exercised his at-home habit!

Needless to say, the hostess was horrified and embarrassed, as his behavior was rude and noticed by others. To make matters worse, another guest asked if she could take extra food home for her children when the meal concluded.

If a guest is picking at the food prematurely, politely ask the guest to wait until all the food can be served at one time. To prevent this from occurring, always have hors d'oeuvres or snacks available at a table in another room *away* from the kitchen.

Unfortunately, scenarios similar to these have become all too common. Proper conduct and simple courtesies have become a low priority. Too many people today simply do not consider how an event is affected by their lack of consideration, nor do they realize that their "at home" behavior is inappropriate.

Frequently Asked Questions

1. *"Should I bring a gift?"*

   It depends on the occasion. Recommended gifts include wine, candy, or flowers. Do not be offended if the wine or candy is not opened and offered to everyone; the host may have selected a wine and dessert that best complements the meal and occasion. Your gift will be greatly appreciated and enjoyed at a later date.

2. *"May I bring an uninvited guest?"*
   If couples are attending and you are single and your invitation was not addressed to you and a guest, call and ask permission to bring one. In this instance, it is proper to ask.

3. *"How should I dress?"*
   If the invitation does not state a dress preference, call and ask how the host will be dressing. Even in sportswear, your appearance should send a professional message. You certainly do not want your appearance to be discussed at work the next day in a negative way. Common sense and modesty should prevail.

4. *"How should I set the table and handle the food service?"*
   If the meal is formal, hire a catering service or someone to assist with the table setup and servings. Or, if it is casual and there will be several tables set up, arrange the dishes, glassware, napkins, and utensils on a serving table and allow the guests to gather their own place settings and then take their preferred seats.

5. *"Should I bring a dish to pass or groceries?"*
   It is not necessary to bring a dish to pass unless it is potluck and you are asked to do so. Never bring groceries to a dinner party. The guest's only obligation is to show up on time, be sociable, send a written thank-you note, and reciprocate. If you do feel it necessary to bring something, do not be offended if it is not offered or served.

6. *"If the invitation is a casual gathering of friends and everyone is to bring a dish to pass and his or her alcoholic beverage, is it proper to take the opened bottle home?"*

No. It is tacky to take an opened bottle home. At the least, it is illegal to drive with an opened bottle of alcohol in your vehicle.

Being invited to someone's home is an honor!

It is also an opportunity for the host to share hidden talents.

Chapter 6
SPORTING EVENTS, GAMES, AND OUTINGS

> Success is a game.
>
> Know the rules, play the game, and win.

Participating in sports, games, and outings are opportunities to relax and enjoy clients and staff away from a work environment; plus they allow you to de-stress or alleviate the intense focus of serious business work. And such an event does not have to be a pre-planned outing; it can be a spontaneous board game in the employee lounge. Whatever the situation, the change of scenery can make employees and clients feel better focused and more efficient.

 The objectives of this chapter are . . .

1. To realize that any kind of corporate outing, especially sporting events, team-building exercises, and retreats, is for the purpose of team building and solidifying relationships;

2. To provide the basic principles for understanding your role as spectator or participator and to cover all the what-ifs and dos and don'ts; and

3. To focus on team-building exercises or events in general and to know that the ground rules involve being open-minded and willing to participate, contributing to a climate of trust, and learning from the experience.

The key to any successful outing or sporting activity is to use this time to solidify friendships and enjoy social interactions in a relaxed and fun atmosphere. This is an investment in your career. Not everyone enjoys the same kind of sport, so make sure the outing is mutually enjoyable. Use it as an opportunity to build trust into a relationship and develop deeper ties.

Long-lasting relationships are built on these four principles:

Trust • Shared Values • Accomplishment • Camaraderie

These basic principles take you from the board room to the game.

Corporate Outings

Enjoying the beauty of nature is a great way to escape stress by taking a break from business indoors. The fresh air, sunshine, and colorful landscape can rejuvenate the mind in a powerful and creative way. Furthermore, it is the best way to break away from glazed-over computer eyes, and it creates camaraderie among peers and clients that you rarely see.

The objective of a corporate outing is to create an opportunity for team building and bonding relationships in a fun environment. Corporate outings, retreats, and team-building seminars have many interpretations. They can range from team building activities to a family-focused leisure activity.

Outdoor Retreats Can Range from Fun Outdoor Activities to Adventurous Escapes	
▪ Hiking or horseback riding	▪ Dinner cruises or cruise chips
▪ Sightseeing tours	▪ Sailing or boating expeditions
▪ Miniature golf	▪ Wilderness retreats
▪ Picnics	▪ Skiing or other snow related activities
▪ Biking (marathons)	▪ Rope courses in the woods
The options are endless. Whatever the selection, well-thought-out planning and courtesy should prevail.	

An outdoor outing also helps us appreciate things we often overlook, like the beauty of nature, freedom from office-related stress, and meeting new people. Whether you are spectator or participator, the ultimate goal is to ensure that everyone has a good time and fair play is the rule.

If the activity is going to be held on a boat or at a forest preserve, make sure that your guests have the necessary emergency information and that there are cell phones available to use. Also, be aware of allergies, fears, sun exposure, and physical limitations. Be sure to have an alternative plan in case bad weather cancels the activity. Consider bringing an extra set of clothing if the weather looks unpredictable.

Respect an individual's right to decline your invitation. There may be a health reason or a personal motive. Important considerations include the following:

- Allergies (wilderness or prairie plants) and asthma
- Fears (of water or heights)
- Sun exposure (skin sensitivities)
- Physical limitations (age- or injury-related)

If you are the organizer of a sporting event, make sure that you have a waiver ready and are aware of the allergies and medical conditions of your associates. As a manager of employees, when we held events and I knew that I had an employee with allergies, I made sure that I knew where his or her EpiPen was. And if there was a diabetic on staff, I knew where his or her insulin was kept.

—Tranda Covington, business operations manager,
Motorola

If you want to be creative and not fall back on the same type of event (e.g., skybox at a baseball game), join the local chamber of commerce, or any such service organization that hosts a wide range of usual and unusual events. This might involve a one-year or extended membership, but it will be well worth the investment. Or you might join a business network that has ties to numerous vendors in the hospitality industry.

When planning, keep in mind that not everyone is going to enjoy the same sporting activity. Be sure to plan alternative activities such as sightseeing tours, guest pass to the spa, or lessons for those who want to learn the game (e.g, golf).

Pool or Beach Parties

Pool parties are a refreshing way to entertain; however, do not assume that all of your guests will want to swim. Not everyone enjoys swimming or knows how to swim, so do not insist that everyone gets into the water just because it is a pool party. Some guests will not even want to don swimwear. Be respectful! If you are sensitive to the sun, ask your host (or the pool staff) to arrange a shaded area for you. Simply say you have a sun allergy or sensitivity. If the host is preoccupied, ask the pool staff.

If you want to save your chair while swimming, it is permissible to place your towel on a lounge chair. A towel on a lounge chair means the chair is taken; do not remove the towel or move the chair if it is not yours! Unfortunately, there are self-serving people who do not abide by this courtesy. You should always set the better example.

A pool party does imply swimsuits, so keep your pool attire selection in good taste and avoid making others uncomfortable: no bikinis for the pool or short shorts for poolside. When out of the water, be sure to wear a beach wrap.

Character, Honesty, and Integrity Should Prevail

Outdoor activities and retreats are wonderful and popular ways to learn about one's character, honesty, and integrity. Perceptions are everything! No matter how hard one tries to be on his or her best behavior, one's true personality will emerge during a competitive game. Unprofessional behavior will dampen career opportunities and business deals. If you cheat, behave inappropriately, or violate the rules of a game, the word will get out. Regardless of the activity selected, do not do or say anything that might cause the company embarrassment.

Also consider the following:

- Whether you are having a good day or bad day, can you stay in control?
- Are you confident and comfortable with your level of play, or are you hard on yourself?
- Do the nonverbal cues of your demeanor reveal your unfavorable opinion of other players?

This chapter will introduce sporting events from a participator and a spectator point of view. Since the game of golf is the most popular international game for solidifying business deals, it will be the featured sport for this chapter.

> Have a good time and play fair.

BASIC PRINCIPLES FOR SPORTING EVENTS

Work hard, play hard, but play professionally.

Sporting events are divided into two categories: (1) spectator and (2) participatory. Being a *spectator* allows you to become emotionally involved in the action. Remember, you are a spectator, not the coach or referee; your behavior will have a direct effect on your reputation.

Being a *participant* allows you to be physically involved in the game. Know and respect the rules of the game. Both require good sportsmanship. There will be times when you will be the spectator and times when you will be the participant. Stay in your role!

When you are entertaining sports enthusiasts, you'll have to decide between participatory sports or observational sports. Golf, tennis, and bowling are some fairly typical examples of participatory sports. Observational sports might include football, basketball, baseball, soccer, lacrosse, ice skating, certain forms of dance, and so on. Of course, one can observe tennis and golf games and participate in ice skating, but it doesn't happen as frequently. Let your client research guide your choices.

—Maripat Quinn, Ph.D., public relations director at Heritage Trust, Mt. Sinai, New York

To avoid embarrassing yourself and your client, do not invite anyone to play a participatory sport, such as golf or tennis, unless you know both of you are competent at the game. Otherwise, stick to being spectators, or consider noncompetitive activities like the theater or a festival. It is about building relationships, *not* winning.

> A person's ability to perform as a team player
> in sports and in the office are interrelated.

Find out the dress expectation and the event requirements, and abide by them. If you are invited to observe a team from a private box, ask if there is a special dress code. For example, it may require more formal clothing than what is appropriate for the bleachers.

Demonstrate respect! When the national anthem begins, remove your hat, place it over your heart with your right hand, and pay tribute to your country. This includes baseball caps! This is not a moment to worry about a bad hair day or demonstrate discontent with your country or politics. A hat of any kind should be removed during the playing of any national anthem. This shows respect toward your country or the country you are visiting. It is the traditional way to begin a game.

Know the Rule of Play

> *Rules* offer us guidance.
> *Rules* make us feel safe.
> *Rules* help us feel confident.

The rule of play (as spectator or participant) should be understood and respected for all activities. This is not the time to show off. It is a time to demonstrate your leadership abilities, flexibility, and sensitivity to colleagues and clients. Your behavior is a direct reflection on your company's name and your reputation.

There are times when discretion is the better part of valor in a close game. Allowing your guest to win might be in your best interest; however, you do not want to insult your guest by making it obvious that you are allowing him or her to win. Winning is a matter of knowing the personality of your teammate. Exhibiting discretion and judgment is always the best course of action. If your guest is so competitive that he can never lose, what would you gain from winning or sparking a temper or bad mood? Instead, ensuring a competitive, close game will meet the return on investment in good feelings for the guest.

Role of the Spectator

Being a spectator allows you to get emotionally involved in the action. Remember, you are a spectator, not the referee; keep over-the-top outbursts in check. Also, your sportswear should be in good taste. Spectator sports often require tickets and are observed in tiered seating or bleachers.

Examples of Spectator Sports	
▪ Golf	▪ Tennis
▪ Hockey	▪ Soccer
▪ Basketball	▪ Auto racing (e.g. NASCAR)
▪ Football	▪ Horse racing
▪ Baseball	▪ Dog racing

Spectators should know the rules of play even if they do not play or participate in the game. Do some research on the players so you know their roles and more about the positions they hold or play. It will make you a better spectator and keep you from asking the person next to you a lot of questions. These questions will interrupt someone's enjoyment of the game. Furthermore, avoid quoting facts unless you are sure of your information and that it came from a reliable source.

If you are meeting for drinks before attending a game, know your limitations so you can control your behavior at the game. Keep in mind that drinks will also be available at the event. Watch your alcohol consumption, especially on a hot day!

Be courteous to those around you. If you have to get up during the game, return to your seat when there is a break in the action, to avoid blocking someone's view of an important play. Also, do not jump up and stand for an extended period of time, blocking the view of those behind you. Always be aware and courteous.

If the person in front of you stands and blocks your view, politely ask him or her to be seated and remember to smile, maintaining a controlled demeanor, and say "please" and "thank you." In the heat of the moment, it is easy to forget to say these powerful words! Keep in mind that people are not intentionally being rude; they are simply caught up in the moment and displaying their excitement. Your tone of voice and facial expression are very important when addressing someone else's rude behavior.

If you are the client or guest, and the team you are watching or supporting is unfamiliar to you (or not your favorite), you still need to show some enthusiasm and support. Stand and cheer with your group. Demonstrate good spectator sportsmanship. Be sympathetic if the team you are expected to support is defeated—even though you may be delighted.

In the excitement of the game, avoid displaying anger or frustration at a play. You are not the one on the field making decisions. You are a spectator! It is okay to yell, but it is not okay to use profane, angry, or abusive language. Do not distract the players or argue with the coach. They are making the best possible decisions at that moment, from their points of view.

Role of the Participant

Being a participant allows you to be physical and competitive. It is also a great way to entertain a small number of guests who prefer an exercise-related activity. Often these activities are part of a fundraising event or a sponsored marathon. Here are some sports in which you are actively involved:

Examples of Active Sports	
■ Biking (Bike-a-thons)	■ Bowling
■ Walk or Run Marathon	■ Golf
■ Tennis or racquetball	■ Hiking
■ Volleyball	■ Lazer Tag or Paintball
■ Swimming	■ Dancing

Participatory sports offer an excellent opportunity to build relationships and are great stress reducers. Again, the focus should be on the spirit of the game and not ego-related. Winning should be based on contributing to the group, integrity, dedication, and sacrifices for the betterment of the team.

If illness or a family emergency prevents you from playing, offer to find someone to take your place or let the event host (boss or client) decide how you will be replaced. This is especially important if a team requires a set number of people. You would not want to be responsible for a forfeit! Never cancel because you simply do not feel like following through on your commitment or because something more interesting came up. Honoring your commitment demonstrates your character and integrity.

Before participating in an event, get in shape. This is no time to take a crash course in exercise, especially if you have been inactive for a long period of time. It may be a good idea to see your doctor beforehand to be sure you are in good enough condition to participate! Then follow your doctor's advice on an exercise routine to get in shape.

Caution: The host or events committee should be watchful of participants who might collapse because their bodies are dehydrated from the heat, or who might experience hypothermia in cold water or cold weather.

Respect your body's limitations and the weather conditions. It is important to make sure that you and your guests are taking all the necessary precautions.

Ask if you will need to bring your own sporting equipment. If you do not have the necessary equipment, check on rental availability ahead of time. Do not assume that the event organizer or your host is going to provide all the equipment or that equipment rental will be available at the site.

Arrive early to allow time for warming up and meeting the other participants, if you have not already met.

> When participating in a run, be aware of the participants alongside you. Do not crowd or elbow someone to gain an edge. Your good sportsmanship (and participant number) is being observed on the sidelines.

In summary

Be honest and realistic about your ability. If you are an exceptional player, be humble. If you are a competitive player, show restraint even when you're trying to gain the edge. If it is a participatory sport, such as golf, and you are a stronger player, simply play to have fun instead of being competitive, and be humble about your level of play. Do not throw a game; it would be more embarrassing for the "winner" and could damage your career. Make it an enjoyable experience for everyone.

> Sportsmanship, like courage,
> is grace under pressure.

CLOSE THE DEAL OVER A GAME OF GOLF

> When asked if his father was the key to his golf success, Tiger Woods smiled and responded, *"I set unachievable goals. When I achieve one, I set another unachievable goal."*

Avid golfers will say that golfing has played a key role in helping them set goals, make new contacts or solidify a contract, expand a client base or negotiate deals. Golf can also play a role in determining if an individual is right for a promotion or the right person to hire. Regardless of the intended business goal, the joy of the game must be part of the equation. Golf is the most popular business sport, both domestically and internationally.

For many companies, golf outings are as integral to corporate life as board meetings, annual reviews, and special events. If you are invited to play a game of golf with a prospective employer or the boss, do not decline because you feel you are too much of a novice or the sport does not appeal to you. It is important to realize that it will help build a stronger relationship, and it will give you the opportunity to display your skills (no matter how weak or strong), tenacity, and sportsmanship. Most importantly, it will demonstrate whether or not you can win or lose with grace and style.

If you are a novice or unfamiliar with the game, take lessons. One cannot simply pick up a golf club and perform well. Learn the etiquette and rules of golf—especially for business golf. Get the answers to your questions in advance, to avoid turning your golf partner (client or boss) into an instructor.

It is essential to know the rules of golf, the proper attire, pace guidelines, and course courtesies. If you are more interested in the game than discussing any business, it should be made clear up front, but you should always remain flexible.

When you are invited to play in a golf outing, be honest about your skill level. If you have not played in a very long time or are new to the game and will be playing with seasoned players, take refresher lessons first, and play a few practice rounds before you join the experienced group. If you have the option, play nine holes on your first few outings before venturing into an eighteen-hole game. An eighteen-hole round of golf should not take more than four and a half hours. This equates to fifteen minutes per hole (eight minutes per hole would be unreasonable).

Whether you are host or guest, be sure to investigate— subtly, of course—the expectations and abilities of the others in your group before you head out to the first tee. What are their handicaps? What is their level of experience? Are they serious or casual players?

Behavior Expectations

Proper behavior is just as important as knowing the basic playing techniques. Some feel they can learn more about an individual with one game of golf than they can in a meeting. Perhaps this is why the game of golf is so highly rated and respected. Set your goals, but do not play at the expense of other players. Good form and courtesy are a part of every professional's game. Be on your best behavior, and let your true personality emerge.

How would you answer the following questions?	
1. How do you handle stress?	6. Are you controlling?
2. Do you cheat?	7. Do you have a sense of humor?
3. Do you use foul language?	8. Are you focused?
4. Are you helpful?	9. Are you disruptive?
5. Are you too helpful?	10. Are you self-absorbed?
The answers will all surface during the game of golf. Like dining manners, it is when the "real you" emerges.	

Do not take cell phones or any mobile technology onto the course with you. Some golf courses have banned the use of cell phones on the course. Many golfers, however, will still receive and make calls or click out e-mail or text messages between shots. This is rude! If you are expecting an emergency call (e.g., medical), put your phone on vibrate—do not let it ring. And when it does vibrate, return the call at a considerate time: for example, at the snack bar or when moving to the next tee.

When Is It Proper to Bring Up Business?

When business is discussed will depend largely on the type of foursome you have. Are they a mix of company people and vendors? Get involved and enjoy the game first, and then bring up business. As in dining, when to bring up business can vary. It all depends on your time frame, the number of holes you are playing, and your golfing partners. Some will start at tee time; however, this is not recommended if it is your first game with the foursome. Tee-time business chat typically takes place with a foursome that meets on a regular basis. If you need a rule that is generally respected, play at least halfway into the game before bringing up any business.

There is an unspoken rule that suggests that you never bring up business before the sixth hole during an eighteen-hole game.

If you are playing with an association or club, you may discover that business is discussed early on the green; however, with a client, the subject of business should be avoided until at least the sixth hole, unless your client brings it up earlier in the game. Some will recommend that you focus on golf and talk business at the nineteenth hole, which is considered the watering hole at the clubhouse.

If your customer or client is using the golf course as an opportunity to ask you key questions that are very important to him or her, simply answer the questions in a concise manner and immediately go back to the game to maintain a casual camaraderie. This is not the time to get into a lengthy discussion; it would be too disruptive to the game. In the spirit of the game, suggest that lengthy discussions be played out afterward. The game of golf is serious business. If someone is trying to use the golf time to monopolize everyone's time discussing business, it is not a good sign and will usually backfire.

Play a Game of Integrity

Integrity is the name of the game. Golf brings together both sportsmanship and etiquette. It is not how far you hit the ball that matters most, but instead how you spend this time with your client or peer. Again, know the rules of golf, the pace guidelines, and the course courtesies, and always dress in appropriate golf apparel and shoes. And, as with any sport, know the sport's etiquette to avoid common missteps.

For non-playing spouses, make tennis or some other activity available and set a time for dinner when everyone can participate. Tee times in this type of setting should be in the 10:00 AM to 11:00 AM range. This allows plenty of time to warm up and finish in time to relax and get ready for dinner.

Checklist: Before You Arrive at the Golf Course

☑ Know the skill of your guests, and choose your course accordingly.

☑ Know how far in advance to make reservations.

☑ Know if the course will have what you need: rental clubs, carts, and restaurant.

☑ Know that there are no special events or activities at the course that will disrupt your round.

☑ Know course policies. (Are metal spikes allowed? Spectators?)

☑ Know what game and rules you will be following.

☑ Know the cart rules, and adhere to them.

☑ Know how to keep the pace of play.

☑ Know good golf course etiquette (raking traps, repairing ball marks, knowing where to stand).

 Avoid the Following Three Common Missteps

1. Lying about your score or handicap
2. Moving or creating a distraction when someone is teeing off
3. Talking when someone is about to swing

Tips and Terms from

Donna Hoffman, President of Women on Course

Dan Hotchkin, Golf Pro, Palatine Golf Club

1. When you are not playing a hole well and find yourself lagging behind or getting frustrated, pick up your ball after ten strokes (or less) and just say, "I've had enough fun on this hole."

2. Do not take your "technology toys" (cells phones, pagers) on the course, or be sure to turn them off.

3. If you are a novice, it is perfectly okay to set your own rules if everyone is playing his own ball (and you are not in a tournament situation). To make the game more enjoyable, you might say that you are going to start play at the 150 marker

or that you will be teeing up your ball on the fairway to make it easier to hit. Your playing partners will appreciate your attempt to keep up the pace of play.

4. Golf is a game of integrity. Never intentionally play poorly. If your partner is a novice, do not overplay your game.

5. The one who invites pays, unless it is understood that the cost will be shared.

6. Do not offer tips or instructions on someone else's play unless they ask for them.

7. Do not mention business if you have not yet reached at least the sixth hole, unless your client does first. Timing is every-thing.

8. Shout "Good sandy" when your partner hits a nice shot out of the bunker.

   Tip: A *sandy* is when a golfer still makes his par after escaping from a sand hazard.

9. Never talk while a fellow player is teeing off.

10. Take only one practice swing in the *tee box*.

    Tip: Teeing ground, tee box, and tee markers: The teeing ground is the area at the beginning of a hole from which the player's first stroke is taken. The area where the stroke will be taken is called the tee box. The boundaries of the teeing ground are defined by a pair of tee markers. Each set of tee markers is a different color. Players then play based on their tee-marker color.

11. Remain in the tee box until everyone in the foursome has teed off.

12. Always replace your *divots* in the fairway.

    Tip: A *divot* refers to the turf area that is scraped up by the golf club or the scarred area in the fairway where the turf has been sliced away. The divot can show whether the shot was made in front of the ball or behind the ball.

A good divot will start just in front of where the ball was at rest, which indicates that your club struck the ball first. After the shot, the divot should be repaired.

13. Don't throw or slam your club onto the ground after a bad shot.

14. Be ready to play at all times ("ready golf").

15. Rake the sand trap after every *bunker shot.*

Tip: Bunker: Also called a sand trap. A bunker shot is a stroke taken in the sandy area.

16. Fix your ball mark on the green.

Tip: Ball marker: When your ball makes a mark landing on the green, you should use your ball marker to fix it. Fixing your ball mark is a courtesy to other golfers. Not fixing it leaves a bumpy green.

17. Don't walk or cast a shadow in another player's putting line.

18. Pick up your ball from the hole once you have reached double bogey.

Tip: A bogey: A score of 1-over par on any individual hole.

Tip: Double bogey: A hole played two strokes over par.

19. Know the golf scoring format (par).

Tip: A par is the standard score for a hole, as determined by its length. The par rating for the course is the sum of all the pars set for each hole.

More Tips from Golf Veterans

The following tips are the result of a survey by Global Protocol, Inc., conducted by seminar participants who spend their entertaining dollars and time on the golf course.

1. The business or host typically pays for everything. This includes green fees, all rentals (e.g., carts, clubs, practice buckets, shoes), a box of balls, plus food and drink on and

off the course. If you are the host, ask your guests if they need gloves or hats at the start of play. Gratuities for valets, caddies, and food for the group are up to the host. (The host should tell the group, "It is covered.") Gifts are optional. (A shirt or visor is a nice takeaway gift.)

2. It is okay to match up the foursomes ahead of time, but the idea is to be socially focused. Match individuals to maximize the fun, not to discuss business.

3. When placing very good players and occasional players together in a foursome or grouping of several foursomes, try to keep the handicap range within ten points. If the participants are occasional players without handicaps, attempt to group them together and have them tee off last. If there are players who are true beginners, team them with better players (ask first) and then play a best-ball type of game, especially on the drives. Remain at the tee box until everyone in the foursome has teed off. Let faster foursomes play through.

4. Never take more than fifteen minutes per hole, never spend more than two minutes looking for a ball, and never take more than one practice swing per shot.

5. Do not stand behind anyone driving, and do not walk across a player's lie on the green.

6. Play ready golf. This requires some judgment in order not to rush the game or interfere with another person's shot, but generally, if you are ready, make the shot.

7. Begin to discuss business in a light manner on the tenth through the sixteenth hole during fairway play. Never bring up business when people are in the tee box or on the putting green. Keep discussions short and light. Plan for a more in-depth conversation at some future time after the game. Remember, the primary goal is to play golf and relax.

8. In a business-related social setting, betting on games is

best avoided, especially with a group that has never played together.

9. Do not rub in a fellow player's bad golf shot or dwell on your own bad shots! If you play once a week or once every two weeks, you are going to hit your share of bad shots.

10. Learn to repair a ball mark on the green before you play your first round. Failure to do is a discourtesy for the other players.

11. Do not hold up a game with conversation, stopping for a drink, taking a cell phone call, or checking your smartphone. Turn your cell phone or beeper off and put away your smartphone to avoid the temptation.

12. Understand that you rake a sand trap after you are out of the trap.

13. Do not walk into your playing partner's putting line. Move away from the green after putting.

14. Do not hit into the group in front of you.

15. Do not drag your spikes on the greens. Spikeless shoes are now worn on most golf courses. Some courses do not allow spikes! Always check.

16. Do not park carts too close to the greens.

17. Never give unsolicited golf tips to another player.

18. On the green, do not let your shadow fall across the line of someone else's putt, and do not step on the line of his putt.

19. Be considerate of others by keeping your round of golf moving—park your cart behind the green or near the next tee, write down your score after you leave the green, and hit when your turn comes.

20. Avoid negative comments toward others on the course. Golf is supposed to be relaxing and fun.

21. Do not stare at a new player while he is trying to tee off.

22. Be humble. Let your golf game do the talking; do not brag.

23. Do not stand behind someone about to swing, and do not

stand on the tee with him or her—that makes the person feel crowded.

24. Do not move or create a distraction when someone is teeing off. Do not talk when someone is about to swing. And do not stand where you will cast your shadow and disturb someone who is putting.

25. Use business language! Do not use foul or vulgar language or tell distasteful jokes.

> ### ▪☞ A Frequently Asked Golf Question
>
> *Q) If I play golf with my boss (or client), should I let him or her win?*
>
> A) Do not patronize your boss. Your boss will surely know if you let him or her win. Likewise, do not show off your skill by winning the game by a wide margin. A close win is better, regardless of who wins.

Do not overtly try to lose; it could be embarrassing or even career-damaging. If you are a stronger player, simply play to have fun instead of being competitive, and be humble about your level of play.

Try to find a balance. Much will depend on the personalities of the people you are playing with. What are their expectations? Your role is to make this an enjoyable experience, whether you are golfing with your boss or with a client.

> Golf is more about bonding and building the relationship than winning the game.

③

THE TEAM-BUILDING REALITY EXPERIENCE

Team-building exercises are typically conducted as part of a corporate retreat, and they involve structured problem-solving exercises followed by informal discussions. People are typically divided into small groups and then come together at the end of the day for a debriefing session.

Do not confuse a team-building exercise (e.g., an outdoor rope course) with an episode on a reality-based television show. While many of these shows have been embraced by the public, some set a bad example for those who believe the shows are reality and not entertainment. Those that model wrong lessons have harmful, long-lasting consequences. Competition is healthy, but do not let it damage relationships with individuals or with your culture.

Vicious verbal attacks, out-of-control egos, and demeaning attitudes contribute to the cultural climate that exists in some of today's television reality shows. Unfortunately, negative emotional ramifications affecting a colleague could last a lifetime. This is not what a team-building exercise or retreat is meant to be.

Retreats or outings are meant to build self-esteem and relationships; these are the real reality shows. Do not say or do things that humiliate or denigrate others. The games are designed to be experiences involving skill, teamwork, and trust in each other.

> *I think that sometimes the stuff we do at employee retreats is kind of cheesy, but it is supposed to be that way in order to get you out of your element for a time. Name games and funny activities keep you going through what would normally be a long day of just information. Cheesy works, and it is good for your soul every so often.*
>
> —Zachary Kimble, director of sales and marketing,
> Denver Marriott

The objectives and ground rules should be clearly defined. If the objectives are not clear, tactfully seek clarification. Keep it professional!

 For example:

- You have to be confident but not cocky, bold but not brash.
- Work hard, play hard, but play professionally and with dignity. Do not exchange your career or image for one moment of indiscretion or bad behavior.
- The intent of many retreats is to build team effectiveness, solve problems, develop new skills, and more. Their success and benefits will depend upon each individual participating effectively and interacting appropriately.
- If you are a woman, do not try to be "one of the guys"; be yourself.
- Display a good sense of humor.

Experiential Learning Activities

There has been a movement toward active training models—generally referred to as experiential training. Many companies are finding that experiential training can have a positive impact on productivity. Experiential programs place people in structured environments designed to reflect situations in the workplace.

Although it is more common with employees, clients may be included. The focus of this type of training is on teamwork, communication, and leadership. It is also fun.

 Some examples of experiential training environments:

- Team challenge courses.

- Rock or wall climbing.

- High ropes courses (uses ropes, harnesses, cables, etc., for off-the-ground challenges).

- Portable initiatives (indoor and outdoor challenges that do not use challenging ropes).

The power of teamwork is explored most often in business simulations (aka initiatives) that provide an environment of "learning by doing." Not only are you having fun, but you are also learning how to work within a team environment through awareness and skill building. This can be a real test of your loyalty, ethics, and trust. Loyalty and trust do not come easily for everyone, especially in a competitive work environment. Developing these attributes needs constant attention and reinforcement.

If a company implements this kind of program, it is essential to debrief people after each activity to ensure that learning transfers back to the workplace. This process is guided by the theory that we learn from disciplined reflection on experience. A facilitator will guide the group discussion so that individual learning can come from the shared experience. Many key points can be drawn to help the participants better connect the experiential training with the real world in which they work.

The following is an example of a "Breakthrough in the Woods" activity conducted by CMI Experiential.

The one activity that I found the most telling was a test of ethics. Of course, I did not realize that at the time. I was focused on the challenge of the activity. The goal was to retrieve the rope hanging from a tree (with a knot for a seat) from the center of the activity area and swing on it to the other side, landing in one of three Hula-Hoops. While swinging, a team member would hand over a cup of water to be delivered to a team member already standing in a Hula-Hoop on the other side.

The individual swinging was not allowed to spill the water or touch the ground with his feet. Once the water was delivered to the other side, you were passed back to your teammates for another push and expected to land in a Hula-Hoop.

If you spilled the water or touched the ground with your feet at any time while swinging or missed the Hula-Hoop when you landed, you were disqualified and had to start over. One of our team members did graze the ground with his feet, but he thought the facilitator was not looking, and he continued. And his team didn't tell on him. Well, the facilitator did see the touch.

When we processed this activity, the facilitator was very diplomatic, so that no one would be embarrassed, but he did point out how easy it is to cheat or overlook an incident when you are caught up in trying to achieve a goal. The individual who acknowledges his error and starts over demonstrates high ethical standards to his team.

Discussion at the end of each activity and at the end of the day is critical to the success of this learning experience.

Bruce Hodes, president of CMI, Chicago, Illinois, suggests that you keep the following eight points in mind when you are participating in experiential training.

1. Be open-minded and willing to try new things. The more you try, the more you will learn.

2. Contribute to the creation of a climate of trust so that everyone feels free to express his or her thoughts and feelings.

3. Value diversity of opinions and ideas—each person's experience is unique and can be a valuable resource to the group.

4. Engage your mind, your body, and your emotions.

5. The bottom line is that you have a say in which activities you want to take part. "Challenge by choice" gives you the power to participate or not participate in any given activity without question or judgment.

6. Stay focused on safety and follow all safety guidelines described by the facilitator.

7. Commit to 100 percent effort in all activities in which you choose to participate.

8. Examine your experiences, and be open to improving your processes and practices.

Corporate outings can be fun as well as wonderful learning experiences. Any activity that helps us learn how to develop better people skills is invaluable training, especially when it is also fun!

> The real reality shows involves skill,
> teamwork, and trust in each other

GOOD SPORTSMANSHIP, INDOORS OR OUT:
Rules for All Occasions

> Winning should be based on contribution to the group,
> integrity, dedication, and
> sacrifices for the betterment of the group.

A person's ability to perform as a team player indoors is related to his or her ability to perform outdoors. Assertiveness, speed, relentlessness, and determination are assets in both sports and business. Meanness, cheating, and arrogance are not.

Electronic, Mechanical, and Board Games

During the 1990s high-tech era, tabletop games found their way from college dorms into the office. It was not unusual to walk in and find employees playing a game of foosball, BattleTech, laser tag, or paintball. Long hours and stress created the need for a fun in-house activity. Today these games are still paramount in many company lounges or cubicles, especially in high-tech circles. Both employees and clients enjoy them because they offer a different kind of relaxation.

> Don't shoot your boss, even with fake bullets!
> —Zachary Kimble, director of sales and marketing,
> Denver Marriott

Foosball (table football) is probably the most popular and is referred to as "soccer guys on rods." Its popularity has led to lunchtime tournaments in the employee lounge. This is another great way to bring people together without taking evening or weekend time away from families. It is the modern chess match. Although foosball is physical and chess is mental, the level of concentration required to play foosball is similar to a game of chess because you have to constantly outthink your opponent and use excellent eye-hand coordination; however, there are also times when you just need to execute the shot as you would a golf swing.

Whether events are held at a corporate headquarters or a private club, often there are designated game rooms, or the games have been situated in the lounge. Create a poster board describing the game, and include the game rules. This information will be appreciated by those less familiar with the game but eager to give it a try.

Be considerate of others who are waiting to play. Do not monopolize the game. Do not get so caught up in the game that you forget your opponent is your client, boss, or coworker. If you have had more experience with the game, assume a teaching position. Help your partner or opponent understand the game, and have a practice game before you begin a competitive game.

 A Checklist for All Competitive Activities

☑ If you are not familiar with the sport or activity, read an instruction book and learn the terminology. Sign up for lessons if you seriously want to compete. Learn as much as you can before the event, and if possible, practice before you participate.

☑ Be on time. Call if you are delayed. Do not cancel at the last minute. If you have to cancel, suggest a replacement if it is appropriate for the sporting event.

☑ Be tidy in locker rooms or changing areas. Leave the facilities immaculate.

☑ Dress in good taste and within the event guidelines. Clothing should not be revealing or skimpy.

☑ Bring proper equipment. If you are the host, bring extra equipment if none is available for rental.

☑ Be honest about your skill level, and do not cheat. Respect your limitations and the limitations of your guests.

☑ Know all the rules of the game or activity. Observe all rules of fair play and safety guidelines. Avoid quoting facts unless you are absolutely sure of your information and that it came from a reliable source.

☑ Smile when you lose. Shake hands to acknowledge a great game or activity.

☑ Never berate your partner or complain about his or her playing method or style. Also do not discuss "how poorly" your team member or past partner performed, and do not dwell on how badly you played.

☑ Abstain from foul language and outbursts of anger, even if the anger is toward yourself. Do not tell sexist, racist, or demeaning jokes. Do not tell a joke at the expense of another.

☑ Do not take liberties with the property, grounds, or equipment.

☑ Do not encourage or allow gambling.

When finished, shake hands with everyone, compliment their playing, and thank them for letting you join them or for having them as your partner.

> Congratulate the winning team or individual.
> Compliment the losing team.

Chapter 7

APPLAUD, CELEBRATE, AND BENEFIT THOSE WHO SERVE YOU

> *There is no accomplishment so easy to acquire as po-liteness, and none more profitable.*
>
> –George Bernard Shaw, playwright, 1856–1950

Employees (past and present) are customers too! There are scores of stories about how a company goes beyond the call of duty to make a customer feel special. But what about the employees? They have the same power of influence as the customers— sometimes more!—and their influence is too often overlooked or devalued.

 The objectives of this chapter are . . .

1. To reinforce the notion that business parties or events are primarily for socializing and for honoring employees, retirees, and special individuals for their achievements and contributions;

2. To recognize that there are expectations when attending special business functions, for CEOs and managers as well as for employees, their family members, and for clients; and

3. To understand that there are specific protocols for organizing and attending family-focused social events, whether they are wedding celebrations, anniversaries, or picnic-style outings.

When planned effectively, employee parties or gatherings foster goodwill between management and staff, especially during stressful times. They can heal wounds, boost morale, and soothe resentments; however, there are issues to consider when bringing different levels of a company together.

An employee party should be for the purpose of socializing. It is a time to help employees get to know each other better by socializing in a non-work environment. It is also a time to bring employees as well as clients and customers together; however, use discretion by making sure you understand relationships and agendas.

Depending on the nature of the business (e.g., construction, high tech, manufacturing, or service), the comfort level of the company circle should be considered. Learn employees' desires and how they would prefer to socialize. For example, in the industrial construction world, the discontent was significantly increased when the union workers' spouses were brought together for a social gathering. The non-union spouses were not hostile, but undercurrents were present.

—Steve Teeple, president, Safe Air Testing, Inc.

Employee parties or gatherings can range from an informal pizza party to a formal holiday party or celebration dinner. Parties offer you the chance to truly have fun with both coworkers and clients, and to get to know the senior staff. (Refer to chapter 3 for guidelines on how to respond to an invitation and be an impeccable guest at an employee party or function.)

If, for budgetary or other reasons, a company cannot fund a celebration event, it must be made clear to the invitees that the party will be a cooperative venture and that there will be a charge to cover expenses. When planning this type of event, you need a guaranteed number of commitments before signing any venue or catering contract.

The event does not have to be a celebration. Providing a work environment that is conducive to relaxation and promotes a healthy lifestyle is a powerful employee benefit.

More and more companies are adding the benefit of a new "relaxation room," a special area where workers can relax for 30 minutes a day. Some also include game rooms, fitness options, an employee lounge or kitchen stocked with healthy snacks or weight-reducing, energy-enhancing food choices, and themed meeting rooms.

It is all about creating an environment where employees can take a break and relax after working hard on a project or working extra-long hours; thus creating a working environment that translates into a healthier culture.

Special Day Celebrations

Observing employees' birthdays, honoring retirements or resignations, and celebrating weddings means a great deal to most employees; however, it comes with risks. These events need to be carefully planned with sensitivity to everyone's feelings. When a celebration is planned, do not omit anyone, regardless of a personal situation that may exist. The result would only be more hurt feelings. It is possible that the invitation itself could heal a wound, while a non-invitation would only aggravate a personal situation.

Company Anniversaries: The most important company anniversaries are the tenth, twenty-fifth (silver), fiftieth (golden), seventy-fifth (diamond jubilee), and hundredth (centennial) anniversaries. It takes good employee relations from all departments to secure and maintain loyal customers; therefore, when a company anniversary celebration is planned, it should include everyone. The celebration is the company's success story. Make it a *class-act celebration*.

When Bergstrom, Inc., celebrated its fiftieth anniversary, all employees were invited to a gala celebration and banquet, which was also attended by customers, suppliers, advisers, and employee guests. This Rockford, Illinois-based designer and manufacturer of climate systems for the commercial vehicle industry boasts a mission to be the best in the business by any measure.

Bergstrom prepared its team members for the event with a seminar covering formal dress and dining etiquette that was delivered to more than three hundred and fifty employees in both the Rockford and Joliet plants.

It concluded with a networking reception exercise for the sales team and management.

The event was voluntary, and participation was well over 90 percent.

We wanted to make sure everyone felt comfortable and did not feel out of place and, therefore, could have an enjoyable evening. —David Rydell, president

One of our measures of performance is being in the "learning mode." Our employees are accustomed to seeking opportunities to learn new things.

—Elaine Markou, director of human resources

Birthdays: Celebrating an employee's birthday is a long-time tradition. Typically, it involves the birthday employee bringing a cake, donuts, or another treat to work for everyone to enjoy. This way everyone looks forward to the next birthday celebration. Some companies sponsor a special monthly birthday celebration in the employee lounge for everyone who has a birthday that month. Birthday recognitions are a perfect way to make an employee feel special and to build morale.

Retirement: A special party or event should be planned for anyone who has been with the company for a long time. Typically, all employees who have had a connection with the retiree are invited. If appropriate, customers and vendors are also included in the celebration. The CEO (or president) makes a few remarks, followed by remarks from a designated manager, supervisor, or coworker, and a memento (gift) is presented. A great finishing touch would be a photo of the retirement ceremony, with a write-up posted in the next edition of the company newsletter and possibly the local newspaper.

Whatever the celebration, it is important to treat everyone with the utmost respect. Recognition at work makes employees feel special. Being left out makes them feel alienated. As previously mentioned, these celebrations have a direct effect on employee morale, enthusiasm, and productivity; therefore, celebrate to maintain workplace harmony. Support your colleagues (or employees), and they will support you when you need them. A sense of inclusion, particularly among team members, is an important asset at any firm. Attention validates importance.

Employees are a company's prize asset.

ENCOURAGING CAMARADERIE, BUILDING MORALE, AND HANDLING PERSONAL SITUATIONS

Managers should always attend special business functions. These are your opportunities as leaders of your company to give your employees the chance to get to know you in a social setting. It is important for employee morale. The management team's participation and behavior should set the example for the staff.

Don't be reluctant to approach senior management at a party. This is an excellent opportunity to take the initiative by thanking them for the wonderful party. It will make a good impression. Employers and members of the management team are always looking for someone to take the initiative and go that extra step.

An employee's presence is always expected. It would not be to the employee's benefit to decline simply because he or she does not like rubbing elbows with the management team or does not agree with a management decision. This is not about work; it is about putting issues aside and socializing! Seek out the clients or people who work in other areas, and get to know the person behind the phone conversation or e-mail dialogue. Make the effort to walk across the room to acknowledge them with a smile, and express your pleasure at finally meeting or simply talking to that person face to face. It will make the tone of communicating long distance on future projects more welcoming and under-standing.

Include retired employees. Inviting a past employee to a special party (e.g., a retirement party or holiday gathering) lets the employee who is no longer with the company continue to feel appreciated. This is especially true if the working relation-ship is like family, which in many cases it is. It is not easy to let go of family. They are not just past employees; they were a part of your family and are now your consumer ambassadors. The ties are strong.

A party is not the time to offer your ideas or plead your case on something specific. This is a social gathering, so stay mindful of others who might want to join the conversation, and invite them to join you. Also, try to keep conversations short and light to give everyone a chance to converse.

Religious Recognition

Be careful not to offend anyone's religious preference or belief system. If you are planning a holiday party, be sure to use the words "holiday party." By the same token, if you are planning a Christmas party, use the words "Christmas party."

> *Believers of other religions are not offended unless a mocking or disrespectful connotation is aimed at their religion or there is an attempt to alienate someone. When you share your religion and honor theirs, it is a step above respect.*
>
> —Steve Teeple, president, Safe Air Testing, Inc.

It is very difficult to know the religious beliefs of every member of a team. During opening or closing comments, acknowledge the beauty of having different cultural traditions represented and thank everyone for their much-appreciated attendance.

Tips for Holiday Parties

Though some companies have dropped their year-end bashes—sometimes out of financial concerns, sometimes over liability worries—the Christmas holiday remains popular.

> At the close of the day before the holidays began, a manager at a small manufacturing company said "Merry Christmas" to everyone and then turned to Mohammed and said "Happy holidays"

> to him." This singled Mohammed out and made him feel like an outsider instead of part of the team. It was a very humiliating experience for Mohammed. In this case it would have been better simply to say "Happy holidays" or "Merry Christmas" to everyone.

The holidays are the favored time to celebrate, and they can bring about their own unique pitfalls in a multicultural workplace and business environment. "Merry Christmas" or "Happy Holidays"? Red and green, or silver and gold? Companies continue to struggle with the religious nature of the holidays. Sometimes it seems like a no-win situation, because when you try to appease one person, another is offended. There is no easy answer. Organizations have good intentions, and people need to be tolerant. Unintentional things happen that are not meant to offend. A professional individual understands and never takes offense. Always respect the intention.

> *I say "Merry Christmas"; you say "Happy Hanukkah," "Happy Kwanzaa," "Happy Holidays," etc. It is that time of the year again when we are all trying to be politically correct, and it can cause awkward moments, if not a strain. It is simply impossible to know the beliefs of everyone we greet during this special time of the year. It is also unfair to yourself to sidestep your convictions through your holiday greeting.*
>
> *Respect is honoring the position of another; therefore, if I say "Merry Christmas" and you respond with your preferred season's greeting (e.g., "Happy Kwanzaa"), we are good! It is a wonderful way to share our holiday preference and at the same time honor the season.*
>
> *Your personal holiday cards should also reflect your religious or cultural beliefs. Do not use "Happy Holidays" as an escape phrase; use it only if it is truly your preferred holiday greeting.*

> *The exception is a corporate or business "Happy Holidays" card that needs to reflect a wide range of beliefs.*
>
> *As the old saying goes, do not walk on eggshells trying to avoid offending another with your personal greeting. Instead, be understanding and flexible! 'Tis the season for sharing and giving.*

The Question of Office Gifts

A popular way to handle the question of gifts is to chip in together (or pass the hat). A collection of money is made and used to purchase a gift; however, this can also cause awkwardness or hurt feelings. If you pass the hat for one, make sure that it is passed for everyone when his or her special day arrives. Some employees claim that even though they chip in for coworkers, no one ever passes the hat for them. Others claim that it creates an awkward situation if they choose not to give. In a sensitive situation like this, and to avoid resentment, the celebration should take place privately, away from the work environment.

An alternative plan is to put an arbitrary limit on the amount to be spent by any one person; make it purposely low to encourage a fun gift. An exception would be a collection that involves a charity; then the amount might be more generous. There is more on gifts in chapter 9.

An Employee's Death

Probably the most awkward moment of all is the response to an employee's death. First and foremost, treat the family with dignity and kindness. Respect their wishes! Next, offer to help with any arrangements, and send flowers and a card from the company to the funeral home or the interment. Make it possible for those from the company who were close to the individual (or family) to attend the funeral. Last, have someone from the company call a few weeks (two to four weeks) following the funeral to see how everyone is doing. If the deceased was an employee, include a nice obituary in the company newsletter. This is normally done with high-level executives. Still, it is a nice gesture for any employee, regardless of his or her rank within the company.

There is a difference of opinion on whether or not to offer condolences days (or weeks) following the funeral. Some feel it would be disrespectful because it serves as a reminder, and others feel hurt if a coworker (or friend) ignores the loss when the employee returns to work or crosses their path at a company meeting or affair. This is delicate! And sometimes it is a cultural norm on how to show respect. If person-to-person is awkward, send a card to the family, apologize for the late response, and state that you just recently learned of the loss. The worst is to be "too busy" to respond! Your acknowledgement of the loss is part of the healing process.

> Attending events and considering special concerns demonstrates you care about your company and your team.

②

STEPS TO ENJOYING A WORRY-FREE SOIRÉE

A soirée (an evening party or social gathering) offers a wonderful opportunity to meet people outside the usual business environment in a fun and festive way. Soirées are most popular around the holidays; however, a soirée can be attached to any event, large or small. These office parties bring people together and allow different facets of one's personality to shine. Sometimes these get-togethers allow you to reconnect with colleagues that you know but have not seen in a while, or with whom you have only shared e-mail dialogues.

The delicate task of navigating the half-social, half-professional occasion of an office party can leave many employees wishing they could stay home. But it is an ideal opportunity to raise your profile at work in a positive way and make connections that help your career. It is also a chance to show that you are a well-rounded person with interests other than work.

The office party can range from a promotion announcement to a holiday celebration. Regardless of the occasion, it can unite a workplace and rejuvenate the team for the coming year. A badly executed party, however, risks alienating employees, tarnishing the company's reputation, and worse yet, costing someone his or her job; therefore, planning should include behavioral guidelines that are shared with employees, and these should include sensitivity to cultural and religious differences among a diversified workforce and client base.

Get Involved in the Planning

If possible, step up and take part in planning the office party. The person who creates and oversees the office party gains respect as someone who makes things happen in a creative and effective way. This is a great message to send to management and to clients.

Once on the planning committee, be sure to define the occasion on the invitation and pay attention to all the details from beginning to end. The party should be an environment where even the shyest attendee feels at ease. You want to transport everyone out of their workday world by offering them a fun, relaxing, and memorable experience. It should not be just about eating and drinking. It is about helping everyone to enjoy himself or herself and learn more about each other.

Attend! Your Attendance Could Open the Door to Advancement

You are invited but have decided you don't want to attend. As previously mentioned, attending is important for both the management team and their respective staff members. Not attending could be detrimental to your career, so you need to have a very good reason for not attending. Missing one company activity probably will not impede your career. Being a perpetual no-show, on the other hand, can cause a company to question your commitment, especially if the position requires you to interact with clients and prospects. If you hesitate to attend because of shyness, focus your attention on introducing others and making sure everyone is connecting. This takes the pressure off how you are going to circulate.

> *If you accept an invitation and then do not show up, you are in essence demonstrating that you lack follow-up skills, you are undependable, and you clearly are not a team player. How you act socially reflects on how you perform in a business setting.*
>
> –Tranda Covington, business operations manager, Motorola

Attending a company party also raises your visual awareness with management and builds a stronger camaraderie with coworkers. Before you attend, find out what is going on in different departments. People like talking about their accomplishments and will appreciate your asking. At the same time, learn about company opportunities by making yourself known to management. This could prove to be an important influence on your position with the company. But do not attend with only your personal agenda in mind. This will be obvious and is self-serving.

Once you arrive, mingle! Do not cluster with the same group of people all evening. Nor should you avoid someone because he or she is culturally different, has an accent, or is physically challenged. This would be counterproductive. When mingling, engage in conversation, circulate, and help others connect. Make sure that your conversations are lighthearted and your topics neutral.

A Party on the Fly

Sometimes the best party is a spontaneous party. Make sure that your spontaneous invitation is targeted appropriately and that you can easily manage the number of invitees. The number of invitations should match the available seating and room size. The location could be a reserved corner of your favorite lounge (reception format), your community clubhouse, or your home.

You will need one great item to serve, such as pizza, and an assortment of munchies (e.g., cheese and crackers or chips). Be sure to include bottled water and sodas along with any alcoholic beverages that are planned. If appropriate, and if you need to keep your cost down, specify BYOB (bring your own bottle) or a snack to pass.

> *Caution:* A BYOB (bring your own bottle) can only be offered if the event is in someone's home or if the establishment has a special liquor license. There is a liability involved.

Protect Your Reputation, and Be Mindful of Consequences

How do you want your behavior to be discussed on Monday? The top "party naughtiness" is typically excessive drinking and inappropriate attire, followed by rowdy behavior and off-color jokes. Have fun, but keep it professional! Be aware that clients are more willing to invest in a person or company that demonstrates proper behavior at all times. You are your company's best reputation builder.

Management must (and does) pay attention to how employees and vendors alike handle themselves in a party environment, to ensure that reputations are protected.

> *True colors can be shown with elegance and conviction. The politically correct statements made by so many are actually offensive to transparent people with good upbringing and the desire to maintain standards. Offending people is rarely the answer. Thinking before speaking is high on the list of answers.*
>
> —Steve Teeple, president, Safe Air Testing, Inc.

It is easy to be comfortable with people you know—so comfortable that you let your guard down too much. To unwind at a party after a busy workweek is great with family and friends; however, proceed with caution if the boss, coworkers, or clients are present. That's because there are spoken and unspoken *rules of behavior* that apply to work-related events.

Inappropriate behavior can result in a promotion tiebreaker that does not go in your favor. It can also affect your performance review. Be aware that some companies have dropped employee-focused celebrations over past inappropriate behavior or liability worries.

Avoid the following:

- Drinking too much—alcohol can have a devastating effect.

- Discussing business in the presence of clients or guests.

- Behaving in a disorderly fashion.

- Telling off-color jokes or jokes at the expense of others.

- Dressing or posing inappropriately, either too sloppily or too sexily.

Concerns over lawsuits involving excessive drinking and risqué behavior have prompted many employers to ban office parties, especially during the holidays. When they are organized, the corporate or outside professional planners are giving employees two drink tickets, arranging cabs, and reviewing the music selection. Other planners are finding creative ways to throw a holiday party without alcohol. For example, some are opting for a coffee or hot chocolate bar, where guests stir cinnamon, marshmallows, mint flavoring, and cream into their drinks.

The following are tips to help you ensure that your behavior is appropriate, undamaging, and on target:

Beware of social media. People who love parties typically are looking forward to an opportunity to "let their hair down"! Beware, however, that in this era of social networks, your party misbehavior can be posted for the world to see. Your company's reputation and your reputation are one and the same. Furthermore, when it comes to social media websites, the comments and photos that are posted are often permanent.

Put your electronics away! It is rude and sends a message of self-involvement when you initiate or take calls on your smartphone or text instead of mingling. Your electronic device is not your date! But that is exactly what it looks like when you stand off by yourself and text instead of mingling with those present.

Avoid personal infringements. Do not take unsolicited photos with your digital camera or cell phone and then post them on the web without their knowledge. This is a personal infringement. Taking photos of coworkers and sharing them as memories may be perfectly appropriate, but how you share them should be approved by management and those who appear in the photos.

Dress appropriately. This is not a time to wear your sexiest ensemble to show off your body. It is still business. Whether the event is casual or formal, if you are uncertain about the dress code or expectation, ask! Your attire is part of your reputation.

Limit your alcohol intake. Do not lose control of yourself! It is easy to feel pressured to order alcoholic beverages at social affairs. Nonalcoholic beverages are just as appropriate. If you do drink alcoholic beverages, drink in moderation, or avoid them if you know your tolerance level is low. A good rule of thumb is to alternate with water or another nonalcoholic beverage.

What happens if you make a fool of yourself at a party? Make an official apology to the people involved the very next day at work, and then move on. Do not over-apologize. If the incident is discussed, comments will surely include your ability to own up to the misbehavior and apologize. Consequently, the end result is less damaging and most likely ignored. It would be worse to try to pretend the incident never happened. In this case, gossip would surely take over and spread about your behavior, damaging your reputation.

Be mindful and careful. Your reputation and the reputation of your company are still under scrutiny. This is not a time to vent about personal discontent or to drink to excess. Do not allow an incident to ruin a reputation you have spent years building. Make things right on the next working day. You will be remembered for how the incident ends, more so than the incident itself.

> You are at your most vulnerable at a party.
>
> Protect your reputation.

③
TIPS FOR
FAMILY-FOCUSED EVENTS

How you prepare each member of your family for attending a social business event will depend on his age, personality, and social skills. Certainly, you can engage in a crash course on appropriate behavior, but sometimes a reminder that simple courtesies and respect of elders are important will suffice.

Brief your spouse on key people, like the members of management, and on your association with specific people, like members of your team. Upon arrival, introduce your family. Do not ignore young children once you have arrived at an event. You cannot expect them to find something to do or another child to play with on their own. Make sure that your children are introduced to other children. If you help them adjust and enjoy the event, chances are that their behavior will be more respectful and less disruptive.

> *Be careful. Do not become so totally concerned with what others think of you that you miss out on the real spirit of the gathering. Most family-focused gatherings are happy occasions—except for funerals. You should make every effort to participate in the festivities, whether they are mixer games, formal theatrics, or simply conversations. Lighten up! Do not be afraid of good, clean humor or stories.*
>
> *—Steve Teeple, president, Safe Air Testing, Inc.*

Walking into a room of strangers creates a certain amount of anxiety for anyone, regardless of age. It is human nature to be consumed with being liked and making the perfect impression, especially with coworkers. At a family-focused event it is just as important to focus on having fun and not to be too paranoid about family behavior. People respect individuality, and manners bring home the family upbringing. Be confident but not cocky or arrogant. A positive attitude breeds a positive outcome.

When you plan activities, have activities with children and activities without children.

Popular family-focused events include the following	
■ Picnics	■ Ball games
■ Pizza parlors	■ Children's theater
■ Beach or pool parties	■ County and state fairs
■ Mini putt islands	■ Amusement parks
■ Circuses	■ Bowling

What to Do with the Children

Children can be great catalysts for mixing; however, they will often act out if they are bored or feeling ignored. Therefore, it is important to have activities planned for the children as well.

At a family-focused event with children divide the ages into groups and plan your activities based on the age group. Also, have a special menu for the kids. Most popular foods are macaroni, hot dogs, corn dogs, French fries, pancakes, pizza.

Plan activities that include the entire family, but also give parents a break so that they can enjoy their activities. However, if your child is disruptive, make your apologies and take corrective steps with your child in a private area. In consideration of the other guests, you should excuse yourself from the gathering if the behavior continues. How you handle the situation will have a direct effect on others' perception of your ability to remain calm under pressure.

 Keep Children Safe with the Following Security Steps:

   ■ Leave your activity agenda with the child care monitors

or chaperones so that the parent can be reached quickly if there is an emergency.

- Ask parents to fill out a permission and information form. This form should include food allergies, medical conditions, and a brief description of the child's personality (e.g., shy, hyperactive, sensitive, aggressive).

- Develop a system that matches the parent to the child. For example, consider having wrist bands in different colors and match the child's colored band to the parent's. Both parents and their children wear the same color wrist band. The band could be assigned an ID name and password or the child's last name. If there is an emergency, the colored wrist bands will make the parents easier to find.

Spouses need personal time as well. Avoid having a spouse responsible for their children during the entire event. Make special child care and activity arrangements.

Child monitors: These monitors make sure that the children are kept busy and help them interact. Child monitors could be older teenagers of employees. They will love the opportunity to be paid.

Babysitting service for babies and toddlers: The safety and security of the children is paramount. Arrange for licensed and screened child care professionals (e.g., care.com). This will allow the spouse more freedom to enjoy the event and peace of mind that their child is well cared for.

Supervised activities for grade school age children: Consider someone who is good with games and crafts. Attention spans are very short. Here are some examples:

- Sports skill class (e.g., child learns the fundamentals of golf, baseball, tumbling)
- Clowns who entertain

- Face painters
- Storytellers
- Arts and crafts

Chaperone for pre-teens and teenagers: This should be an adult who will make sure that the teens stay on the property and interact. Plan activities; however, realize that many teens are very independent and will prefer to spend time in an arcade room or interact in their way.

At the end of the day, have a family banquet meal, and have everyone share what they enjoyed the most instead of having a formal speaker. You can accomplish this by bringing a microphone to each table; ask who would like to share their day or activity. This is a great way to give families the spotlight.

> This is a perfect time to put the spotlight on the family.

WEDDINGS AND THE WORKPLACE
What to Do and What Not to do

—by Angela Gregory

Angela Gregory, wedding consultant for the Riverside Church in the city of New York, offers the following advice if you are invited to a coworker's or client's wedding.

Weddings are a delightful part of the human experience, so it stands to reason that at some point in your working life, you are bound to hear about the impending wedding of a boss, a colleague, or a client. You may be on the receiving end of an invitation, or you may be the lucky one who gets to issue the invitation. Either way, you should exercise good judgment apart from emotion—because, very simply, you never want to do anything that will adversely affect your currency in the workplace. When it comes to social events, offending a boss, a colleague, or a client is easier than you think—so when in doubt, do not be afraid to consult a good etiquette book or an experienced wedding planner.

A Few Tips for Navigating the Waters

1. *Accepting Invitations*

If you are the boss, you are under no obligation to accept invitations from the staff. In fact, if it will set a precedent that you would prefer to avoid—for example, accepting all invitations from staff—it might be wiser to decline. It is always appropriate to send a note of congratulations, and a gift perhaps, particularly if the employee is a close member of your staff and one with whom you have frequent interaction. An invitation

from an important client should always receive consideration and be handled with diplomacy. If you cannot
attend, a note of congratulations and a gift are appropriate. In fact, receiving an invitation is an honor and
should be treated as such.

If you are an employee, you are under no obligation to
accept an invitation that comes from a colleague or
client; you should accept or decline based upon your
relationship. If your interaction is frequent and personal,
accepting an invitation is appropriate. Once again, if you
decline, do so with a note of congratulations. A gift may
be a nice gesture, but one should be sure that the gift is
tasteful and appropriate.

2. *Attending Events*

If you attend the wedding of a boss, colleague, or client, you
should behave in a professional fashion. Yes, it is a wedding, a
lovely social occasion replete with flowers, food, and dancing,
and very possibly an open bar. It is a time of celebration and
merriment—but it is also an arena in which other colleagues
and business associates may be present. Your behavior should
never be the subject of Monday morning gossip or anything
that can adversely affect your reputation in the workplace.
The respect of colleagues can take years to earn, and it can
be tarnished in one inappropriate, alcohol-fueled exchange.

3. *Regarding Same-Sex Weddings*

As we all know, historic legislation has been passed in
several states that now allows same-sex couples to legally
marry. Regardless of your personal position on this subject,
in the workplace, you should exercise the same decorum that
you would when broaching matters of religion or politics—
simply stay clear. Essentially, if you are in favor of same-sex
marriage, you risk alienating coworkers that are not; if you
are not in favor of same-sex marriage, you risk alienating
those that are.

If you are invited to the wedding of a coworker in a same-sex relationship, use the guidelines listed above for gift giving and notes of congratulation. Conversely, if you are not invited to the wedding, don't be offended—coworkers may wish to keep this area of their lives private, and it is their right to do so. If you are uncomfortable attending but know it would be politically prudent to do so, attend with an open heart and joyful spirit; lay aside your views for a few hours, and enjoy. Under no circumstances should you make negative comments during the event; it is a celebration, not an opportunity for public discourse—and you never know who is at the next table or in the next bathroom stall, overhearing you. And of course, be mindful of body language and facial expressions that would let your discomfort be known.

Remember to observe gender-neutral language when referring to same-sex couples. Same-gendered couples do not necessarily wish to be referred to as *husband and husband* or *wife and wife*. Finding gender-appropriate cards is not a problem, and a lovely personalized note is always appropriate. To avoid giving offense, refer to your coworker's significant other by his or her first name, or as *partner* or *spouse*. I have coordinated many same-sex weddings, and at the end of the day, I have come to know that the common theme of these, and of all weddings, is love—real, abiding, and committed love. And love is always something to celebrate!

I'm Getting Married: A Toolbox

1. *Leave the wedding binder home.* Yes, we are happy for you, but don't take up company time and resources surfing the Internet for gown trunk shows and invitation stationery. Furthermore, the last thing your boss needs to think is that you've lost your focus on company business because you are planning your wedding.

2. *Be sensitive.* Yes, your wedding is a wonderful occasion, but a colleague who just had a death in the family may not feel like hearing about magenta table napkins and your calla lily centerpieces.

3. *Electronic invitations?* If the invitation is to attend a wedding shower, perhaps. If it is to attend your wedding, *absolutely not.* A wedding is a sacred, dignified event that calls for nothing less than an actual invitation. Receiving an invitation is an honor; it signifies that the recipient is important enough to be invited to this milestone event.

4. *And speaking of wedding showers,* speak to your human resources department and find out the company policy on parties in the workplace. This is one of those areas in which offending colleagues is almost guaranteed unless everyone is invited. A better strategy would be to have parties and showers offsite—and, please, no public invitations on the bulletin board!

Some Words on Behavior

I have experienced over five hundred wedding events. At this point, I've probably touched miles of tulle and a forest of calla lilies and roses, and tasted a small lake of champagne. It is an honor to accompany couples at this particular moment in their lives, and although I have heard the words hundreds of times, I never get tired of hearing the promises to love, honor, and cherish. It is probably at that moment that I am able to forgive some of the outrageous behavior I often experience on the road to that moment. I'd like to share the following ten tips for those of you on the wedding planning journey.

1. "Bridezilla" *is a TV show, not a how-to manual.* It, and shows like it, are meant to be provocative and over-dramatized. How else would they get you to tune in week after week?

2. *"I want what I want, when I want it."* This is irritating when

coming from the mouth of a five-year-old. It is sad, boorish, and frankly unattractive coming from a full-grown adult.

3. *Be realistic.* The bride and groom create immeasurable wedding angst when they have unrealistic expectations. If you cannot afford something, face the fact, accept it, and move on. Tuna steak cannot be turned into Chilean sea bass—I don't care how skilled the chef is.

4. *It is a privilege to be asked to be a member of a wedding party.* However, bridal attendants are not pincushions; they are human beings. Choose them carefully and thoughtfully.

5. *Keep the focus.* A wedding is a public declaration of a very sacred promise between two people and should be treated with reverence. It is not about the bridal fashion show, it is not about the floral arrangements, and it is not about the Viennese table. The substance of the day lies in the promises. Without those, it's just a church service and a nice party.

6. *Stress is a part of real life.* The stress of planning a wedding is not an excuse to browbeat, belittle, or humiliate family, friends, and the people who are trying to help you, whether you are paying them or not. Personally, I'd be a little concerned about being tethered throughout eternity to someone who loses his or her humanity over planning a church service and a nice party.

7. *Weddings are big business.* We are influenced by powerful marketing, and we are conditioned at a very young age to want the "fairytale." Sit down together as a couple and discuss openly what your wedding means to you. Decide what elements are most important and what things are less important. Be able to clearly articulate your vision, not the one in the latest bridal magazine. Shop around for a good wedding planner, if you need one. There are some great ones out there, but they are not mind readers.

8. *Don't be afraid to seek counsel.* Premarital counseling is mandated by some denominations, but don't be afraid to ask for additional help if you need guidance navigating family, stress, anger, and communication issues.

9. *Don't begin your new life together in a whirlwind of negative energy.* If you believe at all that what goes around comes around, realize that the negative energy you cast out into the universe will return to you. Your behavior may wound a valued relationship in ways that can never be healed.

10. *You will not receive better service with a tantrum.* You will not receive better service if you threaten to sue everyone you meet. The cake will not taste sweeter. The band will not play better. The ice will still melt. What you will do is to succeed in alienating everyone in your midst. Incivility eclipses the beauty of any bride—instead of being the fairytale princess, you have become the wicked stepsister who stole her tulle ball gown.

In 2006, I wrote an article for the *Poughkeepsie Journal* on the "Bridezilla" phenomenon, and a few hundred events later, unfortunately, I am still amazed at some of the behavior of adults in the wedding planning process. The tips listed above are from my original article. They are a reminder that outrageous behavior can affect friendships and family ties. In the workplace, however, bad behavior can derail progress it has taken you years to make, erode respect, damage strategic alliances, and tarnish your personal brand, which in the end is all you actually have. Please, be happy, be wise, and behave yourself—someone is always watching.

Chapter 8

CONFERENCES, CONVENTIONS, AND TRADE SHOWS

> Conventions and trade shows are powerful forums that allow attendees to gather, learn, network, and share ideas.

Conferences, conventions, and trade shows (sometimes referred to as "destination events") are extensions of your business day and a necessary part of an organization's growth. They should be treated with the same level of professionalism. Most importantly, each venue offers an array of networking connections, job opportunities, and work-based training, all in one location. They represent serious business functions built on developing relationships and securing potential new business.

 The objectives of this chapter are . . .

1. To help you realize that your main focus at a major convention, conference, or trade show is to represent your company, that you are your company's reputation, and that you have specific assignments to accomplish;

2. To provide you with the details necessary to navigate a major event successfully, to take care of speakers arranged by your company or organization, to make the most of talks and breakout sessions, to manage a successful booth and attract prospects, and to find time to relax and have fun; and

3. To remind you that there are very specific things you can do to travel and check into hotels safely and protect your ID, your money, and your valuables.

Unfortunately, those who have never visited a particular city or country before tend to view off-site functions as times of leisure and relaxation. Representing your company is the main focus, and obtaining information or securing leads is your main responsibility; therefore, it is important to attend all of the events planned before going sightseeing on your own. It would be a mistake to go sightseeing instead of attending the events, especially if your company is paying for your trip and the event.

The luncheons, cocktail receptions, and after-hours hospitality events are very important to all levels of participants. These events are as much about team building as they are about content. They should not be misused. Keeping this in mind, remember that you are always being observed; you should maintain a professional demeanor each day and at each social function. Proceed with the thoughtful purpose of fulfilling the return on your own or your company's investment.

Staying for the speeches is part of the price of admission, in my opinion, just as staying for the final curtain call and rewarding the performers with applause is part of the price of admission at the theater.

—Hilka Klinkenberg, Etiquette International, Inc., New York

Plan each day with enough time to arrive at each event in a timely and composed manner. Identify the content of interest, and determine the number of tracks or breakout sessions that will make the best use of your time while on site. Review your selected session titles, as well as the presenters for each session. This will help you avoid attending the wrong sessions.

The logistics for setting up a conference have been covered in chapters 1 and 2. A checklist to make it easier can be found in chapter 10.

Check-in Tips

Check in immediately upon arrival to get your conference schedule, agenda, meal tickets, and name tag. Confirmation is required by the hosting organization. Each event allows registered attendees to connect prior to the event and while you are there. Inquire on the event website or at registration.

Not all events provide name tags or badges, for privacy reasons, so do not be surprised if a name tag is not in your packet; however, you might find a list of attendees. This will help you familiarize yourself with names beforehand. As you meet people and receive their business cards, jot down notes on the back after an initial conversation. This will help you remember people and their names.

Furthermore, in formal situations, addressing someone by his or her title and last name is preferred and considered more respectful. Taking liberty with an individual's first name upon a first meeting could be considered too familiar. In a more relaxed environment, first names are more comfortable. Much will depend on the formality of the environment. When in doubt, use titles and last names.

Once you have secured your conference information packet, take the time to review all of the materials you have been given. Get all of your questions answered upon arrival. Ask for a complete layout of the conference hall and convention center or hotel.

Quick Reference

Use the following as your check-in guide:

 Check-in for Attendees

- ☑ Review registration hours
- ☑ Review materials
- ☑ Map out the agenda to include the following:
    - Keynote sessions
    - Concurrent sessions
    - Networking sessions
    - Continental breakfast/afternoon tea/coffee

- Luncheons
- Evening receptions hosted by conference host and outside solution providers (e.g., vendor)
- Exhibition time in the exhibit hall

 Check-in for Exhibitors

☑ Review registration hours

☑ Review setup/tear-down times/dedicated hours

☑ Schedule meetings with potential prospects prior to conference

☑ Map out opportunities to include the following:

- Networking sessions with attendees
- Social functions in the exhibit hall
- Attend any social functions allowing for face-to-face exchange with attendees

Manage Your Time Wisely

Manage your time by mapping out each day and becoming acquainted with the locations of the exhibition hall, general sessions, networking sessions, and breakout sessions. This will help you secure your preferred seating and eliminate the possibility of disrupting the presenters with a late arrival. By being prepared, you will avoid confusion, and you will be certain to attend the appropriate sessions.

> Allow sufficient time to attend the exhibits.
> They are your solution provider.

Note: Larger conferences may provide an *agenda planner* on the conference website; always check.

Be Mindful of Personal Attractions:
You are on a Business Trip

Unprofessional behavior at a conference will dampen career opportunities and business deals. If you behave inappropriately, your career could end.

> A sales executive's team won a company conference trip to the Bahamas as an award for securing a large contract. This was an all-inclusive four-day trip. A married woman on the team met a man who intrigued her, and an affair evolved. She started missing most of her company's events and was questioned regarding her absence. When she tried to end the affair so she could focus on the events, the man started stalking her, and the trip became a horror story. Her reputation was ruined, her marriage suffered, and she lost key clients.

There are many such stories. Discretion is vital. When you are on a company trip attending a convention, it is not a vacation, and it should not take a personal direction. Your integrity and safety, and the integrity of your company, are at stake. Your attitude and conduct are always on display.

> Attend all facets of your conference:
> Gather, learn, network, and share ideas.

SPEAKER PREPARATIONS

Respecting a conference or meeting speaker is a direct reflection on your professionalism. Although they are being paid to present lectures or seminars, they are still your guests. You can help your speaker give his or her best performance by taking care of the majority of the details, allowing him or her to concentrate on the presentation content and delivery. It is also the speaker's responsibility to check with you on all of the planning details.

Although most speakers are self-sufficient and do not require a lot of special arrangements, it is always wise to check. Use the following as a guide for a win-win experience.

1. Inform your speaker about specific details of the program such as theme, objectives, other speakers and their topics, audience interests and concerns, and what kind of presentation is desired. Does your group prefer a how-to lecture, entertainment, motivational speech, demonstration, or interactive session?

2. Give speakers a contact list of meeting planners who are involved in the logistics and introductions, and identity the people who have direct involvement in the preparations.

3. Advise speakers of changes that will affect the timing, attendance count, or location, and mention other speakers who are speaking on a similar topic.

4. Allow speakers to review their biographic details and event announcement before it goes to the printer.

5. Discuss handouts. Will the speaker be bringing handouts, or will you be printing them as part of the agreement? Find out from the speaker when and how he or she would like the handouts to be circulated.

6. If the speaker is bringing promotional material or sale items, discuss how you would like them handled and where they should be placed beforehand. The speaker should *not* include a commercial for his or her products during the presentation; however, a mention that products are available in the back of the room can be made at the close of the speech, preferably by the person who offers closing comments. This is delicate. However, if a speaker is volunteering his or her time or discounting their fee, product promotion is to be expected; just do not overdue it.

7. Do not audiotape or videotape the speaker's presentation unless you have received written permission from the speaker. By the same token, the speaker should not record a presentation without written permission from the planning committee. Without permission, you could be in violation of copyright law or accused of privacy infraction. If permission via a contract has been granted for you to tape the presentation, agree to pay the speaker if the recording is going to be sold.

8. If the speaker is driving, reserve a parking spot or arrange for a valet by the entrance of the event. Your speaker will be bringing equipment and materials. In addition, it can be difficult for a woman speaker in heels to walk a long distance! It is always best to arrange for valet parking. Taxis are not always readily available, so you should make the arrangement.

9. Have the event manager help with details of audiovisual needs. Ask for audiovisual equipment to be sent in advance so that AV personnel can have it ready (e.g., one hour to thirty minutes before it is needed).

10. Future fees can be influenced by how you treat the speaker at this event. Treat the speaker like a VIP, and the next time he or she is invited, you might be able to get him or her to lower their fee. On the reverse side, many speakers feel that they

deflate their value when they lower their fee on a first-time engagement, which is why they might be more willing to offer a break on a next event opportunity or offer a series discount.

11. Handle the speaker's room, beverage and meal tickets, and speaker ID (the speaker packet) in advance. Make sure that the speaker has a copy of the conference folder that all the participants receive.

12. Assign a companion or assistant to each speaker. This person should be stationed at the building entrance to greet the speaker, to check his or her coat, to help with equipment setup, to fetch anything that is needed, to pass out handouts, to show the speaker where the washrooms are located or a private room where he or she can change (if needed), and to assist with equipment and transportation needs at the end of the event.

13. When assisting with equipment, check the placement of the screen, projectors, and sound system. Also, check any computer microphones (lanyard, lapel, or headset). Make sure that the speaker can be heard from the last row and that a large podium or lectern does not hide a short speaker.

14. Be sure to introduce the speaker to the planning committee before the event.

15. Review the speaker's introduction speech with the speaker. Whoever is assigned to do the introduction should be encouraged to practice it so that he or she is not just reading it. The introducer is just as important as the speaker, because this person sets the opening tone. (Refer back to chapter 4 for tips on delivering an impressive introduction.)

16. If a meal is served before the presentation, make sure that the speaker is served first (or is in line first). If it is a buffet, offer to go through the line for the speaker.

17. Offer speakers a secluded place for quiet time before "show time," so that he or she can make last-minute adjustments and

mental preparation. This includes rescuing the speaker from long-winded fans or curious participants. It is important not to drain the speaker of energy before the program starts.

There is a long-time familiar story, told by Earl Nightingale (a famous American motivational speaker and author, known as the "Dean of Personal Development"), about how the comedian Jack Benny would sit in a chair prior to going onstage and collapse his body. He looked unrecognizable and like a little man to the passerby. Then, when it was time to go onstage, he stood up, filled his body with energy as if blowing up a balloon, walked out on the stage, and gave an outstanding performance. He intentionally reserved every ounce of energy for his performance. His audience was that important to him.

18. Set up a signal system at fifteen-minute intervals toward the close of the presentation to indicate how much time is left. Signal the last ten and five minutes as well. This will help the speaker stay on time. If the speaker takes questions during the presentation, the speaker's timing could be thrown off. An experienced speaker knows how to make the timing adjustment; however, the signals do help to end on time.

19. To encourage questions from a reluctant audience, arrange prewritten questions on three-by-five cards with select people in the audience (possibly your planning committee people).

20. Send a thank-you note to each speaker that includes quotable testimonials along with any resulting press coverage, reviews, or photographs.

Contract Fee and Payment

If the speaker's fee is over the company budget, when negotiating the fee, offer things of value to help offset the difference and secure the speaker of choice. This value-added proposition can be a membership directory with permission to add it to the speaker's database, association membership, spouse's travel expenses, a trade journal subscription, ad space, press interviews, a newsletter profile, theater or concert tickets, merchandise, or future workshops. Most speakers will gladly reduce their fee for the exchange. Another option is to get one or more corporate sponsors to offset the speaker's fee.

Most speakers have terms of agreement for their fee. If they have agreed to be paid the full amount or balance on the day of the event, make sure that they receive their checks upon arrival or at departure. If the speaker made his or her own travel arrangements, the travel expenses will be billed.

> Make the speaker feel special!

②

ARRANGING FOR INTERPRETERS:
The Invisible People

> *Interpreter:* A person who translates orally for people of different languages
>
> *Translator:* A person who turns the written word from one language to another language

Unless you have an excellent command of a particular language, an interpreter is your bridge to meaningful communication with an international client or partner. Highly trained professional interpreters translate orally for speakers of different languages, thus becoming the voice of the speaker, whether host or guest. This is extremely important when traveling and attending conventions and trade shows abroad. Never assume that English is the prevailing language!

Selecting Your Interpreter

First, decide what type of interpreting you need. There are three types of interpreting.

1. *Simultaneous interpreting:* The interpreter translates as you speak.

2. *Consecutive interpreting:* The interpreter translates after you have spoken a sentence or paragraph before proceeding.

3. *Escort interpreting:* The interpreter accompanies you in a country where you do not speak the language and oftentimes serves as your guide.

Second, select an interpreter with strong credentials. He or she should have experience in the type of interpreting you require, a personality appropriate for the occasion, and familiarity with the subject matter. In addition to bilingual skills, you may also require an interpreter to have bicultural skills (knowledge in both cultures), a matching level of professionalism, and country-specific knowledge. Plus, your interpreter should be familiar with the jargon used in your field. (Note: if you need an interpreter for a lengthy period of time, you may be required to use more than one interpreter in order to provide sufficient break periods.)

 Your Needs:

- Bilingual or Bicultural
- Professionalism
- Personality Fit
- Knowledge of Subject Matter
- Country-Specific Knowledge
- Number of Interpreters

Provide the following items to your interpreter in advance: your agenda, your speech or any other content to be presented, and an explanation of stories or humor (if used). For your part, test any needed equipment beforehand. Avoid distractions. Instruct others in the party to avoid shuffling papers or making noise and talking simultaneously. Allow for breaks and brief your interpreter during breaks.

 Interpreter's Needs:

- Appropriate, functioning equipment
- Agenda in advance
- Advance copy of speech
- Advance notice of content and an explanation of stories or humor

 Dos and Don'ts:

- Do give your interpreter materials in advance.

- Do give your interpreter regular breaks and brief your interpreter during breaks.
- Do test any needed equipment beforehand.
- Don't shuffle papers or make noise during the exchange.
- Don't speak fast; instead, speak in sound bites (brief pauses between thoughts and/or sentences).

Tip: If you are having difficulty finding an interpreter or discover unexpectedly that you need an interpreter, seek out a student interpreter at a local university.

Positioning Protocol

Once you have made these arrangements, your next consideration is how to interact socially. The challenge is to avoid speaking directly to the interpreter. The interpreter serves as a communication bridge, and should be unobtrusive; therefore, the interpreter should remain invisible to you as he or she relays the conversation. Be sensitive to different cultural styles, and roles of interpreter. Your eye contact should remain with the individual with whom you are communicating.

 You have three choices for positioning:

1. Seat the interpreter between and slightly behind the key parties.
2. Seat the interpreter next to the guest (on the right side of the guest).
3. Use an interpretation booth, if available and appropriate.
   Note: In a dining situation, the interpreter often sits behind you and does not have a meal. They are given their meal either before their work begins or after they have concluded.

In general, be sensitive to different cultural styles and the roles of interpreters in those cultures. Use simple language and avoid idioms, acronyms and sports metaphors. Say difficult words and names slowly and distinctly.

Preparation and careful consideration will ensure that your interpreter serves as a communication bridge and that your interaction is a success.

 Disability Note: Similar guidelines apply for situations that call for a sign interpreter for hearing-impaired participants.

③

MAKING THE MOST OF LUNCHEON AND EVENT SESSIONS

> The speaker respects the audience.
> The audience respects the speaker.

Conferences and conventions are ideal opportunities for networking and career advancement. They are also crucial for gathering new information, learning problem-solving techniques, and designed to be informative and entertaining.

To maximize your experience and get the most out of your investment, attend all of the group meals and sessions. Sit near people you do not know, and strike up conversations. Learn about exhibitors' companies, meet the speakers, and exchange business cards. Gather resources from classes and from exhibitors who hold a special interest for you.

You can have a plan of action, or you can wander around aimlessly. With budgets tight and companies struggling to gain their footing, it is more critical than ever to maximize the potential of conferences. All it takes is a plan of action, prep work, and tech support. But don't only wear your business hat; wear your social hat as well. Sometimes the best connection comes from casual conversation over a coffee or cocktail as you debrief a session.

Prep Plan of Action

1. Before you attend, review your conference brochure very carefully and select the breakout sessions (or tracks) that offer you the best value. Be ready with first and second choices in case a session fills and you are not able to attend.

This happens! Content is most important, especially if you are new to attending conventions.

Experienced attendees might be more interested in social-izing and connecting away from the sessions during tracks involving subject matter they have heard before. In this case, upon arrival become familiar with various social meeting locations (e.g., coffee shops, quiet areas, cocktail lounges).

2. Make a list of people you want to be sure to connect with, and focus on that list upon arrival. Some conferences offer what are called "sidebars." This is where the conference planner can be contacted beforehand to set up meetings between executives or key people.

3. Double-check all the details, from clothing to weather and dates. It is easy to get pre-conference dates and times of activities confused with those of the conference itself. Realize that there is typically an extra charge for pre-confer-ence workshops, and sometimes they are held at a different location.

Conferences do not seem to come alive until dinner, and they don't really swing until after hours. Even those who do not consider themselves partygoers attend. Have caution: this is where it is easy to damage your reputation. Alcohol tends to lubricate conversation and take conversation in the wrong direc-tion. Do not forget to eat and to drink water. It will help offset the effects of alcohol.

Conferences are also about schmoozing. Once you arrive, find out who your resource people are, and learn where to find what you need. During this process, make notes will that allow you to help others connect as you circulate. Realize that everyone has an agenda.

People Movers and Room Monitors

Arrange for "people movers." These are volunteers who are

assigned a segment of the conference to serve as walking concierges or guides. Schedule a briefing time before the conference begins, and have a packet ready at the registration table. Most importantly, if you have never met, make sure that your people movers know who you are and who they are. They should also wear some sort of identifier (e.g., a special hat, T-shirt, or front-to-back slipover panel that ties at the sides).

The people mover packet and briefing should include the following:

- Times and assigned locations.
- Breakout session room numbers for each event.
- A map of the assigned area.
- Restroom locations.
- Eating areas.
- Preparation rooms assigned for speakers or other guests.
- Computer and technology rooms or area.
- A flashlight to use when directing attendees to their conference rooms. (The most effective flashlight has an orange fluorescent cone attached to it as if to mimic a ground crew directing a flight to a gate.)

Room monitors are typically assigned by the event organizers to make sure that each breakout session starts and ends on time. Often they are responsible for introducing the speaker and taking care of the speaker's handouts. It is a good idea to section off the last row or table for late arrivals and for those who cannot stay for the entire presentation. Make sure that anyone who arrives late or leaves early does so with the least amount of noise and disruption to the speaker.

Check to be sure that the room temperature is comfortable. If it is not, the room monitor will relay the concern to the appropriate person. Overall, it is best to keep the room temperature on the cool side. Warm rooms are cozy and make it easy for participants to doze off. Note that the room will be on the chilly side when empty and will warm up once it is occupied.

(Refer to *The Art of Professional Connections: Success Strategies for Networking in Person and Online* for tips on how to be a people mover.)

The Luncheon Program

The conference luncheon is a great opportunity to meet new people, so avoid sitting with people you already know. Assume the role of host, make introductions at your table, and see that the conversation flows. This will demonstrate your leadership qualities. Next, be conscious of your table manners. Eat appropriately and quietly, and demonstrate good dining decorum.

 Be considerate and kind!

- Do not put personal items on the chair next to you. This blocks someone else's use of the chair. Handbags and portfolios go under your chair.

- Do not save seats once the program has started. It is very distracting for the speaker and embarrassing to the individual to go from one table to the next, trying to find a seat, only to learn that it has been saved.

- Do not prop a chair against the table in order to save a seat. This is not only dangerous to people walking past, but it is also rude. If you need to save a seat, stand by it.

(Although these points have already been covered in previous chapters, they are worth mentioning again.)

When the speaker begins, end your table conversation and give the speaker your undivided attention. This means no "sidebar" conversations—a temptation that too often happens when you are bored or not interested in the speaker. This is very rude and distracting behavior to the people around you. Even if the room is noisy, be quiet.

During a presentation, avoid leaving during a speaker's speech. The speaker and other attendees will notice this distraction as you leave the room, especially if you are sitting toward the front of the room. Even if you are bored, remain professional and respectful. (Boredom is not a reason to be disrespectful.) Record your dislike of the speaker or the topic on the evaluation form. The meeting planner needs input, both pro and con.

If you have to leave early, sit in the back row or at the back table so you are not noticed. You should not be in a hurry to leave after the speaker concludes. This could cost you a valuable contact opportunity. Take your time and, if possible, thank the speaker with a handshake; if a handshake is not convenient, make approving eye contact, smile, and nod. Do the same with your table partners. Take an extra ten to fifteen minutes. They might be the most valuable ten or fifteen minutes of the entire luncheon.

Breakout Sessions or Tracks

Your behavior at a luncheon keynote, during a breakout session, or in the lounge is critical to your reputation and the reputation of the organization you represent. Demonstrate courteous behavior at all times. This should be a given, but reminders are always good. As a session attendee, be courteous to other attendees and speakers. Rudeness really stands out and is remembered.

A corporate vice president of a Fortune 500 company was outlining market research data in his PowerPoint slide presentation. A woman, wearing an eye-catching red jacket and seated in the aisle seat in the second row, allowed her cell phone to ring. She answered her phone and left the room, talking as she walked down the aisle. This disrupted the presenter, and we were all affected. Her name tag indicated that she worked for a prominent telecommunications company. Her company's credibility was greatly diminished because of her rudeness. Later I saw her in line at a pay phone!

When several breakout sessions or tracks are planned in the same time frame, participants do have the option of leaving if the topic is not as anticipated; however, be aware that this can be disruptive to both the speaker and attendees who are interested in the topic. So be discreet.

 Breakout Session (or Track) Courtesies

1. Show respect for the speaker. Do not arrive late. If you arrive late or have to leave early, sit in the last row closest to the door. Arrive and depart discreetly. You do not want to distract the other participants or the speaker.

2. If you cannot stay for the entire session, let the presenter or room assistant know before the speaker begins, and take a seat in the back row. Or, if you are not sure of the topic, your decision to leave should be made within the first five minutes of the presentation.

3. If you are sitting in the front row, do not leave! Wait for a break in the program to leave.

4. If the room is packed or there are not enough chairs, halfway through the presentation (or during a brief break) give up your chair to someone who has been standing. This is a wonderful courtesy, and it is noticed and appreciated.

5. Turn off your beeper and cell phone. If you are expecting an emergency call, put your cell phone or beeper on vibrate and discreetly leave the room. Apologize for the brief absence to the presenter at the end of the session.

6. Do not compete with the speaker. Respect his or her format for taking questions. If you disagree with something, do it diplomatically, not argumentatively.

7. If you are asked to participate in a demonstration or activity, do so even if you feel reluctant. Speakers are not paid to embarrass you; they are paid to deliver important information that sometimes requires an interactive activity.

8. Do not take more than one handout or workbook from

the session. If there are extras, ask the presenter if you can take an additional copy. The extra copies may be needed for another session or needed by the event coordinator.

Thank the speaker. Breakout session speakers or presenters often donate their time to the organization or reduce their fees dramatically in order to accommodate the conference budget. Show respect and appreciation.

If you are the speaker or presenter and looking for specific results from your seminar presentation, make sure you ask the audience to share feedback (by calling or e-mailing you direct) after they have put their new skills into practice! It makes a tremendous difference when participants understand that they are not just learning—they are also expected to do something with their new knowledge. It also gives them a chance to get clarity and to boast about their success.

Avoid Burnout, and Take Time to Relax

One of the major complaints about conferences is that they are too intense. Conference planners must have activities running from the early morning breakfast speaker and luncheon speaker to late evening dinners with entertainment. If your convention is three to five days, this can leave you burned out. So plan breaks. You do not have to attend everything. If speakers are not meeting your needs or networking isn't working, try to salvage something out of the time. Set up meetings, listen to other people's conversations for business tips or future contact ideas—anything! Seek out the conference planners and producers and share your thoughts. They love input ... whether pro or con. They are starved for information about the expectations and perceptions of their events. It helps them with the next event to know what worked and what could have been better.

Three days of sessions can be taxing. If there is a track that does not appeal to you, use that time wisely by socializing. Learn what others have learned, share your experiences, and just debrief occasionally. But you should not break away from the conference and take a vacation instead. Even if your boss does not attend, you're still being seen and judged by industry peers, and there's nothing people like to gossip (or tweet) about more than someone's absence from the conference. Have a good time, but keep it in perspective. You are there on company money, not vacation money. If you want to turn it into a vacation, add an extra day or two, or arrive a few days before the conference starts. Do this on *your* time.

The lounge is a great way to relax and to recap with new acquaintances after a mind-boggling day. In addition to alcoholic beverages, lounges also have a selection of soft drinks. If you order an alcoholic beverage, do not drink in excess. Know your limit. A reputation for obnoxious behavior is damaging. Coffeehouses are also available and serve the same purpose.

If your conference is several days long, do not try to attend all the sessions. Take time out from one or two sessions to relax and meet other participants. What you can learn from other participants is just as valuable, and you will feel less stressed.

Beware! Everyone Is Armed with SMS!

Technology reaches the masses in nanoseconds. People are tweeting and facebooking every detail of the event, as well as about people's behavior. If you whine or complain, it will be posted. So be very careful.

> Relax, be approachable, and smile.

EXPERIENCING TRADE SHOWS AS MARKETING EVENTS

If it feels like schmoozing, selling, networking, partying, relationship-building, gift-grabbing, and feet-numbing, it is a trade show. It can have a theater atmosphere, because you are dealing with light, sound, gimmicks, and people saying, "Come see me! No, come see me!" It's a competitive art. Trade shows are also social and cultural events; therefore, understanding each company's and each country's approach to trade shows is indispensable. This starts by learning the corporate culture and traditions of the American company or host country.

A trade show can be your most economical marketing communication tool. Exhibiting accelerates the selling cycle because you meet and communicate with prequalified prospects. Therefore, it is important that you select a trade show that is right for your business and that you handle all aspects of the show in a professional manner.

To get the most out of attending a trade show, you should have an agenda and specific needs in mind. Shop for those items first. Then backtrack to see if there is something new or different that would benefit your business.

Be a "Class Act" Exhibitor

The trade-show exhibit hall is an industry-specific supermarket. Shoppers go up and down the aisles, some seriously seeking a new product or service, and others just window shopping for entertainment. They are the ones that tend to walk by quickly or keep their distance, and this is okay. They came for information or education, or just to pass through and look at the booths to see what people are giving away. If your exhibit catches their eye, they will be back.

Consider yourself your company's ambassador. This is where first impressions are powerful and can make or break your investment. You definitely want appealing graphics and an eye-catching display. Your exhibit booth is also your home away from home, so keep it clean and tidy. If food is allowed behind the booth, throw away disposable plates and uneaten food when finished. While food and alcoholic beverages are discouraged in the booth at most American trade shows, in some countries they are acceptable. If this is the case, select foods with mild aromas so that the scent does not discourage visitors. Make sure not to eat or drink when visitors are present. Bottled water is acceptable.

Your booth should project an image of class and substance, and it should offer an experience. The experience can begin before arrival by having a plan and by deciding on incentives. (If you are an attendee, you should examine the event brochure and make a list of people and companies that you want to meet. Start your rounds with the people on your list.)

Don't just man your booth; be an ambassador for other booths as well. Be an exhibit booth people mover or guide. Before the exhibit doors open and when it is your turn to walk around, visit every booth. Establish a rapport with your exhibit neighbors. If your booth does not meet their immediate needs, recommend another. This demonstrates that your aim is to be helpful. Plus, you might meet the need of another exhibitor. (You will find tips on how to be a people mover and business card follow-up in *The Art of Professional Connections: Success Strategies for Networking in Person and Online.*)

 Tips for the Exhibitor

1. The booth representative should e-mail an invitation to stop by beforehand. Say that you will have something special for them. This could be a unique token to remember the visit.

2. Arrive at your booth early. Wear industry-standard yet comfortable clothing and shoes. You might consider bringing a change of shoes. There is nothing worse than having sore feet from wearing a pair of shoes too long.

3. Greet prospects with a smile, a handshake, and confident posture. Make sure that your name tag is on the right shoulder for easy reading when shaking hands. When your name is *heard* and then *seen*, the chances of being remembered are greater.

4. Ask open-ended, intelligent questions tailored to fit your product or service—for example, "What brings you to the show, and is there anything in particular that you need?" or "May I help you find something?" (This is where it is valuable to know what other booths are offering so that you can make a referral.)

5. Do not eat or chew gum. This should be common sense; however, it happens all the time.

6. Keep yourself energized during breaks by walking around the show, drinking plenty of water, and eating energy foods (not sweets or caffeine). Do not look bored during slow times or when you are tired.

7. Ask for a business card, and remember to mail any promised information afterward. As you collect business cards, remember to make a note on each card about that person. This will help you prioritize cards when you get back to your office. If someone is an important lead, make arrangements to meet for coffee before or after the exhibit time.

8. Instead of having a drawing from a bowl of business cards, add an incentive by announcing that the best potential lead will receive a prize.

9. After the visit, follow up with a handwritten card or an e-mail attachment that you promised to send.

The secret to a successful trade show experience is to maintain a professional demeanor and to show eagerness to share your information. Be sure to have plenty of business cards! Businesses invest time and money in booth space to share their products or services. Treat them as you would like to be treated if it was your booth.

 Three Common Exhibit Booth Pet Peeves

1. *Exhibitor:* People who talk on their cell phone or work on their computers instead of greeting passers-by or visitors. Always be ready to greet.

2. *Exhibitor:* People who break down their booth early. If the exhibit is scheduled to end at 6:00 pm, do not start breaking down your booth until 6:05, even if you do not see any potential customers at the close of the day. Always be ready to receive visitors.

3. *Attendee:* People who visit a booth only to get the freebies and then take several for family and friends. These one-per-visitor gifts serve as a token of appreciation for visiting the booth and learning about the product or services offered. (There is an investment involved that should be respected.)

If a large item is requested or purchased, offer to ship it instead of having the attendee carry it. This is another opportunity to capture a business card and gives you a reason for a follow-up contact.

Tips for Trade Shows Abroad

If your conference is held in a different country, check and respect the customs. It is important to present a positive American image. A trade show in the United States usually lasts for three days. We like to get in, set up, make our sales, and take down in a timely manner. Abroad, trade shows can last up to three weeks.

It would be a mistake to assume that trade shows around the world operate the same. In most countries, a trade show is a grand affair with an international flair.

> *Trade shows in Germany are meeting places of highly specialized experts and decision makers in a particular field. The latest developments and innovations are in vogue, and the experts tend to come right to the point of interest within their specialty. Your exhibit booth should project an image of substance and understated elegance.* —Wallie Dayal, Dayal Resources

The following will help you prepare for a successful experience abroad:

1. Research country-specific business customs and practices. Do not assume that all trade shows are operated the same. There are similarities and differences depending on the culture and intention.

2. Try to get a list of vendors and the names of their representatives ahead of time. (Be certain that this request does not violate privacy laws.) If needed, hire a language specialist to help you practice pronunciation and learn how to properly read names on business cards. In some countries, the family name or surname appears first, followed by the given name.

3. Address someone initially by his family name, or by title and family name. Given names are used only when permission has been granted and the relationship has been established. In some countries, given names are never used. (Refer to step 3 of *The Art of Professional Connections: Seven Steps to Impressive Greetings and Confident Interactions for more details on names.*)

4. Food and alcohol are acceptable at booths in most European countries. In the United States, we discourage food and do not permit alcoholic beverages at booths.

5. The exhibitor's image is always professional; however, Americans tend to be casual in dress as well as conversation. The business suit is your best option internationally. The comfort of tennis shoes and jeans may not be appropriate. American-style small talk is also not popular in some countries. A more serious approach to conversation is preferred.

6. Before attending or participating in a trade show in the Middle East, women need to be sure that their presence will not violate cultural mores and laws. Women should be especially careful to dress appropriately.

7. Rank and status are very important to people in countries outside the United States. It would be very insulting for a high-level manager of one company to be greeted by a low-level manager from another company.

8. In countries like Japan, a trade show is not held as a venue to finalize contracts, but instead as a way to look at samples of new products. Introductions should always include your title; for example, "My name is Jane Doe, president of ABC Company." Your title is a very important part of your name because it communicates your professional standing.

In most countries, relationships develop slowly and require patience. Once developed, contacts and friendships are usually deep and lasting.

Fortunately, English is understood in most countries; however, having a command of basic phrases (e.g., "Hello," "Thank you," and "Good evening") shows respect. If you are going to hire a translator or an interpreter, try to find someone local. Dialects in every country can vary from region to region.

There is much more to know, but you need to seek the counsel of an exhibit professional. Several books on the market can be helpful; check back of the book for resources. Or, you can pick up literature at country-specific consulate offices, world trade center offices, and international trade partners.

Exhibits help finance the event.

Show your support and respect the exhibit hall efforts.

ATTRACTING PROSPECTS WITH BOOTH CHARISMA

Use your personality to give your booth a special charisma. Do not slip into neutral and expect your booth display to do all the work for you, no matter how computer interactive it is. This is show time!

Your company's success and your personal reputation depend on your attitude and behavior. Trade show duty can be tedious, boring, and tiring, but also very beneficial. The secret to a successful booth is to act as if you just arrived and to show eagerness to share your information. All the money and technology in the world will not bring attendees to your booth if the people representing your company make an unfavorable impression.

Your booth should project an image of formality, substance, and understated elegance. It should reflect the company image and personality. Standing out, messaging with a theme and catchy graphics will get noticed. Giveaways or gifts are for the purpose of rewarding prospects for doing something like providing contact info, watching a demo, or taking a survey, not for thanking them for just coming to the booth.

The number-one goal is to get contact information so that a relationship can be developed. Bowls of candy have no purpose at a trade show booth unless the company sells candy. It is a cop-out, and no one ever uses it to engage a prospect. It has become a crazy habit that everyone is following.

—Susan Ratliff, author of Exhibit Like an Expert

Remember that attendees have limited time with lots of options. Your job is to make it easy for them to access you. The exhibit area can be overwhelming. You only have a few seconds to attract an attendee to stop, but you have even fewer seconds to impress an attendee enough to want to listen and take literature.

How to Make Your Booth Successful

You are your company's image. Take your booth seriously, and attendees will too. Do not just stand behind your booth. Be approachable and eager to greet people as they stop by. Be prepared to be of service by acting like a concierge, providing directions and answers to questions regarding the conference that may or may not necessarily pertain to your product or service. You will be remembered for your helpfulness. In addition, it could make things interesting.

If two of you are managing the booth, stand at different sides of the table. Have a twenty-five-word-or-less infomercial prepared. (You can learn more about how to develop an infomercial in *The Art of Professional Connections: Success Strategies for Networking in Person and Online*.) This will help you open your conversation with attendees. Instead of focusing on promoting your business, ask questions. Learn people's needs and hot buttons, and then proceed to educate. People want knowledge. Know that not everyone walking by has need of or interest in your product or service; however, be a friendly greeter. Your best business opportunity could be the person who observed your friendly manner with passers-by.

Have a partner—someone who can relieve you for breaks. You will need to walk away periodically so you can come back feeling refreshed, with renewed enthusiasm. When visiting other company booths, do not help yourself to their giveaways unless you are truly interested in their product or service. Focus more on exchanging business cards and creating relationships. Most will give out extra giveaways at the end of the event. So, if it is something that you want to take to friends or coworkers, revisit that booth at the close of the event and simply ask for extras.

Booth Checklist

☑ Dress professionally. If business casual is the dress code, look professional and not sloppy. You are your company's billboard. How do you want your company to be perceived?

☑ Avoid standing behind barriers in your booth. A table, for example, becomes a barrier between you and your prospect.

☑ Greet each guest with a firm handshake, a smile, good posture, and eye contact. Close each encounter with the same firm handshake, good posture, and eye contact.

☑ Ask questions. Focus on learning about visitors' needs.

☑ Keep a friendly attitude and smile, no matter how tired or bored you may be.

☑ Do not eat at your booth. Put beverages in a discreet place under your table, and only take a sip when no one is looking. You will need water, but do not put your water bottle on the table. It can be an eyesore and distract from your material. If you do have a snack at your booth, eat it discreetly when no one is around, and keep it hidden.

☑ Do not chew gum or smoke.

☑ Do not sit and read. Attendees will not want to interrupt you. You will appear preoccupied and give the impression that you do not want to be bothered.

☑ Stay at your booth, even if it is not busy. When you wander to someone else's booth, an attendee just around the corner may move on if he sees no one present.

☑ Do not use your cell phone at your booth or turn on your beeper. Again, you will look preoccupied and rude. No one is more important than the attendee.

☑ Thank each attendee for visiting your booth.

☑ Do not start dismantling your booth until the exact closing time. The attendee who visits your booth five minutes to closing could be your most promising prospect.

☑ Follow up with promised information.

Booth Giveaways Are Marketing Tools

The booth giveaway gift is another form of marketing and is intended strictly for that purpose. It is typically a logo gift or candy, and it serves as a great way to draw people to your booth and offer a thank-you for visiting. There are mixed opinions on the candy strategy. Many feel that the gift (e.g., candy) should relate to the product or service.

Be prepared! People are going to take liberties. Expect it, and be prepared to handle it professionally and tactfully. Unfortunately, you will have customers or clients who love your giveaway gift so much that they will want to take several home to friends. This can be a very delicate situation. It is your responsibility to be very discreet and courteous in discouraging this liberty. Your body language, tone of voice, facial expression, and choice of words are extremely important. Ahead of time, practice different ways to handle this situation, so you are smooth and natural.

Limit the number of giveaway gifts you have on display. Do not encourage greed by displaying a large number of gifts at one time. Have a small amount on the front table and on the back table.

A senior bank employee asks for five premium items when he is only entitled to one. You don't want to set a bad example in case you run out of giveaways, but the person is relentless and demands that you give them to him. Other people see and hear what is going on.

What do you do?

Thank the individual for his interest, and say that your supply is limited; however, if he should like to stop by at the end of the exhibit, you will gladly accommodate him if there are extras.

Or say, "We are so pleased you like this gift. We will also be using these gifts at another upcoming event. Consequently, we have to limit the number of gifts at this event. Thank you for understanding."

As a passer-by, only take gifts from booths where you are sincerely interested or curious about their product or service. Employees should secure permission before helping themselves to the gifts.

Dismantling Your Booth

When a high-tech corporation debuted its product at a three-day conference, attendees who decided to visit the trade show after the luncheon speaker on the last day of the conference were in for a shock. Unfortunately, the majority of the booths had already been dismantled, and the trade-show area was in disarray. They wasted their time, and the company lost potential business.

Your best prospect may be the person who visits your booth during the last fifteen minutes of the show. Do not dismantle early, no matter how tired you may be or because you are experiencing a lack of visitors. Typically, there is a clause in the exhibitor's contract that will charge a penalty if dismantled early. Always check!

Breaking down your booth early will result in being excluded from the next show. It is usually in the contract that you must not close the booth until the closing of the show or, in some cases, until everyone is off the floor. —Susan Ratliff, author of *Exhibit Like an Expert*

Each booth should look as good at the end of the exhibit as it did as the beginning of the exhibit.

> Keep your booth looking fresh
> from beginning to close.

ENJOYING SAFE TRAVEL

Whether you travel by ground or by air, be mindful of your appearance, safety, and equipment. Make copies of your picture ID, (e.g., driver's license, state ID card, or passport) and credit cards. Put them in an envelope that can be concealed in your luggage, and in your handbag or briefcase. Do not carry only one set in one place.

When traveling domestically or internationally, never let your passport and credit cards out of your sight! This is extremely important. The information could be copied and used against you in an identity theft situation.

> A couple traveling on a business trip allowed their credit card to be taken by the server to the register, not giving it another thought. When their credit card bill came the next month, there were charges for online purchases that they did not make. Their credit card company was contacted immediately. They were able to track the address where the merchandise was mailed, an arrest was made, and the money was restored to the credit card account. They were lucky. Unfortunately, this happens all the time, and many are not as lucky.

You may wonder how a restaurant could allow this. Realize that there is a high turnover in restaurant staff, and it is very difficult to monitor each employee's activities. In most cases, these things happen on the server's last day before returning to school or going to another job.

In a time of high identity theft, it is extremely important to monitor your credit card processing. When it is not feasible to follow the server to the register, check your credit card activity weekly. If an unusual charge occurs, contact your credit card company and the establishment immediately.

Men should keep their credit cards, money, ID, etc., in their front pockets. Women should keep their handbags closed! If the handbag is designed not to close completely, leave it at home. Men and women should take only the cards that they will need for the trip. Typically, this is one credit card and one debit card.

When you travel, go online once a week to check your credit card charges to be sure there are not any surprises. If there is a discrepancy, contact the credit card company immediately. If you do this within 30 days of the suspicious charge, it will be resolved without a lot hassle. The longer you take to make this discovery the longer it takes to get it resolved.

Security

Security is high everywhere. If you do not have a photo ID, you will be denied access to a secured building or airline flight. Have a second ID ready, just in case.

Be Prepared—Consider the What-Ifs

- You forget to transfer your driver's license from one handbag to another.
- Your billfold with all of your identification is stolen.
- You get a speeding ticket and cannot post bond in order to retain your license.

A government-issued photo ID is required for government office buildings and for airlines. These are acceptable:

- Passport
- Driver's license
- State ID card

In most cases you will also be able to use the following to enter high-security buildings:

- A company ID badge
- A student ID card
- A credit card with your photo
- A store discount card with your photo
- Library card with photo

Passports get lost, stolen, or simply misplaced; therefore, scan a copy into your computer. You will need hard copies as well, in case you cannot access your computer file and print. Be prepared for anything and everything.

Print three copies of your passport. (Including copies of your driver's license is a good idea as well.)

1. Keep one in your luggage (preferably your carry-on).

2. Give one to a friend or officemate back home.

3. Place one in your handbag or computer bag.

 Before you leave, check and record the following:

- ☑ US consulate or embassy contact information (the one nearest your destination).

- ☑ Department of State's Overseas Citizens Service. (From outside the USA, call 317-472-2328.)

- ☑ American Citizens Services (ACS) can help you replace your lost or stolen passport, and they can contact your family and friends. (From inside the USA, call 202-647-5225). There is a replacement cost and an expediting fee. If you cannot pay, you can request a temporary passport that is good until you get home.

- ☑ Any other names and phone numbers of people that can verify your identity, both home and abroad. (A family member should also have a copy of your birth certificate in case a copy needs to be faxed.)

- ☑ Medical information.

It is a good idea to have a 6×9 or 9×12 self-addressed, stamped envelope in case something is confiscated. (You will have to guess at the postage.)

Packing and Express Line Tips

1. Dress as if your luggage will be lost, because it does happen. Dress professionally for your travel destination. (Looking professional upon arrival can work to your benefit.)

> I always travel in a professional-looking pantsuit and pack an extra shell in my carry-on luggage. If my luggage is lost, I know that the pantsuit will be comfortable and appropriate. There have been times when my luggage was lost and never found or arrived a day later.

2. Travel the day before your event so that you arrive fresh, and if there is an issue with your luggage, you have time to resolve it. This also allows for last-minute flight changes that delay your arrival.

3. Put plastic dry-cleaner covers over clothes that need to remain on hangers. Ask your dry cleaner to fold instead of hanging your shirts and trousers or blouses and pants.

4. Put shoes, accessories, toiletries, and cosmetics into Ziploc bags.

    If you are someone who perspires easily or who is rushed for time, bring small toiletries with you in a plastic Ziploc bag. As soon as the "fasten your seat belt" sign goes off, go to the rest room to freshen up. Also, carry mouth fresheners. You will feel better, and your cabin mates will appreciate the courtesy.

5. Do not wear clothing with metal buttons or accessories made of metallic parts to airports (e.g., hair accessories, belt buckle, jewelry, shoes). They will trigger alarms and delay your check-in.

6. Place your coat over your arm so that it is easy to put into a bin in the security line. Consider wearing slip-on shoes so that people behind you do not have to wait for you to untie and tie your shoes.

7. Keep your laptop stowed in an easy-to-access area of your carry-on bag. Tape a business card on the underside of your laptop so that it is easy to identify if the person in front of you or behind you has an identical laptop. The wrong laptops do get picked up, especially if you have been pulled out of line for a random scan.

Arranging a Seatmate or Meeting in the Sky

Some new social media websites can help flyers find their ideal seatmates. Two such sites are Planely.com and Satisfly.com; visit these sites to found out how the system works. They connect flyers from all over the world that will be on the same flight or in the same airport. These sites help travelers plan trips and share their experiences. They can help travelers meet, not only online, but also in person—sort of a Match.com of travel. There are more sites in the works that hope to share itineraries on Facebook, so that you could choose to sit next to any Facebook friend. The registration is a combined effort through the airlines' web check-in and Facebook or LinkedIn accounts.

Other sites have their own spin on how to help travelers have a rewarding and exciting experience by utilizing social media postings and boards (e.g., Gogobot.com, TripAdvisor.com). As the popularity of these sites continues, travelers will have more and more options. (Source: *USA Today*, Tuesday, May 29, 2012*)*

Etiquette on Flights with Cabinmates

When on flights, be the example for others to follow. We all have different temperaments and stress levels. Someone has to be in control, so let it be you! You never know who will be seated next to you. Treat your cabinmate as you would want to be treated.

1. If you are having difficulty storing your carry-on luggage, avoid blocking the aisle. Place the luggage on your seat, and wait until passengers have passed and there is a break before resuming storage. If you need assistance, this is the best time for flight attendants to help you. By doing this, you will help the flight take off on time.

2. Be kind, considerate, and courteous to the flight attendants. They have many responsibilities to take care of in a short amount of time.

3. Walk down the aisles very carefully; try not to bump or disturb other passengers. When it does happen, and it will, always say, "Excuse me" with a pleasant expression.

4. Sometimes a passenger will extend his or her foot or arm beyond the confines of the seat. When you see this, say, "Excuse me" before passing. This will alert the passenger, who may not realize that he or she is blocking the aisle.

5. If you are sitting in the window or aisle seat, do not deny the middle-seat passenger an armrest. It is difficult enough sitting in the middle. Only use one armrest; use two only if the other passenger does not need one.

6. It is appropriate today to bring your own food on board. Be sure that the food you select does not have a strong aroma (e.g., onions, garlic, or fish). This aroma will linger in the cabin. Clean up after yourself; keep your seat and tray as tidy as possible.

7. If the person sitting next to you seems nervous, apprehensive, or fearful of flying, start a conversation about a non-flight topic. It will help put him or her at ease. It could be as simple as saying, "Hello, my name is Jane Smith. Welcome to row ten." From this introduction, you will be able to tell if this person would like to engage in conversation.

8. If someone is trying to speak with you and you are tired or want to read, respond with a simple statement, and then

occupy yourself. Do not completely ignore him; he may be nervous and just trying to find a comfort zone.

9. If you are sitting next to someone who is snoring, wiggle in your seat a little in an effort to "accidently" bump him or her. He or she will typically awake with a start and then go back to sleep without the snore. If that does not work, see the cabin crew. If the flight is not full, you might be able to take another seat.

10. If you want to end a conversation, simply say, "It has been a pleasure speaking with you. Unfortunately, I need to do some reading (or take a nap) at this time. I hope you understand."

11. If nervousness causes you to talk, make sure that your cabinmate is interested in having a conversation. If he or she is reading, napping, or preoccupied with his or her technology, that is a sign not to disturb.

12. If your cabinmate keeps looking at or reading your laptop, try to angle it so that he or she cannot read it. Avoid working on confidential data. If you are the one sitting next to someone working on his laptop, do not spy.

13. If you are the restless type or plan to drink a lot of water on your flight, make every effort to get the aisle seat so your trips to the restroom won't disturb those seated next to you.

15. If you are carrying a large business briefcase or tote that you will need to access throughout the flight, select the middle or window seat. The storage area under the middle or window seat in coach is normally larger than that of the aisle seat. If you select an aisle seat, you may have to access your briefcase or tote in the overhead bin, which can be cumbersome.

16. If you will be using your laptop, it may be a good idea to kindly ask the person in front of you before the flight takes off to let you know when he or she plans to recline, so you can keep your laptop from getting jammed between the tray

and seat. (It happens!) Also, extend this same courtesy to the person behind you.

17. If you watch movies on your iPod or laptop, make sure that they are not disturbingly graphic, highly sexual, or overly violent. The eyes around you are also watching.

Do not forget to make a closing courtesy comment to the flight crew. When you arrive, thank the crew for a safe and smooth trip. If it was a turbulent flight, compliment the captain and flight crew on their skill.

Confidentiality

Do not pull anything up on your laptop screen that is confidential. You will unknowingly violate company confidentiality. Airports and flights are not private. People sitting next to you and behind you can often read your screen. The same applies to phone calls. If your call requires the discussion of confidential information, be sure that you are in a private area and no one can hear you.

When using your cell phone, control the volume of your voice. People often raise the tone of their voices in noisy airports, or when nervous.

Ground Travel

When you are in the driver's seat accompanied by clients or colleagues as your passengers, avoid expressing frustration over traffic jams and inconsiderate drivers. Complaining or losing your composure will demonstrate your inability to stay in control. In addition, you do not want to contribute to road rage.

The limo driver is referred to as "Driver" or "Chauffeur." The driver carries your luggage and opens and closes the door for you. Do not open or close your own door! It is an important part of his job. Tip a limo driver 15 percent to 20 percent (ask if a cash tip is preferred). Often the limo fee is handled prior to the reservation by credit card. Always check, and always tip!

If you frequent a city or you use taxis regularly in your home city, consider getting a regular driver. Simply make a connection with a driver that you have found to be reliable. Get his or her business card and record the phone number in your cell phone. Express your desire to use his or her service on a regular basis. Many taxi drivers are hoping for this and will always be available when you call. You can even set up payment options to make the fare easier to process. If you are not familiar with the city, allow the hotel concierge to select a driver for you.

Hotel Accommodations

Before you leave home, make sure that the hotel will provide the personal items you will need in the room at no charge. If they do not, you will need to pack a travel kit. In some hotels (e.g., in Hawaii), there will be a charge for these extras.

 Make sure that you will not be charged for the following:

- Use of hair dryer
- Coffee pot with coffee and tea packets
- Shampoo
- Mouthwash
- Body lotion
- Soap

If you are displeased with the room, call the front desk immediately. Reputable hotels will accommodate you. They would rather that you (and other guests) have a good experience. Most hotels spend a lot of time and energy reading and following up on the issues brought up in a post-trip survey; however, they would rather find out early during your stay so that the situation can be remedied in a timely manner. Consider the times when you had an experience that went from bad to good just because the issue was addressed and fixed promptly.

If you have meals in your room, call and ask for the dishes to be removed when you're finished. It is tacky to place them outside your door on the floor for a long period of time. This also leaves a bad visual for others as they pass through the hallway. Realize that there may be a service charge added to a room service on your bill. If this is the case, you may not have to tip when the food is brought to you, or tip a smaller amount.

Avoid using your room as a meeting or party place unless you have reserved a suite for that purpose. Using your room as a meeting place or for a party can decrease your credibility in the eyes of your client.

When you leave your room, do not leave your laptop or any other electronic devices visible. Hide them! Leave nothing to chance. The hotel is not responsible for anything that is not locked up. Do not mention your hiding place to anyone! Many hotels have laptop safes. If you are going to be gone from your room for a long period of time, it is a good idea to check your laptop. This is a great place to put other valuables too!

Do not take anything from the room as a souvenir (e.g., towels, glasses, welcome portfolio). This reflects poorly on your company; its name is on your reservation! The missing item will be logged in the computer under your name. In addition, you may find an extra charge on your credit card to cover the cost of the missing towel or other item. This is another reason that hotels require credit card confirmation. Your credit card could be charged as much as two hundred and fifty dollars for a missing bathrobe.

When checking into a hotel, remember never to use a debit card. Most times they ask for a credit card for incidentals. Some chains have started to ask if you are sure you want to use a debit card to hold a reservation since it requires an open account and can cause problems. One such problem is that your cash is now tied up for the length of your stay. This could amount to hundreds of dollars, and the difficult part is that it is not easily reversed; sometimes it takes up to three days. This could leave you with no cash to get home. The best thing to do is to hold the room and incidentals on a credit card. Credit cards are different; they do not get charged until you check out and do not tie up your cash.

If you are paying for someone else's room, you will need to fill out and e-mail or fax in a credit card authorization for that person to be able to use your card for his or her hotel stay. It is the same process for paying for a room for a traveling relative or a top recruit. A simple call to the front desk to ask them to e-mail or fax you an authorization form will save you potential time and embarrassment at check-in. Plus, your guest will get right into his or her room and not have to wait around while they track you down, asking you to send a form approving the charges at the point of check-in.

Hotel Security Checklists

If you are new to travel, you may not know all of the security measures that a hotel takes and recommends for your safety. Most importantly, you should incorporate these security measures into your plans!

 When Checking In and While At the Hotel

1. Request a room that is not on the ground floor, facing a parking lot. The best choice is a room on the third floor or higher. With the door open, check the room first to be sure that everything appears safe. Then close the door, lock it, and get comfortable.

2. Put your valuables in the hotel safe. Do not leave them in your car or in an open area in your room.

3. Confirm all deliveries that you are expecting with the front desk. When an unexpected delivery arrives, verify the delivery with the front desk before opening the door. Then look through your door's peephole to see who is there. Do not open the door without checking!

4. Be observant; do not venture into parking lots or darkened

areas. If the lighting is questionable or weak, ask the hotel to provide an escort to the intended area.

5. Only keep the door partially open in your room when you have visitors. Do not keep the door partially open when you are alone, even if you are just going for ice.

6. Ask the front desk to hold your key for you when leaving the hotel, and pick it up when you return. This will prevent losing your keys or having them stolen while you are enjoying time away from the hotel. Too often, hotel guests openly leave their room keys on cocktail or pool-area tables, where they can easily be stolen. Make sure that you have your ID when you go to retrieve your key at the front desk.

7. If a front desk staff member says your room number in hearing distance of another guest, discreetly ask for a different room.

 While You Are Out of the Hotel

1. Never carry all of your valuables in the same place. It is best to put pricey items, such as jewelry and technology gadgets, in a safe deposit box; many hotels have laptop safes inside desk drawers. This is another great place for securing more than just laptops.

2. Never walk alone at night. If you are going for a walk in the daytime, be sure to return before nightfall or take a cab back to the hotel.

3. Protect your identity. Remove your convention ID badge when leaving the hotel or roaming away from the convention area.

4. A woman should carry her handbag with the strap over her shoulder and across her chest. For added protection, place your arm across your bag when on stairways, escalators, and elevators, and when going through revolving doors.

5. A man should wrap a heavy, wide rubber band around his wallet to prevent it from being easily slipped out of his

pocket, or carry just what he needs in his front pants pocket. (Side cargo pant pockets are also risky.)

Safety Tips and Considerations When Traveling Alone

If you are a woman traveling alone, it is safer to have the bellman accompany you to your hotel room with your luggage. Do not try to carry your own bags to save a tip. Your safety is more important. This is also a good precaution if you are traveling with colleagues. It can be awkward having a male colleague walk into your room as he assists with your luggage; his well-meaning gesture may be misinterpreted by others.

Also ask for a room that is near the elevators rather than at the end of a long hallway. Some hotels have one floor (normally the second floor) designated for women traveling alone, as a safety precaution. This floor is monitored more frequently.

Expect to take care of your own baggage. It is not easy to put heavy carry-on bags in the overhead bin. If you need help, ask the flight attendant first. Men are typically very gracious and will jump in and make the offer to help when they see a woman struggling, but do not expect it or make a comment about "incivility" if the offer is not made. Move quickly and confidently. For safety reasons, it is important to look like you know where you are going, even if you do not. If you need directions, always ask a member of the airport or hotel staff.

When you want to dine in a fine restaurant alone, take charge of the situation. Before requesting a table, approach the headwaiter and nicely but firmly explain, "I am a consultant traveling alone on business. I came here because I am intrigued with your restaurant." (Or "the restaurant was recommended to me.") The headwaiter will respect your professional standing and offer you the best seat for single diners.

 Tip: If a booth is an option, request a booth. You will feel less conspicuous.

Traveling with Coworkers

Have a pre-meeting and discuss the responsibilities of your traveling team. Address situations that involve both coworkers and clients. When men and women travel together, meals, taxis, tips, and other expenses are paid separately or split equally. This should be worked out before embarking on the trip so that there are no misunderstandings or awkward moments.

Establish whether or not you are going to talk business on the plane. If you do, keep the conversation general. Avoid any information that is confidential, in case you are sitting next to someone who enjoys eavesdropping.

When two people of unequal rank travel together, the individual of lesser rank often gets to handle all of the details, such as getting a taxi, tipping, making reservations, picking up meal tabs, and other forms of assistance. Typically, this person is a personal assistant. If you are not the personal assistant, ask beforehand how your senior officer or boss would like these details handled.

 Frequently Asked Questions

Q) Should a man be responsible for the woman's luggage?

A) No, each person is responsible for his or her own luggage. This is, however, difficult when a gentleman is acting out of "good form" to help his female companion. It is important for the woman to decline gracefully or accept with gratitude.

Q) What should a female coworker do if a male coworker invites her to his room or to a private dinner?

A) Suggest the lobby, or offer to invite others to join you. Do not allow yourself to be put into an awkward situation.

Q) Should the man take care of the tip for the woman?

A) No. Each person is responsible for his or her own tipping. To avoid this awkwardness, each should travel with at least twenty one-dollar bills and six five-dollar bills (totaling fifty dollars).

When traveling with coworkers or clients with an accent or for whom English is their second language, speak distinctly and listen carefully. The tips in this section cover the most common situations. There are more tips available online and in books on the topic.

Take every precaution and travel safe.

Chapter 9
GESTURES OF APPRECIATION

> *As we express our gratitude, we must never forget the highest appreciation is not to utter words, but to live by them.*
>
> —John F. Kennedy

Gifting is a vital part of the business world because it is an expression of goodwill and a reminder of a productive and special business relationship between the giver and the recipient. It is a way of showing appreciation for a client's loyalty; however, it does not guarantee future business. Gifts make us feel good and think about how the giver took the time to acknowledge the relationship.

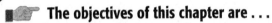

The objectives of this chapter are . . .

1. To help discern the right occasions and the right reasons for giving gifts to business associates and clients; to understand what's appropriate and what's not, and what makes a gift memorable;

2. To show the relationship between showing appreciation and reinforcing a company's brand, and to provide instructions on how to make a gift truly heartfelt; and

3. To provide guidelines on reciprocating gifts, declining gifts, handling inappropriate gifts, regifting gifts gracefully, and above all cultivating an attitude of gratitude and making people feel special.

A *gesture* can be a form of gift when it is offered as a special celebration or an appreciation meal. For example, if you just received a huge order from a client and want to thank him for that order, celebrate over a meal that includes a special toast. Other forms of appreciation might include an elegant dinner, a leisurely lunch, a night at the opera or theater, or a game of golf, to name a few.

A *gift* is a token of appreciation. And a gift should have a theme—"*In appreciation of* ..."—so that the recipient understands the purpose of the gift. For example, a gift should say, "We thought about you," "We appreciate your efforts," "We appreciate your business," "You are important," or "I remember your special day," or the like. The occasion, the appropriateness, and the timing need to be right.

Gifts are not only expressions of appreciation and gratitude, but they can serve as *marketing tools* as well because they reinforce a company's brand or image. However, you need to be careful. Gifts with the company logo are token marketing tools and are best given as souvenirs, grab bag items, or thank-you gifts. They should be avoided as gifts for customer appreciation or for a visiting guest. The exception would be a unique item of great value that only has meaning if the company logo is discreetly *engraved* on the item, thus giving it a special value as a memento.

The Tangible and The Intangible

There are tangible and intangible ways to show appreciation. If you really want to give something valuable, or if budget or policy is a concern, devote some time to a project or to the company's favorite charity. Sometimes a verbal thank you adds the perfect touch.

If your company is in the habit of giving appreciation gifts and policy no longer allows the expenditure, be careful. When clients or customers are used to receiving gifts, they are disappointed when the gifts stop; therefore, minimize your gift giving gradually. Always send something, even if it is a small token of appreciation. It is still appreciated. For example, instead of individual gifts, consider a group or a team gift such as a basket of cheese, crackers, and candy that can be shared. The gift could even be intangible, such as volunteering at a charity in the name of the client.

> Research indicates that there is a strong relationship between gift giving and increased sales. Even a modest gift can significantly enhance a business relationship, because it demonstrates appreciation. A holiday thank-you or end-of-the-year gesture reinforces commitment to current customers and sends a reminder to prospective clients.

Gifting helps bond relationships by demonstrating that you are thoughtful, appreciative, and considerate. Your intention should be honorable. A gift or special gesture should be offered voluntarily, without expectation of a gift or contract. Depending on the situation, though, it is appropriate to reciprocate in kind (e.g., with a dinner or tickets to an event).

Do not give a gift because it makes you look good, or because it benefits you in some way. Gifts are intended to make others feel good and to show appreciation; therefore, it is best to have the gift linked to an occasion.

Honor Company Gift Policies

The appropriateness of office gift giving is determined by company policy, personal relationships, and sensitivity. Check with your human resources department regarding company policy on accepting gifts.

> *It is critical to note the extravagance or perceived extravagance of any activities or meals. Many companies now have ethics policies that discourage gifts or entertainment in excess of a certain dollar amount. Some companies prohibit giving or accepting any entertainment or gifts, regardless of the expense. In some cases, paying for hotels or travel expenses is considered a bribe. Before engaging in any such activity, make sure that you*

have a clear understanding of your company's ethics policy as well as that of your potential or existing client.

–Amy Suess-Garcia, senior director of global customer service, Taylor Company

Business gifts should be signs of appreciation, not rewards for contracts, orders, or assignments. Companies vary dramatically on their gift policies, but it is not easy for the well-intentioned individual to know the gift policy of every customer and company. People will be caught up in the spirit of a special occasion or celebration and want to show appreciation, yet companies have to be careful and make sure that the gift or gesture cannot be interpreted as a gift to guarantee future work or favors.

There may be a gift policy that states limits as to what can be given. A gift is inappropriate if it encourages an employee to act contrary to the best interest of the company or to relax ethical standards. If you receive a gift that could be interpreted as a bribe, be sure to discuss its acceptance with the human resources department or your supervisor.

While some companies do not have a gift policy, others have a dollar limit or other guidelines regarding what their employees can and cannot give and receive. Due to the sensitivity of gift interpretation (e.g., bribing for future business), there is a tendency toward charitable contributions given in the name of the gift recipient. This allows you to send a card to acknowledge your relationship with the recipient and do something beneficial to society in general, without crossing over any ethical boundaries.

With such a diverse population in our workforce, it is also important to learn something about a person's ethnic, religious, and cultural practices (e.g., avoid giving a bottle of wine to someone who does not drink alcohol.) The same applies to any food item (e.g., candy or nuts) that might pose an allergy issue.

Find out what is appropriate and falls within corporate gift guidelines, and then try to learn something personal about the gift recipient. The gift then becomes more than something that will end up in a closet—it becomes a gift with impact. When selecting a *personal* gift, make sure that it is not too personal yet appeals to that individual's sense of style (e.g., a fashion item).

A gift selection is typically made from an established list of gift options and their corresponding prices. Gifts are either stock items or they are ordered from an approved catalog or store. In most cases, you will be required to submit a gift request form. Be sure to know the policy before giving a gift. If your company does not have a specific policy, it will be extremely important to develop one.

 Consider the following when making your gift selection:

- Find out the dollar limit on gifts in the company policy. For example, the gift value norm for most companies is fifty dollars.

- Is it being presented too close to an order being placed or at an unusual time?

- Does the type of gift violate any company policies (e.g., a gift of liquor)?

- Will the gift make you feel obligated to the person or company?

- Does the giver have a reputation for using gifts as an expectation that goes beyond company policy?

Focus on the overall appropriateness of the gift, and make sure that it cannot be interpreted as a favor. Be humble, and offer your token of gratitude without expectations.

This chapter will offer thank you note tips and gift buying guidelines.

The last time you experienced appreciation or gratitude, how did it make you feel?

Pay it forward!

Life is about making people feel special.

CULTIVATE AN ATTITUDE OF GRATITUDE AND APPRECIATION

> *Gratitude is merely the secret hope of future favors.*
> —François de La Rochefoucauld,
> French author and moralist (1613–1680)

Written expressions of appreciation warm the heart and often are valued more than actual presents. Sending a thank-you to event organizers is powerful! They work hard, and knowing that you appreciated their efforts will keep you in the forefront. And never assume someone is above or below receiving a thank-you note from you. Everyone likes to be thanked and appreciated. The purpose of any type of note is to make others feel valued and appreciated. You are making an investment in the other person and creating an atmosphere of goodwill. It is not just about them; it is also about you.

For the employee who worked hard on an event, tell him or her in writing that you appreciated his or her dedication and willingness to help. This note will be kept and cherished! Plus it makes the appreciation tangible.

As a *host*, you should always follow up with your committee and guests to be sure that the event or luncheon was successful and productive. As a *guest*, a written thank-you note shows the best kind of appreciation, an important business *gesture*. Hosts and event planners put so much time and effort into entertainment that they want to know you had a good time. It also demonstrates good follow-up, a critical business gesture.

E-mail Versus Handwritten

A handwritten thank-you note with your *real* handwriting represents the essence of you. It is more than a courtesy; a job or client opportunity could depend on it. It is your signature, and no one else has your writing style. And do not let your fear of bad handwriting hold you back; give it your best. If you feel your cursive handwriting is not legible, then print but sign in cursive. Do not use mailing labels on the envelope. Write! Your handwriting will make your note stand out in a stack of computer-generated mailing addresses.

Also, e-mail thank-yous are easy to delete. A handwritten thank-you is typically placed in your folder. You might not get this opportunity, but when another one surfaces and your file is reviewed, the extra effort just might pay off at a later date.

Sending a written thank-you note is actually less time-consuming than playing phone tag to express verbal thanks, and it is more tangible than e-mailed thanks. A thank-you note demonstrates gratitude and shows appreciation. Small gestures make the biggest impact.

A Notecard or Thank-You Card Is a Gift

> Compliments and thank-yous
> are prized possessions.

When is a thank-you note appropriate? When someone does something special for you, gives you something, or invites you to an event or a meal, or when you just want to express appreciation for someone's efforts or advice, a thank-you note may be called for. If you are thanking someone for a gift that more than one person gave, send the note to the key person (e.g., the organizer), and mention the others. It has your signature, and it has longevity. Some people still save cards!

Office supply and stationery stores have wonderful selections of thank-you cards that are easy to store in your desk drawer or travel case. If the thank-you is more social than business and going to an out-of-town individual, considering sending a scenic postcard.

> *I have a box of "thank-you" and "in appreciation" notecards that go back many years. I just cannot seem to bring myself to discard them. When I am feeling discouraged or feel my efforts are in vain, I re-read my cards, and they reconfirm that I am in the right career and often remind me of important moments that I had forgotten. Save your thank-you cards! When you have that moment, reread them.*

A thank-you note should be sent within a week of receiving a gift, or within a day of having an interview or being treated to a meal or event. Your note should focus on the person who gave you the gift and how special it made you feel. Make it meaningful.

If you forgot to send a thank-you note and a month or two has elapsed, send the note with a delayed response apology. It is still important to make the acknowledgment and show appreciation. Time does get away from us. Your thank-you note needs to be appropriate, and it needs to reflect the appointment or occasion.

Sample #1

Components of a Thank-You Note

- Begin with a sincere opening: "Dear Kathryn."
- Say thank you for the gift, appointment, or gesture.
- Write how you plan to use the gift, or comment on the gesture.
- Follow with a compliment or a note on how you will be following up or how you were affected by the gesture.

- Mention that you hope to see your host again or attend the next event.
- Close with warm regards and your name: "Best regards, Jane Adams."

Sample #2
No-Frills Formula: Name It, Highlight It, and Sign Off
A *hand written* note only takes three lines:

- *First sentence:* Reference the event, the name of the gift, or whatever prompted the follow-up.
- *Second sentence:* Say something specific about the event, the conversation, or the gift.
- *Third sentence:* Thank the person for the event, their thoughtfulness, or for the gesture.

Sample #3
Phone: Thank You Script

- "Thank you for a wonderful event. I know that a lot of time and planning went into it."

  (Wait for a response.)

- State something specific that made it spectacular or beneficial for you.

  (Wait for a response.)

- When you debrief, you might want to . . . etc.
  (Offer a helpful suggestion.)

This gesture creates a "warm fuzzy" connection and demonstrates professionalism. It is a key follow-up. Furthermore, it has an effective chance of erasing any discomfort that may have occurred during the event or the interaction and solidify what was helpful.

Goodwill Professional Notes

Anita Brick, director of career services at the University of Chicago School of Business, has done extensive research into the value of sending notes or responding with thank-you notes, which she refers to as "professional notes." She divides the giving of professional notes into the following three categories:

 Anita's Three-Step Professional Note

1. *Acknowledgment:* Paying back

2. *Encouragement:* Paying forward

3. *Gratitude (Thank you):* Showing appreciation

Your thank-you or professional note is a goodwill gesture and does not have to be fancy or expensive; however, it should have a professional look. It should be simple and specific. Purchase a professional-looking box of preprinted thank-you notes at a card shop, or purchase a box of blank notecards in various colors. Select a color that commemorates the event or is your signature color.

When you handwrite your note (instead of using e-mail), you are giving it a personal touch by sharing your signature. It is not about your penmanship; it is the essence of you on paper.

> Send a note as a way to make your networking event tangible. The note can let the individual know that you enjoyed meeting him or her and that you will be calling or following up in a few days. Certainly, these notes can be e-mailed, but a handwritten, mailed note offers a more personal touch and is more impressive.

Do not expect something in return; however, when something positive happens because of your note, consider it a gift, or simply smile because you did something that made someone want to respond in kind.

What to Write and What Not to Write

Use the KISS technique (Keep It Super Simple), and be sure to be specific. Debrief the event or lunch in your mind (or on paper). What stands out? This shows you paid attention and focused on the person. Better yet, make a note during or immediately after the event so you do not forget. Make sure that you are writing the note for the right reason. It should not be used to manipulate nor have strings attached. It should not be self-serving or selfish.

Be specific. Show how you have paid attention and acknowledge something. What did you learn or gain from the encounter? You are not just sending a card; you are giving a gift of words. Also, avoid sending the same note to several people. Remark on something specific that is special to the recipient.

The most awkward note to write is one that expresses sympathy or responds to a sad event. The important thing to remember when sending this type of note is to be sincere.

 Tips for the Expression of Sympathy

- Acknowledge the loss: "I was so sad when I heard …"
- Express your sympathy: "I'm thinking of you and your family. I'm so sorry about this difficult time."
- If you know the person, add a personal note: "I will always remember (*express a fond memory*)."

Do not say, "I know how you feel," because most often you *do not* know how an individual feels. Just express sadness at his or her loss.

Stamped with Style

Depending on the nature of the event, you may want to affix an interesting stamp to mail your card, something that will reflect the mood and catch the eye. Alternatively, use a stamp that reflects the recipient's special interest (e.g., if he or she is a gardener, use a floral postage stamp). This adds that extra special touch that will be remembered.

Creative stamps and unique envelopes captivate people. It is like sending them their favorite photo on a special canvas. If you know that your client or customer loves antiques, select a vintage stamp. Vintage postage plus a unique envelope equals a special message. This is an envelope and note that will be kept and remembered, and it is a great way to let your client know you will always go the extra mile.

The post office carries a wide range of stamps, envelopes, and packaging materials. Taking the time to select a special way to mail a note is another way of making your client feel very special. If the postage will require more than one stamp, create a mosaic theme on the envelope. If your client is a stamp collector, he or she will appreciate the artwork. E-mailed notes cannot do this.

Avoid political or religious stamp themes for the same reason that you would avoid conversations on politics or religion. It could send a risky message. The recipient's opinion or belief may differ from your viewpoint or belief system.

Know your client! If he or she is very conservative and has a "no frills" attitude, stay with traditional business envelopes and stamps. If your client is flamboyant or involved in the arts, give your note a creative touch.

> Be appreciative.
> Show gratitude.

GIFTING AND LASTING MEMENTOS

> Deposit a good feeling; it leaves a lasting impression, and you will reap benefits when you least expect it.

People love to leave with a token to remember an event; small gift bags are greatly appreciated and popular. The gift bag should consist of items that relate to the theme of the event. (Adding a gourmet chocolate mint is always a nice touch.) Focus on a "tangible memory" item, and try to avoid logo items. For example, a group photo taken and sent in an attractive frame offers a wonderful memory. If possible, select a frame that can have the company logo embossed on it.

The most memorable gift is a memento, a keepsake—something that has a special meaning. Whether the gift is for a colleague or a client, the worth of the gift should not be judged by how much it costs; it should be more about the individual's personal interests or tastes and what gave you joy when selecting the gift. Furthermore, the gift should be based on your relationship to the individual.

When to Give

Most gift giving is centered on calendar-specified holidays (e.g., Christmas), corporate special occasions (e.g., a retirement party), and employee birthdays; however, be original and create your own occasion. For example, if an individual has gone above and beyond to help his or her peers with a big project that is outside his or her own work, an appreciation gift from the group would be a wonderful surprise.

Popular Occasions for Gifting

- Holidays
- Birthdays
- Special anniversaries
- Employee celebrations
- Weddings
- Baby showers
- Get well or encouragement
- Grand opening

"Be original, and create your own occasion."

If you are giving a *gift of appreciation*, explain the purpose of the gift in the card so the receiver will not feel confused or embarrassed. For example, you might say, "This is in appreciation for all the special help you gave me when I was on a deadline."

If the gift is for a special occasion (e.g., a wedding, a birthday, or an anniversary) and there is a gift registry, you are not obligated to buy from the registry, especially if the items selected are pricey. Instead, select something that has a special meaning or is unique in nature. If you are selecting a pricey item, have several others join in on the gift. In other words, make it a group gift.

Sometimes an employee's personal celebration creates gift-giving awkwardness. When are you obligated to send a gift, and when is it appropriate to decline the invitation?

An Employee's Wedding: As an employee, you are not obligated to invite the boss to your wedding. The invitation should be based on how well you know your boss or on your length of service. As the boss, you are not obligated to accept wedding invitations or send gifts. If you choose not to attend or send a gift, you should send the couple a note of congratulations.

An Employee's New Baby: As the boss, you are not obligated to send a baby gift to an employee; however, you should send a personal note of congratulations.

An Employee's Birthday: Human resources or senior management should make a policy regarding employee birthdays. If the celebration is held at the office, it should be held in a private area, such as the employee lounge. Gifts are best given as group, department, or team gifts. (Realize that some employees feel that their birthdays are personal and therefore do not want them acknowledged at work. Birthdates are protected personal information. One's right to privacy should always be respected.)

What to Give and to Whom

The worth of a gift is not always judged by its dollar value. Learn an individual's interests and needs, and then select something within your budget. Do not get hung up on the idea that you must spend a certain amount of money. It is the thought and effort spent on the selection that counts. Respect your budget when creating your gift-giving list for clients or prospects.

 The business gift list follows this order of priority:

- Major customers (primarily high-ranking individuals)
- Their employees (individuals with whom you have been in direct contact)
- Other customers
- Prospects

Gifts can be related to a hobby or special interest; donations to a favorite charity; tickets to an event; or gourmet baskets of coffee, tea, or chocolates. When social and business friendships overlap, it might be wise to give or exchange such gifts outside the office at a special coffee, lunch, or dinner.

Office Gifts

When giving a gift to a coworker, make sure that it is not of a personal nature; for example, cologne is very personal, and a garment requires the right sizing. A garment exception would be a polo shirt or T-shirt with a company logo or a customized design that reflects an achievement. Otherwise, you might risk a misinterpretation of intent. The best gift is a gift that is related to the individual's job or hobby.

A gift to your boss is best given as a collective gift from the department or team. In most situations, a gift to a boss from one individual is not recommended, in order to avoid the appearance of trying to secure favoritism. Take up a collection from coworkers in your department or group, and buy a group gift that reflects your boss's hobby or special interest. If a gift from the department is unfeasible, simply give a card with a note of thanks and appreciation for a great working relationship.

You should never expect a gift from your boss or the management team. The company party or holiday bonus is the gift from the company. Show your appreciation by attending the party.

The best way for coworkers to exchange holiday gifts is by drawing names for a gift exchange or grab bag. Do not alienate someone because he or she prefers not to participate in a grab bag or gift exchange; he or she may already be involved in several through other departments, organizations, or friendship circles. Be sensitive to everyone's budget!

It is fun to open a gift in front of the giver so that the excitement of the gift can be shared; however, do not expect or insist that a gift be opened immediately. There are times when it is appropriate to open a gift later. This keeps the gesture more personal. The risk in opening a gift in front of others is that someone observing the exchange might misinterpret the gesture or feel slighted. On the other hand, if you are the recipient, ask if they would like you to open the gift when you receive it, and do not be offended if the giver of the gift prefers that you open the gift in the privacy of your office or home.

The Gift of Time

Do not underestimate the wonderful gift of time. Use your giving spirit as a volunteer. This never violates a company policy. Volunteer at your client's or prospective client's favorite charity, participate in fund-raising activities, or provide a community service—the possibilities are endless!

Wrapping and Sending a Gift

A gift's outer appearance speaks volumes. When you wrap a gift, use quality gift wrap, and include a card that explains the gesture. If it is being mailed, be sure to double-check the mailing address—find out if there is a special mailroom or box number— then send it by certified mail. Follow up a week later to make sure that the *intended* person received it.

> *During one holiday season, I sent my clients a basket of Stony Mountain Chocolates. When I did not hear from one specific client, I called and learned that she never received the basket. I checked my certified mail receipt and learned the name of the person who signed for the basket. It had been delivered to the wrong building, and since they did not know the intended recipient, they shared the basket within their department. I explained what happened to my client and sent her a gourmet coffee gift card of the same value.*

Ready-made gift baskets of candy, gourmet coffees or teas, wine, or cheese and crackers are easier to send, because all the work is done for you; however, you still need to call to be sure the item was received.

> *When Chocolate of the Month sends out gift baskets, we spot-check different recipients to see if they received their baskets and find out how they stood up in shipping. I can then call my clients and tell them that during a quality control check, the person they sent a basket to asked me to tell them that they just loved their gift! This also gives us another opportunity to thank our clients for their order.*
>
> —Jackie Sanborn, instructor, Fullerton College

Always follow up to be sure that the intended recipient received the package. If you are the recipient of a gift, always let the sender know that you received the gift. This is common courtesy.

Special Occasion Gifts

It can get tricky when giving gifts within the office or department during holidays or special occasions. As mentioned previously, it is better to give a gift to the boss from the team than from an individual. Gifts among employees and peers are best done with a grab bag that has a designated dollar limit. Keep the grab bag gifts unisex, or have a male grab bag and a female grab bag.

If you enjoy giving holiday ornaments, make sure that it is a stand-alone ornament and not one that must be hung from a Christmas tree. Not everyone puts up a Christmas tree or practices the Christmas tree tradition.

The holiday party or bonus is the company gift to the employee. A hand-signed card by the company president or CEO is also a gift.

What if a colleague gives you an expensive gift for your birthday, and you just know he will expect one in return? How do you nip this in the bud? The answer is simple: reciprocate in a small way.

> *I became fast friends with a new coworker from a different department. My birthday came shortly after we met, and she gave me a high-dollar gift certificate. I certainly did not want to start the cycle of expensive gifts, so I reciprocated on her birthday with a lunch and a modest gift. She continued to give me gifts for no real reason. It had to stop, because now I felt like she was buying my friendship or favor. Each time I remarked on how thoughtful the gift was but told her that the gift was not necessary. I also weaned myself from that personal friendship and kept the interaction at a business level. Eventually, the gift gestures stopped; however, the camaraderie did remain. It was a delicate situation, but our relationship stayed positive.*

If profits are down and you cannot be generous with a customer this year, send him a hand-written card, saying, "We want you to know how much we have appreciated your business this past year, and we look forward to many more years of serving you." It is the acknowledgment that is so important. The worst thing you can do is ignore a customer or individual because the budget is tight. This is a time when everyone *will* understand and appreciate your restraint or limitations.

Reciprocating a Gift

Just because someone gives you a gift, you do not need to give a gift in return. This gift is an extension of a special kindness. If you are the recipient of a gift, respond immediately with a written note of thanks, a phone call, or by e-mail, whichever is more appropriate.

When the gesture is a special meal, consider reciprocating at the same level. For example, if a client treats you to a fine dining experience, you will return the favor with an equally fine dining experience when the right opportunity presents itself.

Gifts are not meant to create a feeling of imbalance. When you are given a gift, it does not mean that you have to reciprocate with a gift. Receiving a gift should not be treated as accepting an obligation. Instead, it should be a graceful act of acceptance.

If someone gives you an unexpected gift, do not be embarrassed or feel obligated to return the gesture with a gift. This often happens during the holidays. Just smile and say, "Thank you. I was not expecting anything." Some people just enjoy giving and would be embarrassed or possibly even offended if the gesture were returned with a gift. If you feel the need to reciprocate, take this person to lunch as a special thank-you.

And finally, knowing how to gracefully refuse a gift is just as important as knowing how to accept one.

Declining a Gift

For ethical reasons, you may have to decline a gift. Gracefully refuse gifts that are excessive, inappropriate, or against corporate policy. The main thing to consider when deciding whether or not you should decline a gift is "How will the gift be perceived by others?" It must pass the appearance test (is it extravagant?) and the motive test (could it be interpreted as an expectation of future favors?).

When you make the decision to decline a gift, you should return the gift within a few days, and the sooner, the better. Acknowledge immediately with a phone call, e-mail message, or hand-written note, saying that the gift is greatly appreciated but that company policy does not allow you to accept the gift. A gift return has to be done very carefully so as not to offend the client or vendor.

 You have a few options:

- Offer thanks for his or her thoughtfulness, and state that the gift was too generous and that, as a result, company policy does not allow the gift to be accepted. Be sure to state that you appreciate how much thought and time was spent selecting the gift.

■ State that your company policy does not allow you to accept gifts, and ask if the gift can be donated to the giver's favorite charity, or simply explain that the gift is being given to a charity on his behalf. If it is donated to a charity, make sure that this gesture is noted in company gift-giving records. Since the gift was intended as a business gift, it could have tax implications.

■ If it is a non-food item and appropriate, you can state that the gift will be displayed in the company library or lounge for all to enjoy.

■ If it is a lavish gift of food and beverage items, state that it will be shared with the entire team or department.

■ If it is a large basket of nonperishable gifts, state that it will be broken down into individual grab bag gifts to be shared at the next special event or given to a church to use in a fund-raiser.

Inappropriate Gifts

Avoid controversial gifts or gifts of a personal or intimate nature, such as religious or political books, intimate apparel, or fragrances. Avoid humorous gifts that take the risk of offending. What is humorous to you may not be humorous to the recipient. Gag gifts are also risky.

If you are the recipient of an inappropriate gift, use tact and good judgment. As much as you feel offended, do not offend in return. You might respond by saying, "Thank you for the thoughtful gift. However, I am not comfortable accepting it. I hope you will understand."

If you are unable to accept a specific gift for personal reasons (e.g., wine or any other liquor) simply say thank you and comment in a friendly tone that you do not drink alcohol but that you will offer it the next time you have guests who do drink wine. You do not need to say why you do not drink alcohol. It is extremely important that you do not show displeasure. Understand that it was a well-meaning gesture.

> I had known for a long time that a personal acquaintance was a recovering alcoholic, but in my excitement of giving wine gifts in cute wine blankets one holiday season, I forgot. I will never forget the shocked look on his face when I presented the wine as a gift. Once I realized my misstep, I apologized and asked that he share the wine with his holiday friends. I did not ask for the wine back, as most people would. The next day I bought a box of gourmet chocolates, wrapped them in beautiful holiday paper, and gave them to him so he could have a gift from me to enjoy with his family or staff. As for me, I ended up double gifting to save face, which was the right thing to do, since it was my misstep.

Realize that these things happen! And be sure to make a note once you realize that a friend, colleague, or business associate has dietary, religious, or other restrictions.

Regifting: The Practice of Recycling Gifts

Simply stated, *regifting* refers to receiving a gift that you do not want or need and then passing it on as a gift to someone else, so as not to waste the gift. Depending upon how it is handled, it can be a good gesture or a hurtful experience. Certainly, much depends on the motive behind the gift exchange.

The White House takes advantage of regifting, as do many government agencies. It is not surprising! They receive an amazing number of gifts throughout the year from all over the world. These gifts are tagged upon receipt (with who gave the gift and when) and regifted discreetly and carefully to avoid offense.

Having worked for Clare Boothe Luce and Jackie Kennedy, we regifted all the time.

Regifting is okay, provided that ...

■ *the gift is a very nice one;*

■ *there is no possibility of the donor ever finding out what you did; and*

■ *there is no possibility of the recipient ever finding out what you did.*

During the days when I received lots of great gifts that were duplicates (the same scarves, the same perfume, the same talking Santa, etc.), I would carefully regift.

One must never regift just because the gift is ugly or gauche. You must be careful to have the gift on hand when a relative, your former boss, or anyone connected to the gift comes to see you during the year after you received it. After that, you're off the hook. Of course, perfume (which is ruined after a year, no matter how well it was sealed), candy, and food packages can be regifted at will within the holiday season.

When I received duplicate gifts for my office, I would always send the duplicate to a friend three thousand miles away. Always, always inspect the gift to make sure that it hasn't been monogrammed with your initials or personalized in some other way.

And never do what I did—I sent my former secretary in Chicago the same beautiful crystal paperweight she had sent me the year before! In other words, when you put away something to regift, put a note on it saying who gave it to you and when and where.

—Letitia Baldrige, author *New Manners for New Times*

People have mixed feelings about regifting, so be careful. Never regift just because the gift is ugly or not needed, especially if it came from a coworker, personal friend, or family member with whom you have a lot of contact. To avoid hurt feelings, there should be no possibility that the original gift giver will find out that you passed the gift on to someone else.

Keep in mind that when you wrap a personal (regifted) gift, the recipient assumes that you purchased the gift especially for him or her. This is where it gets touchy. There is less risk with food or beverage gifts that can be shared.

For those who are opposed to regifting, you might want to consider extenuating circumstances and how to properly handle a gift that one cannot use or does not need. Much depends on the type of gift that is being regifted and how it is being given. The emotional challenge comes when you put a lot of thought into a particular gift and later get it back as a regift. This happens!

If you are going to regift something that you cannot use, ask a coworker or family friend if he would like it. For example, if you received alcohol as a gift and you do not drink alcohol, give it as a host gift or thank-you gift, or offer it when entertaining your friends or family. Of course, be sure that the gift did not originate from the same circle of friends or coworkers. Or consider regifting to your newspaper carrier, hair stylist, delivery person, babysitter, etc.

 If you must regift, ask yourself the following questions first:

1. *Is the gift regiftable?* Never regift signed books, monogrammed items, or a gift that has been used. Some gifts that are good candidates for regifting include unopened bottles of good wine or a desk item (e.g., decorative letter opener).

2. *How is its condition?* Only new, unopened gifts in good condition should be considered for regifting. Never give partially used gifts or items that you have owned for a long time.

3. *What are your intentions?* The gift should be very nice and something that you are certain the recipient will enjoy. Do not give a gift just to give a gift. Be sure that the recipient will appreciate the item. Remember, if you feel that an item is undesirable, the recipient probably will too.

4. *How should it be wrapped?* While gift bags in good condition can be reused, wrapping paper is a one-time thing.

Finally, if you suspect that a gift you have received has been regifted, take comfort in the fact that the sender truly feels that the gift is something you would really like.

A better alternative would be to give the gift (unwrapped and unopened) to a charity or shelter, or to someone as a token of thanks. Alternatively, give it to your church or other organization to use as a raffle or attendance gift.

International Gift-Giving Considerations

If you are purchasing gifts for international guests, be sure to do your research. What might be an appropriate gift in one country may be offensive in another. Most countries have rituals or ceremonies attached to their gift giving. This not only involves the selection of the gift, but how it is presented as well. If you are entertaining international visitors, learn the gift-giving protocol of that culture. This information is easily available online, through your local consulate's office, and in books. To get you started, consider the following:

- Gift giving is part of doing business in most countries.
- The presentation is extremely important. The wrapping may be more important than the gift.
- Every culture differs as to what is appropriate. It is extremely important to research the gift-giving protocol of the specified country.
- Status gifts like designer or name brands are important. Designer labels and "Made in USA" labels are recommended.
- A gift should not be too costly, or the recipient may consider it a gift for a future favor. This will go against company policy.
- Make sure that you know enough about the individual who will be receiving the gift to choose appropriately.

- A gift should *not* always be opened in front of the giver, so do not expect it to be opened. And be sure that it is appropriate before you open a gift for yourself in front of your international partner. People in some countries are more humble about the exchange and prefer that gifts be opened privately.

Internationally, gifts with the company logo are typically inappropriate and can be considered an insult.

Whether the recipient is domestic or international, a gift will have more meaning if it communicates the thought process that went into its selection, and the same is true with greeting cards. Expensive gifts can make recipients feel very uncomfortable, because they may not be able to reciprocate in kind, or they can set the wrong tone. Thoughtless or inappropriate gifts can make the recipient feel unimportant.

> Respect policies and customs.
> Give because you want to give.
> Accept gifts gracefully with thanks.

GIFT SELECTION AND SHOPPING TIPS

Shop on your own time or on your home computer. Your office computer belongs to your employer. In addition, employees should not use their employer's time or equipment to shop, even during the lunch hour, unless permission has been granted.

 Considerations

- Give in good taste; you will be remembered for your choice of gift.

- Company logos should be discreet or avoided. This means that you do not send a gift that has the logo all over it or the logo dominates the gift. If you give a book, place your logo on the inside cover with a note. Also, a logo gift that can be used year round will keep your company name visible.

- Avoid improper and controversial gifts—any gift of a personal or intimate nature—and gag gifts.

- The gift should complement one's company image, be useful, and be relevant.

- A personal gift should relate to the recipient's hobby or special interest.

- Package gifts attractively. Include a card. Presentation can be everything.

- A gift should not be too cheap or too expensive.

- The best gifts are gender-neutral and in impeccable taste.

- Make sure the gift is in the spirit of appreciation; do not expect a gift in return.

- Personalize a gift with a note; however, be sure the note

is not too personal. Misinterpretation is a risk, so clearly state the intent.

 Gift Selection Ideas

- A bottle of wine with a funky corkscrew or wine outfit and a book on the history of wine
- Membership to a wine or food of the month club
- Store or restaurant gift card
- Concert or sporting event tickets
- Gourmet shop item
- Wine basket or wine in a wine blanket
- Magazine subscription
- Desk item
- Unique leather business card holder
- Computer item
- Books
- Gift basket
- Favorite food item (e.g., specialty donuts, candy, gourmet coffee beans) gift-wrapped in a whimsical fashion
- Sports or hobby item
- Electronics
- Gifts relating to your city and location
- Traditional gifts that reflect the corporate culture
- Donation to a favorite charity in their name
- Memorabilia

 What's In and What's Out

This list will vary with the times and trends. As some trends go others will return.

- Out with gift certificates—in with *gift cards*

- Out with personal items—in with *theater, sports, event, or dinner tickets*
- Out with a set of crystal—in with a special commemorative crystal or a universal flute
- Out with a set of white wine or red wine glassware—in with a set of balloon (wine) glassware or stemless glassware

This list will change, so be aware of what is in and what is out.

> Call a department store's giftware personal
> shopper to learn about gift trends.

Chapter 10

CUSTOMIZE YOUR CHECKLISTS AND JOURNALS

Because everyone's needs are different, the planning process for hosting a successful event depends greatly on the personalities and professionals involved. This chapter contains a variety of checklists designed to help you create your own plans to ensure a successful event.

☞ The objectives of this chapter are . . .

1. To impress upon you the need to foresee and plan for every detail and every contingency when planning an important event;

2. To provide you with tried and tested guides for successfully planning and executing a successful business event; and

3. To remind you that evaluating an event afterward is just as important as all the preparations that go before.

I developed these checklists as a protocol adviser and overseer of logistics in cooperation with Fortune 500 companies and municipalities that were planning major events or receiving international visitors. The planning included all the details for the events, from planning to execution, as well as preparing their staffs for receiving international guests and traveling abroad.

These are tried and true checklists, but they are not meant to be definitive. You may well use all six checklists in their entirety, or you may decide that only certain segments of each one match your needs.

Every event has its own unique set of circumstances that requires specific guidelines. Let these checklists serve as your initial planning guide, and adapt them as your needs dictate. You will find some repetition among the lists, but the purpose for that is to ensure that you cover everything in a logical sequence. You will need to adapt (or customize) the checklists to reflect the size of your event , level of formality, and caliber of guests (e.g., dignitaries). The following is based on a large event:

> Leave nothing to chance: create comprehensive checklists.
> Make your event worry-free and fun!

Checklist #1: *Option A*–Establishing Communication to Finalizing Details

Checklist #2: *Option B*–Information Gathering to Wrap-up

Checklist #3: Audio for AV Professionals, Planners, and Speakers

Checklist #4: Food and Beverage Planning

Checklist #5: Gathering Data for Domestic and International Visitors

Checklist #6: Event Journals and Calendars

> *Note:* Checklists #1 and #2 are very similar and offered as Option A *or* Option B. You should select the one that works best for your team and your needs. Checklist #3 and #4 expand on Option A and Option B recommendations.

To make record keeping easy, use the sample checklist forms at the end as a guide to create your own event binder.

Checklist #1: *Option A*
ESTABLISHING COMMUNICATION TO FINALIZING DETAILS

When starting your planning, select individuals who will serve as great resources, and select planners to help you with the initial steps. Use the following checklist as a comprehensive guide for tackling the logistics:

Step 1: Gather Information and Establish the Communication Process

- ❑ Determine the date of the event.
- ❑ Calculate the number of guests.
- ❑ Know the nationality of the guests.
- ❑ Will you need interpreters and translators?
- ❑ Establish your objectives.
- ❑ Establish budget parameters. (Identify revenue sources and expenses.)
- ❑ Brainstorm event ideas.
- ❑ Decide on event theme and activities.
- ❑ Determine the type of group and purpose.
- ❑ Will there be entertainment? (If yes, what type? And what will be needed?)
- ❑ Will there be special needs (e.g., wheelchair access, seating, dietary restrictions)?
- ❑ What are the audiovisual requirements (e.g., microphones, screens, projectors)?

❑ Identify committee responsibilities.

❑ Designate a smoking area.

Step 2: Identify Logistics and Assign Responsibilities

❑ Select and contract event venue and food service.

❑ Design room setup, type of service, and theme.

❑ Create a timeline (timing outline between speaker, planner, and food staff).

❑ Designate responsibilities for special tasks (e.g., sponsorships, invitations, logistics, site contract).

❑ Assign lead people, and identify vendor and facility contacts.

❑ Create an event specifications book or record using an accompanying checklist for each task.

❑ Schedule a pre-event inspection and meeting with facility staff.

❑ Schedule a pre-event meeting with volunteers.

❑ Check safety and security measures.

❑ Will you need to arrange for or hire a parking valet service?

Step 3: Food and Beverage Options: Breakfast, Lunch, Dinner, and Breaks

❑ Design meals with food staff (or catering) offering healthy alternatives, creative choices, and chef specialties.

❑ Request a tasting to help determine meal selection. The tasting should have a wide selection of menu options. The individuals involved in the tasting should represent a cross section of food preferences and diets (e.g., dietary restrictions, health-related diet programs, cultural considerations).

❑ Determine where and how food and beverages will be served during breaks and if there will be seating.

❑ Determine the timing for breakfast, lunch, or dinner and the number of servers (e.g., one server per three tables of eight or ten).

❑ Have one or two alternative foods (e.g., vegetarian) available.

Step 4: Food Service Preparation

❑ Will there be food restrictions or special orders?

❑ Will you need foyer or hallway food service (outside the event room)?

❑ What is the type of food service (breakfast, lunch, dinner, reception)?

❑ What do you want served at breaks?

❑ Is the meal to be a buffet or sit-down lunch or dinner?

❑ If there is a cocktail session prior to the dinner, what kind of beverage service will you need (glass, plastic, paper)?

❑ Sterling silver or plastic utensils?

❑ Stir sticks or spoons and claw tongs?

❑ Plain or logo napkins?

❑ Be sure that paper or glass plates, glassware, utensils, and napkins are available.

❑ Are drip trays (for coffee) and discard bowls (for wrappers) provided?

❑ Decide on beverages and condiments and how they should be served or displayed (artificial sweeteners, cube or granulated sugar, milk/cream dispenser, powdered cream packets, lemon wedges, honey, jams, tea bag assortments, regular and/or decaffeinated coffee, hot water, water pitchers or bottled water).

❑ Select hors d'oeuvres that are easy to handle and eat, especially if this is a stand-up event.

❑ When and how frequently are beverages to be replenished?

❑ Have a conference-size table (rectangular) set up with tablecloth and skirt.

❑ Beverages should be placed on the table at the far end or at an alternate location.

❑ Food should be placed next to the tableware setting and before the beverages.

❑ Dishes, utensils, and glassware should be displayed at the beginning of the table (opposite the beverages). The movement proceeds like this: dishes, napkin, utensils, food, and beverage.

❑ Tray jacks (restaurant serving trays used for serving meals and for cleanup) should be available and possibly covered with linen.

❑ Schedule continuous cleanup. Be sure to have disposal trays available at opposite ends of the room for ease of cleanup.

Step 5: Alcohol: Consider Liability and Safety

❑ Will you be placing a bottle of wine on each table, or will you have a server pour wine by the glass for each guest?

❑ Ensure that the hotel or catering service is licensed, and ask to see a copy of their certificate of insurance.

❑ Always arrange for a trained and certified bartender to serve alcohol.

❑ Consider providing a limited number of drink tickets instead of having an open bar.

❑ Consider having the waitstaff offer each guest red or white wine while seated (prior to eating the main course) rather than placing full bottles on the table. This way each guest is provided with a glass of wine with his or her meal while it limits the number of glasses any one guest consumes.

❑ Close the bar one hour before the event ends, and serve coffee, tea, and sodas.

Step 6: Select Bar and Liquor Plans

❑ *Paying by the bottle (or by the drink):* This can be your cheapest alternative—but you need to know your group. It is important to take an inventory of the bar before and after the event and have the bartender initial the inventory sheet. In some cases, you may bring your own liquor; however, be prepared to pay a corkage fee.

❑ *Hosted or Open Bar:* The sponsor pays for private room setup and all drinks. Ratio of bartenders to guests is one to fifty. *Beware: people drink more at an open bar.*

❑ *Limited Open Bar:* Offer one selection of red wine, one selection of white wine, and two types of beer. This limits the cost of a fully hosted bar.

❑ *Cash Bar:* This is a bar setup in a private room where guests pay for their own drinks, either with cash or by purchasing tickets.

❑ *Package Bar:* Buying drinks "per person" for a designated number of hours can be the most expensive option, but it depends on the group.

Step 7: Finalizing the Event

- ❏ Examine all the checklists to be sure that everything is covered.

- ❏ Distribute gratuities, if warranted.

- ❏ Write thank-you notes or letters.

- ❏ Process and pay invoices. If paying the invoice at the event, make sure to ask the facility's manager to signal you when the bill is ready, so that you may go to a private location to pay. It is inappropriate to study and pay the bill in the presence of your guests.

- ❏ Debrief with your committee (staff and volunteers).

- ❏ Record everything in the event specifications book.

> *In some cases, depending on the type of event, it is a good idea to solicit feedback by offering a survey or critique of your event. This feedback is invaluable in planning for future events, and it is a compliment to the guests that you value their opinions enough to ask if they were satisfied.*
> —Amy Suess-Garcia, director of communications and training, Taylor Company

Once your ideas are in place, it is time to make and finalize your arrangements.

②

Checklist #2: *Option B*
INFORMATION GATHERING TO WRAP-UP

This checklist will help you ensure that all arrangements have been made, resources scheduled and finalized, communication equipment ordered and delivered, and name badges printed.

Step 1: Information Gathering

- ☐ Event goal and objective.
- ☐ Name of event.
- ☐ Date and time.
- ☐ Selection of caterer.
- ☐ Location and directions.
- ☐ Event theme.
- ☐ Event activities.
- ☐ Anticipated attendance.
- ☐ Backup plan if weather will be a factor.

Weather Alert!

If you are receiving out-of-town guests, send them a five-day weather report. Although they can access this information on the Internet, it may not occur to them to dress accordingly. Make business and casual dress recommendations. For example, if you are located in a desert city and the visit is planned for January, it may not occur to your visitors that they will need jackets for the evening hours. The desert does get cold at night.

❑ Budget parameters: Revenue sources and overall expenses.

❑ Committee roles and responsibilities.

    ○ Project manager, site contact person.

    ○ Invitations: mailing and handling responses.

    ○ Raffle items, services, etc., solicited from community.

    ○ On-site staff.

❑ Identification of new members, sponsors, volunteers.

❑ Audiovisual requirements.

❑ Interpreters or translators (if needed).

❑ Photographers or videographers. (If needed, state how photographs or videotaping will be handled.)

❑ Creation of a resource list or file to share.

Step 2: Formulation of Event Plan

❑ Create "Event Specification Book".

❑ Establish timeline.

❑ Call possible event locations.

❑ Conduct site inspections.

❑ Select event location.

❑ Sign contract.

❑ Pay deposits.

❑ Identify vendors (photographer, printer, flowers, entertainment, rentals, etc.).

❑ Design and order invitations.

❑ Create and update attendee list.

❑ Address and send invitations.

❏ Schedule reminder cards and follow-up phone tree.

❏ Receive and count RSVPs ("respond by") cards.

❏ Address safety and security.

Step 3: Logistics

❏ Room setup and furniture arrangement.

❏ Rental furniture and equipment.

❏ Sound system and entertainment power needs.

❏ Staging requirements.

❏ Setup days and times.

❏ Tear-down days and times.

❏ Flowers and decorations.

❏ Signage and name badges or tags.

❏ Registration table.

❏ Menu.

❏ Table decor and linen.

❏ Number of waitstaff and bartenders needed.

❏ Waste management arrangements.

Step 4: On-Site Event Management

❏ Pre-event meeting with site.

❏ Pre-event meeting with volunteers.

❏ Day of event walk-through and inspection.

❏ On-site contact meeting with faculty staff.

❏ Distribution of gratuities, if appropriate.

Step 4: Food and Beverage Arrangements

❏ What is the estimated attendance?

❏ What are the table linen color choices?

❏ Are centerpieces and decorations needed for the head table and buffet tables?

❏ How many places are required at the head table?

❏ Will the head table be on a platform?

❏ Is a floor or table lectern needed? Where should it be placed?

❏ Are microphones needed? How many? What type? Where will they be positioned?

❏ Will there be a visual presentation requiring a screen and projector?

❏ How much time is needed for setup?

❏ When will the room be accessible?

❏ Where will dignitaries or VIPs be served?

❏ If service is buffet style, are head table guests to serve themselves, or are servers to prepare their plates?

❏ Establish protocol for visiting the buffet line. Will everyone serve themselves on their own, or will tables be directed to the buffet line at specific intervals?

❏ If meal tickets are to be collected, who will collect them and where? At the door or at the table?

❏ How are late arrivals without tickets to be handled?

❏ Are tickets required for head table guests?

❏ Is a registration or supply table needed outside the function room?

❏ Is an award table needed behind the head table?

❏ Are programs or menus to be placed on tables or chairs or distributed at the door?

❑ Is a room needed for VIPs prior to the function?

❑ Must special arrangements be made for guests with dietary or cultural food restrictions?

❑ Are there banners that need to be placed?

❑ Is a coat-check room needed? If so, will an attendant be needed, or will it be self-check?

❑ If awardees are seated in the audience, how will they approach the lectern?

❑ Will a spotlight be used to illuminate their approach to the platform?

❑ Is the master of ceremonies to be spotlighted?

❑ Is the national anthem to be played? (If so, the American flag is required in the United States, and it must always be displayed to stage right, with state flags to stage left.)

❑ Will there be an audiovisual presentation? What type? Are extra extension cords needed?

❑ Is background or dance music planned?

❑ Will there be entertainment for which an additional stage or platform is needed? If so, what size and height?

❑ Are platforms and stages to be skirted or carpeted?

❑ Are there lighted stairs with handrails?

❑ Is a rehearsal planned? If so, when and where?

❑ At what time will the doors be opened?

❑ What is the timing for all aspects of the event (pre-program music, entertainment, meal service, formal program and presentations, dancing, etc.)?

❑ Where are the restrooms? What arrangements should

be made to allow guests to reenter the function room if door controls will be in place?

☐ Where is the designated smoking area? This is especially important with international events where smoking is still socially acceptable in public.

Step 5: Key Security and Safety Checklist

☐ Notify security staff and request them to be a part of your team.

☐ Communicate current visitor information: names, titles, and state or country.

☐ Identify risks both during tours and on site and when visitors are on their own.

☐ Plan for risks, with protective measures outlined; use a "what if?" approach.

☐ Communicate plans to team and security.

☐ Identify fire exits and weather shelters.

☐ Brief visitors on safety and how to protect themselves.

☐ Provide visitors with relevant emergency contact information: local and state police, sheriff's department, fire department, hospital and clinics, dentist, optometrist, chiropractor, primary-care physician, local pharmacies, nursing and health services, poison control center, coast guard (if there will be boating or fishing), corporate and hotel security desk, and city and state government offices.

If you are receiving international guests, also include contact information for local foreign embassies and consulate offices. You may also want to consider contact information for the FBI, Secret Service, and various US government offices.

❑ Provide each visitor with a pocket-size handbook. You may want to include a small first-aid kit of aspirin, bandages, antibacterial ointment, gauze, and a small pair of scissors.

❑ Collect each visitor's emergency contact information sheet, which should also list any allergies they have or special medications they require.

❑ Provide visitors with corporate team and security contact information and a map of the facility and the city.

Step 6: Event Wrap-Up

❑ Receive and pay vendor invoices.

❑ Finalize expenses.

❑ Gather and record participant and guest evaluation form comments.

❑ Debrief with committee (using evaluation form).

❑ Write and send thank-you letters.

❑ Organize and schedule a volunteer post-party.

Checklist #3
AUDIOVISUAL CHECKLIST FOR AV PROFESSIONALS, PLANNERS, AND SPEAKERS

—by Greg Nosek

Greg Nosek, known as "Your Show-Ready Audio/Visual Specialist," offers the following guidelines for a worry-free and successful business, educational, social, or musical event.

When meeting for the first time before an event, I can't tell you how important it is to conduct a site survey with your video team. That is how your idea begins to be "show-ready." It provides a clear picture of your design theme, goals, budget, and how that fits into your production timeline. This holds true for the individual professional speaker as well as for the business conference or live musical event.

I believe your audiovisual team should offer you a "show-ready," worry-free audiovisual atmosphere so that you can focus on your attendees, business partners, and colleagues. Keep in mind that much will depend on your needs and desired outcome.

When you are looking for a videographer to shoot your next web message, keynote presentation, or business or educational conference, you would like it to be done well the first time. You want your video team to be "show-ready." Be mindful that you may want to repurpose the footage for a highlight or a promotional message for an upcoming event, or to share with your attendees, sponsors, vendors, and volunteers to celebrate the success of the gig.

For those in the arts and entertainment world, the same attention to details is essential. Capturing a live event of any kind with strong technique, audio, and lighting will contribute to the success of your show, and will allow you to build on what you are creating today.

 Tip: "*Show-ready*" means that all equipment is functional and backups are in place.

Being worry-free comes from complete vendor and team support and having a clear objective through the planning stages, rehearsal, and the show.

This all carries over into the editing room, where your message is skillfully tailored through your vision.

A "show-ready" atmosphere will allow you to tell your story from the heart and enjoy your meeting, conference, or special event using your skills as a performer, presenter, or musician. Remember most of all to have fun and grow your business through strategic planning.

Step 1: Cameraman and Presenter Considerations and Responsibilities

- ❑ Visit the location together at the same time of day as the presentation.

- ❑ Identify all power needs, the performance or presentation area, and camera position.

- ❑ Ask to see the hotel podium, markers, and flip chart(s), and confirm availability.

- ❑ Ask to see risers and stair units. In addition, ask to see furniture (e.g., chair, stool, or tables) that will be used if there is to be a panel discussion.

❑ Take pictures of the meeting room, lobby, foyer, and podium for your event signage. This process will help ensure the branding of your event in all photos and video footage.

> Brand your media content!

❑ Identify an area for back-of-room sales and/or a book signing area for your attendees and cameras.

❑ If a book signing is to be staged in the lobby, the same process applies.

❑ The cameraman should bring the camera to the site survey to check room light levels and focal distances and to determine if additional lighting is needed.

❑ When creating vinyl banners or signage for your event, consider using a *flat* look instead of a *shiny* look that will reflect light. You may *not* want to include a date, so it can be reused for the next event.

❑ Discuss postproduction. Does the client want videocassettes, DVDs, or an electronic file on hard drive?

Step 2: Select Camera-Friendly Clothing and Avoid Grooming Distractions

❑ Wear clothes that breathe! When a room gets warm, you do not want to show signs of perspiration. Avoid wearing 100 percent synthetic shirts or blouses; they cling to the body and are uncomfortable. (For men, it is highly recommended that you wear a 100 percent cotton T-shirt under your dress shirt. The cotton T-shirt protects the dress shirt from perspiration stains.)

❑ Check air conditioning. If the room is cool, you might want to wear a jacket. Also realize that a cool room will warm up as the room fills with attendees. Be sure to wear an outfit that looks professional with or without a jacket.

❑ Always bring a backup shirt and tie (or blouse) in case you perspire or spill food on yourself.

❑ Be mindful of the color of the room and your backdrop if no drape is being used. (For example, if the room is beige, don't wear a light brown or beige suit or dress. You will blend into the background.)

❑ If using a drape to define the presentation area, try to plan for uplighting the drape to increase the depth of focus for the camera and to have the presenter *pop* from the backdrop.

❑ Avoid dressing in monochromatic colors (wearing all one color scheme). Try an understated pattern (small-scale geometric patterns are more professional), or mix colors (e.g., a bold-colored blouse or shirt with a neutral jacket).

❑ Power dress! Wear clothes that make you feel strong and confident and are best worn in contrast (a light color paired with a dark color).

❑ Carefully select your jewelry to avoid distractions. A quality camera will catch the sparkle of a diamond stud earring. The distraction and noise of jangly bracelets, earrings, and necklaces can interfere with the ability of a lavaliere microphone and could be heard through the PA system.

❑ Wear appropriate clothing to accept a lavaliere belt pack. You will need clothing with a waistband or belt, and a collar or lapel that is strong enough to support the microphone. If you are going to wear a dress without a belt or pocket, be sure to add a jacket. The pocket can be used to hold the lavaliere.

❏ Remove your name badge while presenting and for photographs. Wearing a name tag on stage and in photographs detracts from a clean, professional look.

Step 3: Microphones, Video, Photography, and Equipment

❏ Supply a dedicated wireless microphone for the camera on channel one, with an additional microphone for audience response and ambience on channel two. Do not depend on the house system to do everything.

❏ If you're spending hundreds of dollars on quality equipment and labor, don't penny-pinch on good audio.

❏ Arrive early enough to set up a merchandise table, change clothes, and perform a sound check for your cameraman and the house PA system. (It is best to do the sound check when wearing your presentation attire.)

❏ Assign or request a production assistant to facilitate video testimonials before and after the event.

❏ Select (or hire) someone to take as many pictures as possible to help illustrate attendance and the overall size of the event. (Again, remove name tags for photos.)

❏ Bring your own computer, power supply, hand remote, batteries, and adapters.

❏ Bring what you need for your presentation. (If in doubt, bring it.) Make sure your equipment is labeled in some way, so that it does not get confused with other equipment. (A suggestion for cables is to wrap colored tape or tie a colored ribbon around the cable.) This will also help you identify it so that you do not leave it behind.

❏ Discuss embedded audio and video in the presentation, and confirm audio and video playback during sound check.

❑ Discuss postproduction. Again, does the client prefer videocassettes, DVDs, or an electronic file on hard drive?

❑ Discuss shooting a conference teaser video for social media to increase public awareness, attendee registration, and overall anticipation for the event.

Step 4: Conduct a Site Survey

❑ Make sure that cell phones work and you have good cell coverage. If cell phone coverage varies, inform your staff of the areas for the best coverage.

❑ Meet with the facility's lead staff members who are directly involved with *show day*.

❑ Check the location for cleanliness and maintenance of the carpet, walls, power outlets, and lighting.

❑ Is there Wi-Fi Internet access? If so, is there a connection fee?

❑ Can you meet with the in-house AV contact in case of an emergency?

❑ Identify the location for crew parking and the loading dock and the best hours of operation so you don't conflict with regular deliveries. Ask to meet the dock master.

❑ Identify the parking locations for all attendees' cars and the fee schedule, if there is one (e.g., free parking, fee for validation parking, fee for ticketed parking). Request a parking map.

❑ Identify handicapped parking availability.

❑ Measure the room, and draw a picture; don't depend on hotel diagrams for dimensions. Identify large potted plants, fixed countertops, floor and wall outlets, light switches for every fixture, drapes that open and close correctly, and an in-room thermostat control.

You can save money by using your own AV person. Hotels charge high fees, especially at upscale resorts. Although there may be policies regarding the use of outside equipment, you always have the option to negotiate the use of your AV team for labor and equipment. You are looking for the greatest flexibility for your event.

❑ Consider the *load-in* (setup) and *load-out* (strike) schedule. Do you have enough time? Is there a meeting booked right before or right after your event? Can you set up the night before?

❑ If you have a room in the middle of three rooms, ask about the other groups. If you have an awards lunch or dinner, make sure that your music and microphone levels won't disturb the other meetings; also make sure that their music and PA system will not disturb your event. This is a courtesy. If possible, always ask for a room at the end of a hallway.

Tip: Airwalls are freestanding curtains or accordion sliding walls that serve as room dividers. It is very important to be aware that there are no electrical outlets in an airwall, so power needs to come from one end of the room. Therefore, additional power cables may be needed.

❑ Check for clear food service entry and egress, to prevent servers from walking behind the projection screen or through the AV equipment. Check for the availability of fake plants to disguise or cover speaker stands. Check to see if you can dress up the corners of the screen or stage with the use of black drapery.

❑ Check the condition and availability of riser platforms.

Are risers extra, and are they in good shape with a good skirt? Are the stair units safe for women wearing heels?

Step 5: Considerations for Events Held Outdoors

❑ If meals will be served outside on a patio, identify the electrical power and a good place to position the PA or head table.

❑ Consider the direction of the sun based on the time of day. Will you need shading?

❑ If the event is held in a tent and a storm is predicted, will the sound of the rain interfere with the sound equipment? If so, have a backup plan.

❑ If the event is outside (not in a tent), have a backup room arranged in case of inclement weather.

Step 6: Power Needs and Adjustments:

❑ Will the air conditioning be on for the load-in (setup) and load-out (strike)?

❑ Large-scale shows will often have the loading dock doors open for hours at a time.

❑ Identify if there is sufficient power for everything. Does the hotel provide electrical service for a fee? Lights, sound, projection, cameras, and FOH (front of house) should all have their own dedicated circuits.

Tip: FOH is where audio, lights, video gear, and crew (including the technical director) are positioned in a concert or ballroom setting as they run the show.

Tip: Videoland refers to a situation where all the video gear is set up backstage and the technicians are able to communicate with audio, lights, and the technical director by headset.

❏ A2 (the audio assistant) is also positioned backstage on headset so that he or she can mike up the presenters as they come up and down from the stage.

❏ Have your AV team talk to the hotel engineering staff about electricity needs (especially if airwalls are being used) and how to *breaker off* certain lights in the room or to have a centrally located room lighting control panel. If a control panel is unavailable, unscrew the bulbs behind and directly in front of the projection screens.

Step 7: Business Needs

❏ Does the event site or meeting place have a business center with Internet and a reliable printer? This is important for the speaker, the meeting planner, and all attendees.

❏ What are the hours of operation for the business center, and is there an attendant?

❏ Where is the nearest office supply retail store (e.g., FedEx office, UPS store, OfficeMax, Staples)?

Step 8: Traveling Crew/AV Staff

❏ Inquire about alternative food choices for crew besides hotel options. Is there an off-site restaurant or fast food nearby?

❏ Request a list of less expensive hotels that are within a few miles.

❏ Inquire about transportation for off-site or traveling crew.

Step 9: Tips for a Press Conference or Rally Held Outside

❏ Check for construction concerns.

❑ Will you be inviting local media to cover the event? If so, consider a *press box* that will provide a quality audio signal for all invited media coverage.

❑ Will neighboring businesses, residences, or parking be affected?

Checklist #4
FOOD AND BEVERAGE PLANNING

—by Larry P. Canepa and Haydee Pampel

Part I:
Selecting the Right Caterer within Your Budget

Larry P. Canepa, certified culinary educator and the director of training and development, Dinner at Eight, offers the following guidelines and considerations when selecting and working with catering professionals. You have a lot of options and decisions to make.

Types of Catering

☐ *Mobile Caterer:* Serves food directly from a vehicle at outdoor events.

☐ *Drop-off Caterer:* Provides box lunches (sandwich, chips, fruit, dessert) and beverages.

☐ *Event Caterer Staff:* Helps set up the dining area; does not prepare the food.

☐ *Catered Event:* Provides food and drinks.

☐ *Catering Company or Specialist:* Works with the event theme or color scheme, prepares the food, and serves the food.

☐ *Personal Chef:* Specialty catering that does special event dinners (e.g., celebration, romantic, special guests) in remote locations (e.g., in the home).

☐ *Full-service Catering:* Provides food services and decorations and handles settings and lighting.

Types of Rental Quotes

There are two types of quotes:

- ❏ Anytime weekday delivery (more economical).
- ❏ Exact-time delivery.

Pricing

There is typically a per-person flat price; however, there could be an additional charge that is not associated with the plate charge.

Pricing should include the following:

- ❏ Flat plate price.
- ❏ Extras such as permits for lighting, fire, liquor, special event, parking (if needed).

Proposal

A sample of a full-service catering proposal would include the following:

- ❏ Rental arrival time.
- ❏ Staff arrival time.
- ❏ Meal service time.
- ❏ Bar close time (includes a "last call").
- ❏ Rental pickup.
- ❏ Out-of-venue time.
- ❏ Menu considerations: Specific dietary or religious needs such as halal, kosher, vegetarian, vegan, and food allergy.
- ❏ Hors d'oeuvres: Will they be passed or stationary or both?

❑ List of meal rentals (e.g., tables, chairs, plates/utensils/ glassware, serving equipment), and added cost for breakage.

❑ Table takedown. (Is it included with setup?)

❑ Staffing needed. (Note that a plated meal requires more staffing than a buffet.)

❑ Overtime. (If needed, what are the additional costs?)

❑ Service charge. (This can include sales tax, gratuity, permits, and any extras.)

Part II:
Planning the Food and Beverage Count

Haydee Pampel, international meeting planner, uses the following tips and formulas when planning food and beverage service based on number of guests. This is why advance registration is critical to the success of any event. When you're unsure of your party count and want to play it safe, think about foods that will stretch to accommodate unexpected guests—for example, cheeses, tarts, veggies, or focaccia pizzas. These go a lot farther and are less expensive.

> When buying alcohol, find out if you can return an unopened bottle of alcohol if the label is intact. This will allow you to overbuy (playing it safe) and get money back if you do not need the extra bottles.

Count on serving ten to fifteen one-bite hors d'oeuvres per guest, and serving one drink per hour per person. Buy about a third of each of hard liquor, beer, and wine, and don't forget soda and water.

Breakfast

- ☐ Coffee: twenty cups per gallon.
- ☐ 65 percent hot beverages and 35 percent cold beverages.
- ☐ Serving staff: One per one hundred guests.
- ☐ Buffet tables: One per one hundred guests. (If 120 are expected, set up two tables.)

Banquets

Wine

- ☐ Three bottles per table of eight: two white and one red.
- ☐ Five drinks per bottle is average.
- ☐ One-half bottle per person with 10 percent buffer.

Serving Staff

- ☐ One per twenty (optimal).
- ☐ One per thirty-to (standard).
- ☐ One per sixteen (with wine or upscale service).
- ☐ One wine steward per five tables.

Tables

- ☐ Eight people to a sixty-inch table.
- ☐ Ten people to a seventy-two-inch table.

Receptions

Serving Staff

- ☐ One bartender per one hundred people (if arriving at intervals).

❑ One bartender per fifty, if arriving as a group.

❑ One cocktail server per fifty people.

Food

❑ Five o'clock PM to six o'clock PM—food consumption is lower.

❑ Six o'clock PM to seven o'clock PM—food consumption is higher, more relaxed.

❑ Less food but more drinks if reception precedes dinner— six pieces per person per hour prior to dinner.

Beverages

❑ 50 percent hard and 50 percent soft (including water or bottled water).

❑ Twenty-one to twenty-five drinks per bottle of liquor.

❑ Wine consumption two and a half to three glasses per person during a two-hour reception.

❑ If participation is mostly women, plan on more wine than hard liquor.

Space

❑ Five to ten square feet per person, plus space for bars and buffet tables.

❑ For a cocktail reception where people tend to stand, plan on seating for 20 to 25 percent of attendees.

Checklist #5
GATHERING DATA FOR DOMESTIC AND INTERNATIONAL VISITORS

When preparing to receive international guests or when traveling abroad, form a committee of nationals or individuals with country-specific experience and discuss the following questions. Record the responses and use them to create a Q&A binder.

1. Where should I sit or stand upon arrival at a meeting? Who may enter and leave a room first? Who should direct others?

2. Do the people from this country expect to bargain? If so, where does the bargaining take place—at a table, or behind the scenes?

3. How do they view emotion?

4. Does this country stress the individual approach, or is it better to stress the group? Do these individuals make decisions based on a consensus, or is one person empowered to make decisions on behalf of the group?

5. How do they view work? Are they workaholics, or do they place other activities ahead of work? When and where should work be stressed or avoided? When does their business day begin, and when does it conclude?

6. How much attention should I pay to rank and position? Should first names or titles be used? Do they tend to be casual or formal?

7. What is the protocol for the business card expectation and exchange?

8. What is the best way to reach them? Should I make a direct call or have someone introduce me?

9. Are there special religious customs or taboos that I should be careful to observe?

10. What gestures are considered acceptable, and what gestures are offensive?

About You

1. In addition to your organization, what other companies or organizations will be involved?

2. List names and titles in order of rank and a summary of each person's role.

2. How much time has been allocated for the visit?

About the Visitors

1. List names and titles of visitors. Be sure to include name pronunciation guidelines.

2. What is your history with your visitors? Have they visited your city before?

3. What is the purpose of their visit?

4. What is their travel itinerary?

5. How do they expect to be greeted at the airport?

6. What is the length of their stay?

7. What types of activities are planned? What are their preferences?

8. Do they have a personal agenda?

Additional International Conference Tips

1. Arrange for translation facilities and for interpreters.

2. Prepare conference literature in all languages that will be represented.

3. Do not schedule a formal meal function on the arrival date. Instead, make simple sandwiches and snacks available.

4. Note religious and dietary restrictions or ethnic preferences for food and beverages.

5. Prepare a guide sheet identifying menu items and their ingredients.

Consider including a protocol and cultural etiquette guide sheet in the attendee binder. This will help all cultures relate and avoid unintentional missteps.

This guide sheet should address the following:

❑ Assign planning committee ambassadors for each country, with contact info, or appoint special committee members or reference in cultural matters.

❑ Use correct forms of address when greeting and speaking.

❑ Note how names will appear on the name tags. Make name tags that have the attendee's first name in upper- and lowercase and the last name in all caps. (For example, in Spanish a woman's married name is her second name, and her maiden name comes first. Hence, Roberta ORTEGA de Mendez's official family name is actually Ortega.)

❑ Note the risk of making jokes when the humor is not understood.

❑ Make notes on cultural mannerisms.

❑ Note how translations will be handled at conference educational sessions. (Make the same arrangements for anyone who is medically challenged.)

❑ Give embassy information.

❑ Are flags going to be displayed? If so, it's important that the flag of each country is represented and according to the correct protocol. (Contact the embassy of the specific country for placement protocol.)

There are many factors to consider when planning an international conference—domestic or abroad. The above are simply suggestions to get you started. Consult (or hire) an international meeting professional.

⑥

Checklist #6
JOURNAL AND LOG

At the end of each event, keep a journal or log of what went well and what did not. It should include all of the "whos, whats, whens, wheres, and whys" of the event, plus what you wore. Also, include personal information about your guest or guests so that you can ask specific questions when you follow up or prepare for the next event. This kind of inquiry makes your guests feel important and demonstrates your ability to pay attention to detail and to be thorough. This journal will be an invaluable reference guide for future events, especially when receiving international guests. It will also serve as an invaluable aid should someone else be assigned to the next event.

If this is a new event, create a three-ring binder with tabs. (If it is a repeat event, check last year's folder for what went right and what went wrong.) Depending on the size of your event, your tabs might include the following: ✳ Venue, ✳ Contracts, ✳ Correspondence, ✳ Budget and Expenses, ✳ Food and Beverage, ✳ Insurance, ✳ Decorations, ✳ Entertainment, ✳ AV Equipment Needed, ✳ Timeline, and ✳ Table Arrangement and Seating.

Use the following as a guide when creating your event journal or event recap. The steps are very similar to the steps used to plan your event (see Checklists #1 and #2); however, your event journal includes more specific information about your guests. Anything you recorded of your conversations will also be helpful.

Step 1: Details of the Visit and People

❑ Name of organization and/or sponsoring organization.

- ❏ Number of visitors.
- ❏ Name of individuals and titles. (If possible, include a brief bio of each visitor.)
- ❏ Originator or key contact person's phone number, e-mail address, and fax number.
- ❏ Travel accommodation information (hotel, car rental, flights).
- ❏ Letters of invitation for visas prepared. (Many countries will require someone in the host country to write a letter of invitation so that the guest may obtain a visa.)
- ❏ Concierge and technology services used.
- ❏ Locations visited.
- ❏ Dates (tentative and confirmed).
- ❏ New product or service, demonstration of specific interest.
- ❏ Sales potential (new or current customers).
- ❏ How charges will be handled and expense accounts arranged.
- ❏ Strategy and comments.
- ❏ Notes on any past experiences with group or customers.
- ❏ Sample of working agenda.
- ❏ Full name. (If the name is gender neutral, indicate Mr. or Ms.)
- ❏ Title.
- ❏ Family members (if accompanying guest).
- ❏ Smoking or nonsmoking.
- ❏ Languages. (Will interpreters or translators be needed?)

- ☐ Special needs and restrictions.
- ☐ Dietary or culture-related food restrictions.
- ☐ Gift expectations or recommendations.
- ☐ Repeat visitor(s)? (Yes/No).
- ☐ Leisure activity preferences.
- ☐ Visit and meeting agenda.
- ☐ Welcome packages prepared. The welcome package should be left at the front desk of the hotel so the guests have all pertinent information for the event when they arrive (guest list, a welcome letter, name badge, pen or pencil, event agenda, speaker biographies, discount tickets, and drink tickets, etc.).

Compile a complete report reflecting the visit as well as expenses. This report can be used for tracking costs. Have all those involved in the visit review the report to ensure that it reflects everyone's experience.

Step 2: Closing the Event

- ☐ Log account reference number (if issued).
- ☐ Name and address list. (Include e-mail address and fax and phone numbers.)
- ☐ Department to be charged—accounting details.
- ☐ Number of guests.
- ☐ Names of greeters and/or planners (everyone involved in caring for the visitors).
- ☐ Dates of event.
- ☐ Hotel and car rentals used.
- ☐ Business objective and sales potential.

- ❑ Technology used.
- ❑ Sites and other locations that were included as part of the event.
- ❑ Contractors and outside services used.
- ❑ Gifts appropriated.
- ❑ Special instructions or notes.
- ❑ Additional comments and strategies.
- ❑ Sign-off area for manager or planner.

Sample forms (Pre-Meeting Preparation, Visitor Information, Event Journal, and Post-Meeting Analysis) are provided next to help you keep excellent records. Again, use them as guides, and customize your own journal.

SAMPLE PLANNING FORMS

Form A: *Premeeting Preparation*

This form will ensure that the visit is a smooth and productive interchange. The information listed should be gathered and documented. Someone should be assigned to coordinate both the premeeting preparation and post-meeting analysis, plus all the details in between.

Form B: *Visitor Information*

Keep the visitor and staff informed of the entire travel itinerary. Will there be a display of the visitor's country (or state) flag in the meeting room? A flag display sends a strong message that you respect your visitor. Flags can be displayed in the conference room or scheduled meeting places.

Assign tasks prior to the visit, and make sure that each person understands his or her responsibilities and details about the visitors. Here are some examples:

- Who will pick up visitors at the airport?
- How will they be transported to their hotel?

Make sure that everyone on your team, from setup to cleanup, has a clear agenda of the visit and knows his role. Be sure that you know if your visitors are smokers and if special arrangements are needed. Not every country is as sensitive to nonsmoking areas as the United States has become. If the visitors' agenda includes "free time," make sure that they know their transportation, restaurant, and sightseeing options.

Form C: *Event Journal*

Be sure to add any topics or points that are pertinent to your event.

Form D: *Postmeeting Analysis*

Always debrief, no matter how small or large the event. Review what went well and what went astray. Include details about the entire event (e.g., names and titles, location and logistics, activities and entertainment).

Form A

PREMEETING PREPARATION

Date of Arrival: _____

Number of Visitors: _____

Names and Titles of Visitors: _____

(Pronunciation Guidelines): _____

Nationality of Visitors: _____

Organization or Company: _____

Country: _____

Type of Event

- ☐ What is the purpose of their visit?
- ☐ Business objective:
- ☐ When will they arrive?
- ☐ What is the length of their stay?
- ☐ What types of activities have they requested?
- ☐ What types of activities have been scheduled?

History

- ☐ What is your organization's history with these guests?
- ☐ Have there been issues or difficulties in the past?

Details

- ☐ Are there sensitivities or special accommodations to consider?
- ☐ Do they know how to dress for the weather or certain occasions?

❑ Will they need equipment or technology?

❑ What are the three most important points that your organization should focus on?

Security for the Visitor

❑ What steps can be taken if the visitors' belongings or important papers are stolen?

❑ Give visitors a list of emergency contact names and numbers (e.g., hospital, fire, police, US Customs). Include what to do and whom to notify for illness or injuries.

❑ Give visitors their host's office, home, and cell phone numbers.

❑ Issue visitor badges.

❑ Consider all areas of risk; once identified, create risk elimination strategies.

❑ Gather visitors' emergency contact information.

Form B

VISITOR INFORMATION

Keep contact information for each visitor in a file (name, city/
state, phone, e-mail).

A small bio on each visitor includes the following:

Full Name: _____

Title: _____

Smoking Preferences: _____

Native Language: _____

Languages: _____

English Proficiency: _____

Interpreters Needed: _____

Special Diet: _____

Medical Alert: _____

Repeat Visitor (Y/N): _____

Gift Considerations: _____

Full Flight Itinerary: _____

Leisure Activities Requested: _____

Facilities Requested to Visit: _____

Nonbusiness Requests and Concerns: _____

Additional Notes:

_____

Form C

EVENT JOURNAL

Date: _____

Name of Company: _____

Names of Guests/Visitors: _____

Theme: _____

Date/Time/Location: _____

Attendance: _____

Type of Invitation: _____

Entertainment Selected: _____

Logistics: _____

What went right? _____

What went wrong? _____

Questions or Confusions: _____

Improvements: _____

Contractors Used: _____

Dress: _____

Summary of Event: _____

Company Facilitators/Organizers:

Other Comments:

_____

Form D
POSTMEETING ANALYSIS

Date: _____

Names of Visitors:_____

Country: _____

Names/Titles of Visitors: _____

Visitors' Expectations:_____

City and Organization Expectations: _____

Sites and Companies Visited:_____

What did they enjoy the most?_____

What did they enjoy the least? _____

What went right? _____

What went wrong? _____

What were typical questions or confusions?_____

How can their next visit be improved? _____

Company Sites Visited:_____

Entertainment Selected: _____

Contractors Used: _____

Summary of Visit:_____

REVIEW QUIZ AND SUMMARY

REVIEW QUIZ FOR
PLANNING YOUR EVENT

Use the following review quiz to help plan your event and establish comfort when attending an event. Take your cues from the chapters referenced.

- Chapters 1 and 2 help you consider and plan the purpose, theme, and logistics for small to large events.
- Chapter 3 takes you through the components of an invitation, the guest list, and name tag considerations.
- Chapters 4 through 9 help you select the type of event and identify expectations unique to that event.
- Chapter 10 offers you a large-event checklist and sample planning forms.

1. Determine the personalities needed and the expertise involved in building a cohesive team. What are the *three* most popular ways to determine the type of event that helps you achieve your entertaining goals? *(chapter 1)*

2. Identify the "Five P's" that are important to the planning process, and the "Five W's" that are needed on invitations and promotional materials. *(chapter 1)*

3. Create a planning strategy and start your planning by identifying your purpose, goals, theme, and size of event. *(chapter 1)*

4. Will this be a small private-company-sponsored retreat or a large event? *(chapter 2)*

5. Identify distractions that could impede the success of your event. *(chapters 2 and 3)*

6. Identify the qualities and considerations you need to be a gracious host (or planner). *(chapter 4)*

7. Identify the qualities you need to be an impeccable guest (or participant). *(chapter 4)*

8. As a participant (or guest), what are your behavior account-abilities relating to cultural events, home entertaining, sporting activities, company parties, and conventions? *(chapters 5, 6, 7, 8)*

9. Are you planning a cultural, sporting, or employee apprecia-tion event? Or are you planning a convention or trade show? Once you have identified the event, outline the rules of behavior, any special considerations pertaining to that event, and anything else necessary to make that event successful. *(chapters 5, 6, 7, 8)*

10. Identify food service needs, room logistics, and table setup. *(chapter 3 and 10)*

11. Address your AV and food needs. *(chapters 2 and 10)*

12. Create your invitation making sure that it includes all the information a guest needs and that it makes responding easy. Indicate the dress code on the invitation. Then determine how name tags will be handled? *(chapter 3)*

13. Decide if your event requires outside professional assistance and if it involves special needs. *(chapter 4)*

14. Will you need a welcome packet, goodie bags, appreciation or thank-you gifts? *(chapter 2 and 4)*

Now that you have completed your research, what have you and
your planning committee decided?

Type of Event   _____

Theme: _____

Size of Event: _____

Logistics and Meals: _____

Invitation List: _____

Gift Considerations: _____

Planning Notes: _____

_____

_____

_____

_____

_____

_____

_____

_____

_____

_____

Use the forms in chapter 10 to help your organize and capture
every detail and to serve as a reference for future events.

Strategize for a Successful Event

- Determine the Purpose
- Control the Logistics
- Prepare Proper Invitations
- Avoid "What to Wear" Issues
- Create Memorable Events
- Consider Cultural Experiences
- Know the Basic Principles for Sports
- Utilize Conferences and Trade Shows Wisely
- Celebrate Those Who Serve You
- Cultivate an Attitude of Appreciation

Make it Special and it will be Rewarding!

—Gloria Petersen

RESOURCES

RESOURCES

SME (Subject Matter Expert)
Training Module Companion

This book is designed for university career centers, corporate trainers, and independent consultants who need a how-to guide for planning parties, conferences, and other events.

This book is designed to assist in the planning of small or large events. (Training module companions are available for the first three titles: *Seven Steps to Impressive Greetings and Confident Interactions*, *Success Strategies for Networking in Person and Online*, and *Dining Strategies for Building and Sustaining Business Relationships*.)

To request more information about *The Art of Professional Connections* book series and training modules, contact Gloria Petersen (gpetersen@globalprotocol.com).

This is the fourth of four books and modules in *The Art of Professional Connections* series. Check our website for information on the other three books, which cover networking, greetings and interactions, and meeting over meals.

Blogs on current issues and thought-provoking commentary can be found on our websites GlobalBusinessProtocol.com and GloriaPetersen.com.

Books Help You Expand Your Knowledge Base

There are many excellent books on the market—too many to list—that cover interpersonal skills and protocol. Much depends on what you are seeking. If you want to know about the protocol for particular kinds of interaction, I recommend any book by my personal mentor, Letitia Baldrige, an etiquette and protocol guru whose career included overseeing presidential inaugurations that date back to the President Kennedy years. If you are attempting to build interpersonal skills, look for books recommended by the Association of Training and Development and by best-selling authors. There are many wonderful options.

People Offer You Real-Time Experience and an Opportunity to Perfect Your Technique

A team of business professionals and industry experts offered input in the development of this book. My experience and research combined with their knowledge and expertise contributed to the content. However, the following resources will aid in helping to further expand on an area that may not be covered in this book or to take an idea a step further.

Recommended Resources:

- *Exhibit Like an Expert: Sell More, Look Great, and Make Money at Tradeshows, Consumer Shows and Events,* by Susan Ratliff (only available on the author's website: exhibitexpertsaz.com)
- *Global Etiquette Guide to (name of country),* by Dean Allen Foster
- *Protocol: The Complete Handbook of diplomatic, Official and Social Usage* by Pauline B. Innis
- *How to Get the Most Out of Trade Shows,* by Steve Miller
- *New Manners for New Times,* by Letitia Baldrige
- *Passport* series, by WorldTradePress.com

Recommended Websites:

- Flag Protocol: usflag.org/flag.etiquette.html
- Receiving Lines: ediplomat.com/nd/protocol/entertaining.htm
- Electronic invitations: evite.com
- National Concierge Association: ncakey.org
- Special Needs:
    - ada.gov *(Americans with Disabilities Act)*
    - nfb.org *(National Federation for the Blind)*
    - rid.org *(Registry of Interpreters for the Deaf)*
    - nad.org *(National Association of the Deaf)*
    - amcin.org *(Association for the Mentally Challenged)*

INDEX

This index does not include Chapter 10:
Customize Your Checklists and Journals

INDEX

A

Activity exercise, xxiii

Aggarwal, Dr. Neelum T.
  Applause at cultural events, 179
  Attire worn at rock concerts, 186
  Cell phone use at cultural events, avoiding, 175
  Concierge use, 136
  Fact checker, xvii
  Seating at outdoor concerts, 190
  Unwrapping cough drops at cultural events, avoiding, 178

Air flights, arranging a seatmate or meeting in the sky, 309

Applaud, celebrate, and benefit those who serve you
  Generally, 241–246
  Birthdays, celebrating, 245
  Company anniversaries, 244
  Death of employee, responding to, 250–251, 333
  Encouraging camaraderie, building morale, and handling personal situations, 247–251
  Family-focused events tips, 259–262
  Holiday parties, 248–250
  Office gifts, 250, 338–339
  Religious recognition, 248
  Retirement parties, 245, 247
  Soirées, steps to enjoying a worry-free soirée, 252–258
  Special day celebrations, 244–246

Weddings and the workplace, what to do and not do, 263–268

Appreciation gestures. *See* Gestures of appreciation

Arts and theater, *see* Cultural events

At-home entertaining
  Generally, 192–209
  Buffet and open seating, 202–204
  Casual coffee meetings, 204–205
  Cultural experience, as, 170–171
  Formal dinner party, 205–206
  Frequently asked questions, 207–209
  Guest etiquette, 206–207
  Guest responsibilities, 199–202
  Home preparation suggestions, 195–199
  Telecom muting, 204–205
  Webinars, 28

Attire
  Accessories count, 119–121, 124–127
  Active wear, 116
  Addressing in invitation, 15, 99, 113–127
  At-home entertaining, 196, 197
  Black tie/tuxedo, 122–123
  Business dress and formal attire, 121–127
  Casual dress, 115–117
  Checklist, 123–124, 371–372
  Cocktail attire, 121, 123

Seating for latecomers to dinner events, 76

Soliciting feedback by survey or critique of event, 361

Welcome package suggestions for themed events, 53

Summary, 409–410

Symposium or conference characteristics, 32

T

Table and chair selection, 58

Tablecloth and placemats, 60–61

Tablescapes (table cover): place settings and utensils, 59–60

Tasting session, 21–22

Team approach to event planning

Generally, 12–16, 133–134

Accommodating guests with disabilities, 159–166

Being a gracious host of impeccable guest, must-knows for, 146–153

Checklists and journals, *this index*

Concierges, 135–138

Conference meetings planning, 33–35

Establishing protocol and procedure, 13–14

Pacing yourself to avoid burnout, 26

Receiving line protocol for formal events, 143–145

Sample planning forms, 392–402

Security team at event, 43–45

Selecting and engaging your team, 12–13

Selecting the introducer

and master of ceremonies, 139–142

Socializing solo at a predominantly couples event, 156–158

Spousal participation, 154–156

Using a professional event planner, 24–25, 36–37

Utilizing parking-lot flipcharts, 34

Team building, 31, 212-213, 233,

Teeple, Steve

Boosting morale at employee events, 243, 248, 255, 259

Christmas party designation, 248

Fact checker, xx

Thank-you notes, giving, 328–334

Theater events (live performance)

Armrests, using, 182

Arrival and seating, 173–174

Auditorium seating and policing challenges, 180–182

Backstage tours, 183

Behavior, 177–178

Clapping and applause, 177, 179

Coughing, 178

Dressing for, 118, 176

Escort and usher seating, 180–182

Etiquette for, 172–184

Flashing lights as seating signal, 176

Hats off, 176

Illness of attendee, rescheduling, 180

Late arrivals, 175

Lost and found, 180

Treats (candy) in meeting room, 40

Shania Twain, xx, 192

U

Unwrapping candy or cough drops, avoiding, 40, 178

V

Venue
  Availability, 14
  Large events, relationship with facility staff and vendors, 38
  Rock concert venue, selecting, 186
  Security arrangements, 43–45

W

Warm rooms, 286–287

Webinars
  Generally, 27–28
  Educational seminar, 31–32

Websites
  Invitation through websites such as MyRSVPLive, 97
  Special needs guests, equal opportunity rights and helpful websites, 165–166

Weddings and the workplace, what to do and not do, 263–268

Welcome arrangements, 20, 53–55

Welcome packets and baskets, 53, 137–138

West, Paula, xx

Women
  Purses of women guests at seated events, 84–86, 287

Seating men and women, 78, 81–82

Traveling, 317–319

ABOUT GLORIA PETERSEN

Author, Speaker, Trainer

 Gloria Petersen is founder and president of Global Protocol, Inc., the premier resource for personal performance enhancement and professional leadership development. Since 1985, thousands have learned to project personal power, poise, and presence to attain success in business. With her guidance, individuals have built self-confidence and promoted a dynamic business culture based on teamwork, relationships, and productivity.

Audiences are energized by Gloria's down-to-earth style because she inspires them to take control of their careers and to serve as role models for others. Her customized seminars, workshops, and training programs have a proven track record for teaching individuals how to develop the social intelligence necessary to inspire, lead, and succeed. These are the ultimate business skills for building long-lasting relationships with coworkers, management, and customers. Her seminars and training programs introduce techniques for projecting confidence and controlling difficult business situations.

History and Training: Prior to founding Global Protocol, Inc., Ms. Petersen spent sixteen years in civic and corporate roles, developing her business protocol and international etiquette experience. Credentialed as a certified protocol professional (CPP), she is a graduate of the Protocol School of Washington, the Professional Image Institute, and Dale Carnegie and Associates. She continues to focus on keeping her knowledge current by conducting surveys, attending frequent symposia, and monitoring the business climate for emerging issues.

Media: Gloria Petersen hosted the Fox television series *Image of Success* and has made network television appearances on CNBC's *The Power Lunch, Fox News, ABC News, CBS News,* and *NBC*

News. She served as an etiquette judge on the Learning Channel's reality television show *Faking It* (a segment was featured on *The Oprah Winfrey Show*). And she served as an etiquette instructor for Common Threads, a program for underprivileged children that was televised on the *Today Show.* Ms. Petersen continues to serve as a contributing columnist for newsstand magazines, trade magazines, online blogs, and corporate newsletters.

Gloria Petersen
has authored the following four-book series

The Art of Professional Connections:
Seven Steps to Impressive Greetings and Confident Interactions

The Art of Professional Connections:
Success Strategies for Networking in Personal and Online

The Art of Professional Connections:
Dining Strategies for Building and Sustaining
Business Relationships

The Art of Professional Connections:
Event Strategies for Successful Business Entertaining

To order books:

by Gloria Petersen

Book #4:

The Art of Professional Connections
Event Strategies for Successful Business Entertaining

To order books visit:

www.GlobalBusinessProtocol.com

www.GloriaPetersen.com

www.ArtofProfessionalConnections.com

Make your challenges work for you, not against you
by communicating with personal power, poise, and presence

To bring a customized training program
to your facility or event contact:

Gloria@GloriaPetersen.com

Telephone: 602-553-1046

or Toll free 866-991-2660

SIA information can be obtained
www.ICGtesting.com
ted in the USA
0W06s1610070717
8427BV00015B/50/P

Cl
at
Pri
BV
48